Monetary Theory as a Basis for Monetary Policy

This is IEA conference volume no. 131

Monetary Theory as a Basis for Monetary Policy

Edited by

Axel Leijonhufvud
University of Trento

palgrave

in association with
International Economic Association

First published 2001 by
PALGRAVE
Houndmills, Basingstoke, Hampshire RG21 6XS and
175 Fifth Avenue, New York, N. Y. 10010
Companies and representatives throughout the world

PALGRAVE is the new global academic imprint of St. Martin's Press LLC Scholarly and Reference Division and Palgrave Publishers Ltd (formerly Macmillan Press Ltd).

ISBN 0–333–74892–1

This book is printed on paper suitable for recycling and made from fully managed and sustained forest sources.

A catalogue record for this book is available from the British Library.

Library of Congress Cataloging-in-Publication Data
Monetary theory as a basis for monetary policy : papers of the IEA conference held in Trento, Italy / edited by Axel Leijonhufvud.
p. cm. — (International Economic Association series)
Papers of the conference held on Sept. 4–7, 1997 at the University of Trento.
"In association with International Economic Association."
Includes bibliographical references and indexes.
ISBN 0–333–74892–1
1. Monetary policy—Congresses. 2. Inflation (Finance)––Congresses. 3. Money—Congresses. I. Leijonhufvud, Axel. II. International Economic Association. III. Series.

HG230.3 .M666 2001
332.4'6—dc21

2001021744

10 9 8 7 6 5 4 3 2 1
10 09 08 07 06 05 04 03 02 01

Printed and bound in Great Britain by
Antony Rowe Ltd, Chippenham, Wiltshire

Contents

Part II Monetary and Financial Instability

The International Economic Association

A non-profit organization with purely scientific aims, the International Economic Association (IEA) was founded in 1950. It is a federation of some sixty national economic associations in all parts of the world. Its basic purpose is the development of economics as an intellectual discipline, recognizing a diversity of problems, systems and values in the world and taking note of methodological diversities.

The IEA has, since its creation, sought to fulfill that purpose by promoting mutual understanding among economists through the organization of scientific meetings and common research programmes, and by means of publications on problems of fundamental as well as current importance. Deriving from its long concern to assure professional contact between East and West, and North and South, the IEA pays special attention to issues of economies in systemic transition and in the course of development. During its nearly fifty years of existence, it has organized more than a hundred round-table conferences for specialists on topics ranging from fundamental theories to methods and tools of analysis and major problems of the present-day world. Participation in round tables is at the invitation of a specialist programme committee, but twelve triennial World Congresses have regularly attracted the participation of individual economists from all over the world.

The Association is governed by a Council, comprising representatives of all member associations, and by a fifteen-member Executive Committee which is elected by the Council. The Executive Committee (1995–98) at the time of the Trento Conference was:

President:	Professor Jacques H. Drèze, Belgium
Vice-President:	Professor Anne Krueger, USA
Treasurer:	Professor Erich W. Streissler, Austria
Past President:	Professor Michael Bruno, Israel (deceased 26 December 1996)
Other members:	Professor Anthony B. Atkinson, UK Professor Vittorio Corbo, Chile Professor Karel Dyba, Czech Republic Professor Jean-Michel Grandmont, France

Sir Austin Robinson was an active Adviser on the publication of IEA Conference proceedings from 1954 until his final short illness in 1993.

The Association has also been fortunate in having secured many outstanding economists to serve as President:
Gottfried Haberler (1950–53), Howard S. Ellis (1953–56), Erik Lindahl (1956–59), E. A. G. Robinson (1959–62), Ugo Papi (1962–65), Paul A. Samuelson (1965–68). Erik Lundberg (1968–71), Fritz Machlup (1971–74), Edmund Malinvaud (1974–77), Shigeto Tsuru (1977–80), Victor L. Urquidi (1980–83), Kenneth J. Arrow (1983–86), Amartya Sen (1986–89), Anthony B. Atkinson (1989–92), and Michael Bruno (1992–95).

The activities of the Association are mainly funded from the subscriptions of members and grants from a number of organizations, including continuing support from UNESCO, through the International Social Science Council.

Acknowledgements

I thank the members of the Programme Committee, Daniel Heymann, Niels Thygesen, Thomas Sargent and Ignazio Visco, for their recommendations and advice. Regrettably, in the end, the two last mentioned were not able to attend. Discussions and correspondence with most of the participants, and with several people who would have liked to, but could not, attend also helped to shape the programme. Even if I have not listed them all, I have not forgotten their assistance.

Professor Michael Kaser, as General Editor of the International Economic Association, undertook the final editing of the manuscript – a hard job that I am infinitely grateful to have escaped.

The core funding for the conference was provided by the University of Trento, through the Department of Economics, and I am grateful to Rector Massimo Egidi, Chairman Geremia Gios and to my colleagues for their generosity in supporting the initiative. The foundation of the Cassa di Risparmio di Trento e Rovereto (CARITRO), through the mediation of its chairman, Professor Giovanni Pegoretti, and the European Financial Group, through its chairman, Dr Spiro Latsis, were major sponsors of the conference, as, thanks to Dr Ignazio Visco, was Banca d'Italia. Contributions were also received from Monte dei Paschi di Siena and Consiglio Nazionale delle Ricerche.

Finally, I come to a group of friends without whose ideas, initiatives and hard work, nothing would have worked as it should, and did! My colleagues Roberto Tamborini and especially Elisabetta de Antoni were of great help as members of the local organizing board. Although 'unlisted', Daniela Silvestri and Earlene Craver-Leijonhufvud also deserve credit as such. Morena Carli and Rosa Doneddu not only ran the secretariat with the faultless, cheerful efficiency that so many participants have remarked upon subsequently, but they also assisted for many months with the logistical planning, the correspondence and the accounting for the conference. I am deeply grateful to them all.

List of Contributors*

Carluccio Bianchi, University of Pavia, Italy
Luigi Bonatti, University of Trento, Italy
Michael Bordo, Rutgers University, New Brunswick and NBER, USA
John W. Crow, Former Governor, Bank of Canada
Jacques H. Drèze, CORE, Université Catholique de Louvain, Belgium
Sylvester Eijffinger, Tilburg University, Netherlands; College of Europe, Bruges, Belgium; and Humboldt University of Berlin, Germany
Francesco Farina, University of Siena, Italy
Jean-Paul Fitoussi, Institut d'Études Politiques de Paris, France
Giorgio Fodor, University of Trento, Italy
Jean-Luc Gaffard, University of Nice Sophia-Antipolis, France
Jean-Michel Grandmont, Centre de Recherche en Economie et Statistique, Paris, France
Dale W. Henderson, Federal Reserve Board, Washington DC, USA
Daniel Heymann, United Nations Economic Commission for Latin America, Torcuato di Tella Institute and University of Buenos Aires, Argentina
Seppo Honkapohja, University of Helsinki, Finland
Otmar Issing, Deutsche Bundesbank, Frankfurt, Germany
Lars Jonung, Stockholm School of Economics, Sweden
Martin Kaufman, International Monetary Fund, Washington DC, USA
Jinill Kim, University of Virginia, Charlottesville, USA
David Laidler, University of Western Ontario, Canada
Axel Leijonhufvud, University of Trento, Italy
Robert E. Lucas Jr, University of Chicago, USA
Ramon Marimon, European University Institute, Florence, Italy and Universitat Pompeu Fabra, Barcelona, Spain
Jacques Mélitz, University of Strathclyde, Glasgow, UK and Centre de Recherche en Economie et Statistique, Paris, France
Robert A. Mundell, Columbia University, New York, USA
Mustapha K. Nabli, The World Bank, Washington DC, USA
Luigi Pasinetti, Catholic University, Milan, Italy

*Including contributors to the companion volume, *Monetary Theory and Policy Experience*.

Heracles Polemarchakis, CORE Université Catholique de Louvain, Belgium
Pedro pou, Central Bank of Argentina, Buenos Aires, Argentina
Pier Luigi Sacco, University of Bologna, Italy
Pablo Sanguinetti, University Torcuato di Tella, Buenos Aires, Argentina
Kumiharu Shigehara, Organisation for Economic Co-operation and Development, Paris, France
Hans-Werner Sinn, University of Munich, Germany
Luigi Spaventa, University of Rome La Sapienza, Italy
Erich W. Streissler, University of Vienna, Austria
Roberto Tamborini, University of Trento, Italy
Niels Thygesen, University of Copenhagen, Denmark and Centre for European Policy Studies, Brussels, Belgium
Juan Urrutia, Universidad Carlos III, Madrid, Spain
Albert M. Wojnilower, The Clipper Group and Craig Drill Capital, New York, USA

List of Abbreviations and Acronyms

AEA	American Economic Association
AL	Alesina's central bank legal-independence index
CAPM	capital asset pricing model
CB	central bank
CBI	central bank independence
CD	certificate of deposit
CEPR	Centre for Economic Policy Research (London)
CIS	Commonwealth of Independent States
CORE	Center for Operations Research and Econometrics (Louvain-la-Neuve)
CNRS	Centre National de la Recherche Scientifique (France)
CREST	Centre de Recherche en Economie et Statistique (France)
CPI	consumer price index
DC	developed country
DM	Deutsche Mark
d.o.n.i.	degree of nominal indeterminancy
DP	Drèze-Polemarchakis
E15	European Union (15 member states)
ECB	European Central Bank
ECU	European Currency Unit
EEC	European Economic Community
EMI	European Monetary Institute
EMS	European Monetary System
EMU	Economic and Monetary Union
ERM	Exchange Rate Mechanism
ES	Eiffinger and Schaling (central bank legal-independence index)
ESCB	European System of Central Bankers
EU	European Union
FMP	Federal Reserve–MIT–University of Pennsylvania econometric model
FOI	financial opposition to inflation
FOMC	Federal Open Market Committee
G-7(10)	Group of Seven (Ten)
GCB	group central bank
GDP	gross domestic product

GMT	Grilli, Masciandaro and Tabellini (political and economic independence index)
GNP	gross national product
HKS	Heymann–Kaufman–Sanguinetti
i.i.d.	independently identically distributed
IGE	intertemporal general equilibrium
IMF	International Monetary Fund
IT	inflation targeting
LDC	less developed country
LVAU	unweighted legal-independence index
LVAW	weighted legal-independence index
MCI	monetary conditions indicator
Mercosur	Southern Cone Common Market
NAFTA	North American Free Trade Agreement
NAIRU	non-accelerating inflation rate of unemployment
NBER	National Bureau of Economic Research (Cambridge, Mass.)
OECD	Organisation for Economic Co-operation and Development
OLS	ordinary least squares
OPEC	Organization of Petroleum Exporting Countries
POI	public opposition to inflation
PPP	purchasing power parity
PSI	political system index
RPI	relative price inversion
REIT	real estate investment trust
SDR	Special Drawing Right
SUMLV	sum of legal-independence variables
TOR	turnover rate of central bank governors
TSLS	two-stage least squared regression
VAR	vector autoregression
VAT	value-added tax

Introduction

Axel Leijonhufvud
University of Trento, Italy

The present volume is one of two resulting from the conference on 'Monetary Theory as a Basis for Monetary Policy' held in Trento in September 1997. The second, entitled *Monetary Theory and Policy Experience*, is being published separately in the International Economic Association–Palgrave series.

The planning for the conference began in the summer of 1996, well before the Asian plunges into depression. But even if the theme did not adumbrate such dramatic developments or their further ramifications in Russia and elsewhere, it concerned related issues.

The conference was intended to start a debate over the relationship between current economic theory and central bank practice. Monetary neutrality has gained a stronger hold over theory since the inflationary 1970s, starting with the monetarist doctrines that the Philips curve is vertical and that inflation expectations explain nominal interest rates, later becoming embedded in more fully articulated models of intertemporal general equilibrium. The theory resulting from this development leaves central banks with nothing useful to do except to stabilize the price level. It is not an altogether unwelcome doctrine among central bankers, as it would make their lives easier: in giving them only a single goal variable, it frees them from responsibility for difficult trade-offs and, in addition, it has become the basis of the recent fashion for giving central banks independence from political authority.

All this takes for granted, however, that central banks can control only nominal magnitudes and have no useful powers to affect real variables such as output, growth and employment. Earlier theories of monetary policy, on the other hand, were based on the belief that they were able to affect the real interest rate and to regulate the real volume of credit. They also presumed a need on occasion for policy to dampen the credit cycle or, that having failed, to step in as a lender of last resort. Implicitly at least, both central banks and financial markets still pay some heed to these earlier theories, as the use of Bank Rate is back in fashion and the markets react to its use in the belief that real growth, and not only inflation, is at stake. And, obviously, recent events have driven home the lesson that it is not altogether safe to relinquish all responsibility for the credit cycle.

These issues are spelt out at greater length in my introductory essay in Chapter 1, which also argues that, in the context of monetary regimes that give the authorities some leverage over real interest rates, the vertical Phillips curve is an oversimplified hypothesis that needs to be reassessed.

The three chapters in Part I are all written from a general equilibrium perspective. Jacques Drèze and Heracles Polemarchakis investigate the scope for monetary policy in a complete markets Arrow–Debreu model with inside money which is demanded for its convenience in making payments. The monetary authorities control the nominal interest rates that constitute the opportunity cost of holding this money. A state-contingent policy rule for setting these rates will not suffice to control the variability of inflation. The authors go on, therefore, to explore 'empirically relevant departures from neutrality' that would give more leverage for policy.

Ramon Marimon takes the 'fiscal theory of money' as his point of departure. In this theory, which is associated above all with the names Sims and Woodford, the price level will stay constant as long as the government obeys its intertemporal budget constraint in the sense that the present value of expenditures is covered by the present value of taxes. If expenditures were to exceed taxes, the price level must move so as to bring in an equivalent inflation tax. Marimon applies the same reasoning to the theory of the firm and shows that, in a model which allows for the possibility that the firm will not honour its intertemporal budget constraint, the Modigliani–Miller theorem will not hold.

Robert Lucas revives Milton Friedman's optimum quantity of money idea and explores the possible welfare gains from deflating at a rate sufficient to push nominal interest rates to a level near zero.[1] The welfare gains are found to vary considerably, depending on how the necessary extrapolation of empirical demand curves into the near zero interest rate range is carried out.

Financial instability commands the attention of the first two chapters of Part II. Both have one thing in common: namely, that they see the dangers of financial instability as stemming from economic reforms, changes in regulations or rapid financial development which create an environment with which market participants and policymakers have not had sufficient experience. Albert Wojnilower reviews financial developments in the USA over the past twenty years. Although generalized credit crunches have been avoided during this period, he finds that the structural changes that have taken place in American financial markets give little assurance that they will not recur in the future. Indeed, he concludes that, when they do, central banks may find them more difficult to deal with than in the past.

The chapter by Daniel Heymann, Martin Kaufman and Pablo Sanguinetti is motivated by a number of Latin-American boom-and-bust episodes that have followed a roughly similar pattern. The booms were initiated by comprehensive economic reforms, including inflation stabilization. For a period, increases in both investment and consumption could be sustained by trade deficits financed by capital inflows, but eventually a slowdown in growth would induce a cessation or reversal of capital flows and trigger sharp recessions. The authors focus on the difficulties of forming correct expectations of investment returns and wealth following an abrupt structural break such at that represented by the reforms. They go on to demonstrate how even fairly sophisticated expectations-formation schemes may easily produce the kind of overshooting and subsequent sharp setbacks that are the stylized facts of these historical episodes.

Jean-Paul Fitoussi reviews European macroeconomic developments and the policies of the E15 since the beginning of the 1980s, but focusing particularly on unemployment problems and the disappointingly 'soft' growth in the 1990s. The evidence, he finds, points to high real interest rates (and a negatively-sloped real term structure) as the proximate cause, and too restrictive monetary policies as the ultimate culprit. Alternative explanations are carefully considered but rejected. Fitoussi's conclusion: 'the battle against inflation must be terminated, because the phenomenon has disappeared'. Subsequent to the conference, of course, France and the other member countries of the European Monetary Union have come to enjoy the monetary conditions that Fitoussi pleaded for, and their growth rates have picked up, so far without inflation.

One of the aims of the conference was to restart a debate on the role of credit in monetary theory and on the role of central banks in the regulation of the (real) price and volume of credit. In this ambition, the conference did not quite succeed. But it did bring together a number of outstanding monetary economists from around the world, and the reader will find much stimulus from their contributions.

Note

1 This chapter is based on Lucas's Presidential Lecture to the Econometrics Society and is reprinted here with the permission of the editor of *Econometrica*.

1
Monetary Theory and Central Banking

Axel Leijonhufvud
University of Trento, Italy

1 Policy doctrines: changing context, changing content

In the 1970s, in the waning days of the so-called Keynesian consensus, macropolicy was still stabilization policy. It was believed that the private sector was unstable, but that the discretionary policies of a benevolent, competent and consistent government could maintain high employment and reasonable price stability.

This pessimism about the private sector and optimism about government of that earlier time has turned into optimism about the market and pessimism about democratic government. This great, underlying shift in beliefs and attitudes has changed the context in which monetary policy is being debated – and therefore, also the content of the debate.

At the time of writing, policy theory has become the art of constraining governments, of fashioning institutions to prevent politicians from violating intertemporal budget constraints, and more generally from engaging in short-sighted, time-inconsistent policies that in the end produce only inflation. The current vogue for independent central banks pursuing low inflation targets is largely motivated by this view that governments must be restrained forcefully from mismanaging public finances. The arguments for independence meet with little dissent from within the central banks.

At the same time, in modern theory, the stability of the private sector is supposed to take care of itself. Stabilization policy, in the old sense, is regarded as a misguided ambition. This doctrine would relieve the monetary authorities of any responsibility for unemployment and the cycle. Yet, it is not one they would be wise to embrace.

This great change in the prevailing political economy did not occur without reason. It is in large part a response to the great worsening of the fiscal position of so many national governments in the 1970s and 1980s. Governments saddled with large debts and running chronic deficits cannot entertain Keynesian ambitions. Keynesian economics had its beginnings in a world of failed banks, bankrupt businesses and foreclosed farms – and perfectly sound public finances. Governments of undoubted creditworthiness, with peacetime records of always spending well below their capacity to tax, were in a position where they could borrow and spend to ease the liquidity constraints of an over-leveraged private sector, and thus stimulate aggregate activity. They would be able to do so without adding to the money supply and without necessarily causing inflation. The 'functional finance' of Abba Lerner, which envisaged government surpluses in booms repaying the deficits of recessions, also kept the maintenance of the solvency of the government firmly in view.

In the 'rigid wages' brand of Keynesian economics, it was envisaged that real activity could be stimulated (or dampened) simply by inflating (or deflating) nominal aggregate demand. In Monetarist theory, the real effects of monetary policy also depended on the stickiness of nominal wages. In macrotheories of these varieties, the issue of the creditworthiness of governments was lost from sight. It had to be rediscovered. The work on intertemporal monetary general equilibrium models by Sargent and Wallace at Minnesota[1] brought it back into focus.

The importance of government solvency was, however, also being forcefully demonstrated in practice by the experience with high inflation in a number of (at the time, mostly Latin American) countries. What these experiences showed was that impecunious governments, lacking credit, cannot stimulate aggregate activity. Printing money will not only produce high inflation, but also actually depress real activity so that disinflation and stabilization generate a growth spurt (see, for example, Heymann and Leijonhufvud (1995)).

The governments of Western Europe and North America have not been in this situation, of course. But while governments with high outstanding debts and additional large unfunded liabilities may not be utterly powerless in this sense, they are in the risk zone. If the markets come to conclude that the polity of a country is unlikely ever to deal effectively with chronic deficits, interest rates on its debt will increase and the acceptable maturities shorten. In this risk zone, additional deficit spending will raise the rate of inflation and cause exchange depreciation, but have little or no effect on aggregate activity and employment. And a monetary policy that monetizes past deficits will do no better.

The deterioration of the public finances of many industrialized countries up through the 1980s is thus one reason – one good reason –

why we hear less today about macroeconomic measures to combat unemployment. But it is not the only good reason.

The industrialized economies are far more highly integrated today than they were a few decades ago. Foreign trade looms much larger in relation to GDP, while capital moves freely around the world, and moves more readily, perhaps, in response to lower taxes than lower wages. For small, open economies, therefore, the room for independent macroeconomic policies is all but non-existent – and every country is 'smaller' in the relevant sense than it used to be.

Other developments have contributed to changing the context, and thus the content of debate. The constraints on the macropolicies that are feasible have tightened at a time when the pressures for structural change are unrelenting. Manufacturing as a source of employment is going the way that agriculture has already gone in the twentieth century – and it is probably receding even faster, although the pace is impossible to foresee. The same forces of technological change are eliminating many traditional white-collar jobs as well.

But, if the response to the European unemployment problems since the 1980s has been little more than pleas for more labour market 'micro flexibility', the tightening feasibility constraints on macropolicy are not the only reasons. It is also, of course, that monetary theory has changed, and changed drastically.

2 New theory and old

Traditionally, monetary policy theory has had two main preoccupations: nominal anchoring and the stability of credit. The first set of questions concerns how the nominal scale of relative prices is determined, and how to assure that the anchor does not drag or let go, causing inflation. These questions were more or less neglected in the older central banking literature that took a metallic standard for granted. Concern with the golden anchor that might let go prompted Wicksell's 'pure credit economy' model of 1898, but the theory of inconvertible fiat money became of dominant importance, first with the great inflations of the 1920s. The monetary theory since the 1970s has advanced our understanding in this area very considerably. The 'monetarist arithmetic' and related capital theoretic developments have, in particular, clarified the fiscal conditions of monetary stability.

At the same time, modern monetary theory represents a break with the main tradition of central banking doctrine, which was concerned with controlling the credit cycle to avoid financial crashes and bank panics, and with managing the system's reserves so that the convertibility of bank money into the standard commodity could *almost* always be defended. Today's theory may have rediscovered the importance of the solvency of governments, but has rather lost sight of the solvency of the private sector and more particularly of the banking system. In assuming that the economy is in intertemporal general equilibrium (IGE), it in effect assumes away the problems with which older central banking theories sought to cope. The following properties of the IGE model are germane:

(i) physical assets and financial claims are seen as objectively knowable probability distributions of future cash flows; agents with rational expectations know these distributions;
(ii) real interest rates co-ordinate consumption and production plans to maintain the economy on the intertemporal efficiency frontier;
(iii) discounting the correctly perceived prospects (i) at the equilibrium real rate (ii) means that the wealth of the system is correctly evaluated;
(iv) consistent pricing of all assets and claims means that a generalized form of the Modigliani–Miller theorem holds: the value of the economy's income prospects is independent of financial structure; only those physical and human capital assets that would appear in the economy's consolidated balance sheet are relevant to the determination of the price level and to real aggregate demand; thus 'inside' money, and more generally the volume of credit in the system is of no macroeconomic consequence; and
(v) the nominal scale of the economy is determined by (the time-path of) the stock of outside money.

Within such a conceptual framework, the only sensible function remaining for a central bank is to provide nominal stability by control of the 'outside' money supply (in so far as government fiscal policy makes such control possible). Attempts to regulate real activity are as senseless as they are futile. The bank has no power over real rates of interest and no sensible purpose would be served by attempts to regulate the volume of credit.

Whatever it is Greenspan thinks he is doing, this is not it.

3 A brief retrospective

Contrast this modern theoretical framework to some older, once influential theories:

3.1 Wicksell

In Wicksell's 'cumulative process', competition between banks with excess reserves depresses the market rate below the real intertemporal equilibrium ('natural') rate. The result is inflation fuelled by expansion of inside money.

Wicksellian theory therefore differs from the modern theory on two critical points: (i) that the market real rate of interest may differ from the equilibrium rate; and (ii) that inside money plays a crucial role in explaining the time-path of the price level.

3.2 The art of central banking

The central banking doctrine that evolved in the gold standard world presumed that the gradually growing world stock of gold, and the private sector's gradual learning to economize on gold reserves, determined the trend of the price level. But general expansions of trade and bank credit may drive prices above this trend, just as credit contractions may drive them below it. The 'trade cycle' consisted of alternating periods of 'high' and 'low' prices (relative to the equilibrium level or trend). 'High prices' would stimulate output and employment, but high prices in one country relative to the rest of the world would cause an 'external drain' of reserves that in severe cases could precipitate a banking crisis.

The primary function of the central bank in this setting was to moderate the trade cycle so that the exchange rate could always be defended, and banking crises avoided. The instrument for doing so was the Bank Rate. But the bank should also provide an 'elastic currency' so as not to prevent output growth. The judgement of how much 'elasticity' could be allowed without inflationary overheating of the economy made central banking an 'art'. A secondary function was that of lender of last resort, especially in those instances when an external drain was amplified by an internal drain, threatening a general bank panic.

3.3 Mises and Hayek

The monetary cycle theory of the Austrians hypothesized that the lowering of the real rate of interest associated with a Wicksellian inflation must raise the level of investment, especially in durable capital, and thus distort the allocation of resources.

In this overinvestment theory, while monetary expansion is inflationary, it is not neutral. Although Austria had suffered through an outside money hyperinflation after the First World War, this Austrian cycle theory was set in a gold (exchange) standard context. It is inside money that expands in the cyclical upswing. The gold anchoring of the nominal scale should sooner or later force reversion to the longer-term trend of the price level. Rational expectations within such a regime imply that expansions and contractions of the banking system's monetary (demand) liabilities have their counterpart in expansions and contractions, not only of the nominal, but in large part also of the real volume of credit in the economy.

In an over-investment process, realized returns will be lower in real terms than initially projected. Thus much of the credit extended may in fact be unsound. For some periods, unanticipated inflation may make creditors carry part, all, or more than all of the losses. But in anchored monetary regimes, the demand for base money will begin to recover as soon as inflation slows. This will slow inflation further and in turn reinforce the incentives to restore liquidity positions. Prices are then likely to fall below the level at which credit was granted, which will cause widespread solvency problems.

For several decades of Keynesian and then Monetarist domination, the over-investment theory was taken seriously only by devotees of Austrian Economics. Recent events in Asia should give it new life!

3.4 Fisherian debt-deflation

In Irving Fisher's debt-deflation theory of great depressions, a deflationary shock to the system becomes endogenously self-amplifying. If, initially, the economy had the equilibrium volume of inside credit, a fall in the price level will make its real value larger than either debtors or creditors desire. The attempt by debtors to improve their cash-flow to avoid default will increase excess supplies in all goods markets. This, in turn, exacerbates the deflation and the real value of outstanding debts grows still larger. The feedback is deviation-amplifying, carrying the system further and further away from a Modigliani–Miller equilibrium.

Fisher's original theory pertained to a closed system with a single currency. A variant, updated for our times, would put debt-deflation in a multiple currency, flexible exchange rate context. Consider the case where the capital inflow to a particular country reverses so that its exchange rate starts to depreciate significantly.[2] This may happen for a number of reasons – one being fears about the solvency of the private sector in the wake of an over-investment boom. If at this juncture the private sector has large dollar-denominated indebtedness, a scramble for dollars in order to liquidate it before the exchange rate falls further may ensue. This will amplify the decline of the exchange rate and make matters worse. Foreign lenders, acting individually and watching the solvency of debtors erode, will not stabilize the situation. '*Sauve qui peut*' –

and the Devil take the hindmost. This process will take the exchange rate (of the baht, rupiah or won, for instance) far below the level consistent with longer-term trade fundamentals.

3.5 Keynes

Keynes's theory was fundamentally adaptive (Leijonhufvud (1998)). Agents would adapt their quantities demanded and supplied to not always anticipated changes in prices; they would change prices in response to not always foreseen excess demands or supplies. This collective learning process could fail to home in on a full employment general equilibrium if conditions were such as to cause effective demand failures.

The first type of effective demand failure was intertemporal. Present saving is not an effective demand for future consumption; it may therefore fail to call forth corresponding investment. Similarly, investment may exceed saving, causing excess demand for goods and labour, and thus inflation. The central hypothesis was thus that, because of speculation or central bank intervention, the real interest rate might fail to co-ordinate transactor plans to maintain the system in intertemporal equilibrium.

Monetary policy is useful in this context in so far as it can be effective in nudging the real interest rate towards its 'natural' value (to use the Wicksellian term).

The second type of effective demand failure was at the root of Keynes's multiplier process: an excess supply of labour will not constitute an effective demand for consumer goods if the unemployed are without liquid means. Once the (downward) multiplier has been allowed to take hold, moreover, conventional monetary policy measures will be of limited use, at best.[3]

The distinction between inside and outside money was in general not clearly drawn in the Keynesian literature. In Keynes's *Treatise*, cyclical variations in the money supply are clearly changes in inside money, but in the *General Theory* the money supply is treated on the whole as an exogenously fixed stock of outside money. Except in the work of James Tobin, this ambiguity runs through *both* the later Keynesian[4] *and* the monetarist literature.

3.6 Keynesian economics

In later Keynesian theory, the analysis of intertemporal saving–investment co-ordination disappears entirely. It focuses instead on the relationship between nominal aggregate demand and the ('sticky') money wage.

The Keynesian analysis of monetary policy was carried out in the IS–LM framework. An increase in the money stock would depress the interest rate and stimulate current investment and consumption spending. If money wages are sticky, real output and employment rise.

This analysis is conceptually consistent *if* the monetary regime is operated to resemble a gold standard (albeit an attenuated gold standard). In such an institutional context, the central bank's open market purchases should be seen as injections of inside (reserve) money enabling a more general expansion of inside credit; moreover, rational expectations are that the price level will show reversion to trend. Equilibrium wages and prices in such a regime will not vary in proportion to the money stock (whether measured as M1 or M2).

3.7 Monetarism

Monetarist theory postulates an exogenously controlled or controllable money stock (in which outside and inside components are aggregated). Nominal income is determined by the condition that the amount of M1 (or M2) demanded equal this supply.

From Friedman's 'restatement' of the quantity theory (1956) onwards, credit has nothing to do with it. Early monetarist theory had a quite explicit polemical thrust, not only against theories emphasizing unmeasurable 'liquidity' or 'credit conditions' (Radcliffe Report, 1959) but also, for example, against Tobin's insistence that open market purchases did not have the same wealth effects as helicopter drops of currency.

From Friedman's AEA presidential address (1968) onwards, another element enters in: namely, the hypothesis that the real rate of interest is determined entirely by real factors over which the central bank has no control (and that observed variations in the market rate of interest should be interpreted as revealing changes in the Fisher expected inflation premium).

Even before the rational expectations development, therefore, monetarist doctrine was conceptually 'close' (on some admittedly undefined metric) to theories assuming intertemporal general equilibrium and generalized Modigliani–Miller.

3.8 Rational expectations monetarism

In Lucas's formal and more restrictive version of Friedmanian monetarism (Lucas 1972, 1975), changes in the stock of money may temporarily disequilibrate perceptions of the real rate of return, and thus affect activity levels. This transitory effect evaporates as the true value of M becomes known.

A whole literature of game-theoretical exercises purporting to constitute a political economy theory of monetary policy has been built on this Lucasian foundation.[5] In these models, central banks try to create 'unanticipated' inflation as often and as much as seems worth the loss of credibility and so on. Whether any central banker will recognize this as 'what goes on behind closed doors', I am not privileged to know (but I would be very much surprised if it were so.)

3.9 Intertemporal general equilibrium

Consistent centralized accounting (at equilibrium intertemporal prices) implies Ricardian equivalence and the ineffectiveness of open market operations. It also implies that the traditional quantity theory proposition that the equilibrium price level should vary in proportion to the contemporaneous stock of money is false (in this modelling context). Instead, the price level should vary in proportion to a present value measure of outside money (Wallace (1981), Sargent (1987)).

This requirement holds independently of the size of the outside money stock – that is, even if the outside money component is vanishingly small.

The apprehension is growing in some circles that smart cards may soon drive the demand for government-produced currency to the vanishing point. At the same time, the pressure is mounting to abolish reserve requirements (as in Canada, for example) to avoid keeping banks at a competitive disadvantage.[6] The combination of these two developments would mean that the denominator of the standard base money multiplier is tending to zero. That would spell the realization, one century postponed, of the conditions envisaged by Wicksell (1898) in his 'pure credit economy' analysis (Leijonhufvud (1997)). But modern theory denies that there is a problem – beyond, perhaps, the choice of a new unit of account.[7]

4 The natural rate of unemployment

That 'the long-run Phillips curve is vertical' has long since become a widely accepted cliché[8] among economists. But it is at best a half-truth. As with most half-truths, it makes a dangerous habit of mind. It has become the linchpin of the current policy passivity doctrine which dictates that monetary policy should not be used to attempt to 'steer' real variables, such as unemployment or the rate of growth.

The half that is very nearly true – or almost always true – states that inflation will become expected, that expected inflation will shift the short-run Phillips curve, and that purely inflationary policies, when fully expected, will not have significant, predictable effects on employment. Suppose for simplicity that outside money is not just neutral, but superneutral, and consider inflation driven by outside money. If we now imagine that the history of the economy was to have been one of *x* per cent outside money inflation higher than what in fact took place, we should also imagine the scatter of Phillips data points to have been *x* per cent higher. In this type of counterfactual conceptual experiment, every point in the scatter gives rise to a 'vertical Phillips curve'.

At base, the argument stems from the conviction that, as long as money is neutral, no significant social problem can be solved merely by printing the stuff. This is not always true, however, since situations can occur in which purely inflationary policies will actually help – although these may also be the situations in which it proves peculiarly difficult to inflate (or reflate): namely, in the aftermath of a great financial collapse such as that of 1929–33 or, more generally, in cases of depressions primarily or largely caused by large overhangs of 'bad loans'.

The half of the cliché that is untrue – almost always untrue – speaks of the vertical Phillips curve in the singular, as a unique locus located at the 'natural rate of unemployment' (NAIRU). The natural rate hypothesis is obviously not a necessary condition for inflation to shift the short-run Phillips curve, but in his famous presidential address (Friedman 1968), which became the beginning of the end for Keynesian aggregate demand management policies, Friedman introduced it as an integral part of his particular explanation of the expectational dynamics of the process. His theory presupposed that all deviations in the historical scatter of the actual from the natural unemployment rate arose from accelerations and decelerations in inflation that were not fully and symmetrically anticipated. Note that these should be outside money inflations in which the ratio of inside to outside money remains constant. Inside money inflations, which is to say credit inflations, cannot be extrapolated confidently and are not neutral. In Friedman's theory, this inside–outside distinction is not made. But we have no reason to suppose that all price level changes in the historical Phillips scatter were caused by nominal impulses of the pure 'outside' variety.

The NAIRU doctrine implies that unemployment will converge on the natural rate as soon as wages have caught up[9] with previous changes in the money supply. This is not generally true. Yet the idea that the achievement of full employment depends only on adjustments in the labour market was not one to which 'sticky wages' Keynesians were apt to take exception. Their response, rather, had to be 'stickier than thou, Milton'. But it marks a relapse of macroeconomics into the kind of pre-Keynesian partial equilibrium thinking that treats the 'rest state' of the labour market as being independent of the state of all the other markets in the system.

The simplicities of early Keynesian theory should have sufficed as mental inoculation against the NAIRU doctrine. Ages ago, the Keynesian Cross used to be the vehicle for demonstrating that, if at the full employment rate of output, X^*, saving exceeded investment, real income and employment would have to fall until $S(X) = I$, at some level $X < X^*$. Flexible wages will not suffice the restore full employment in this situation.[10] Friedman's proposition, Keynes would have said, is true if, and only if, we restrict ourselves to cases of perfect co-ordination of saving and investment intentions. We can translate Keynes into Wicksellian language to underscore the point: $S(X^*) > I$ implies $r > r^*$; that is, when full employment saving exceeds investment, the market rate of interest exceeds the natural rate.[11] Intertemporal prices are wrong.

The natural rate doctrine, in other words, carries with it the implicit assumption that the system is always in intertemporal equilibrium.[12] This is a strong assumption, to say the least.[13] Keynes once pointed out that Ricardo had reached the conclusion that the rate of profit uniquely determined the (real) rate of interest because he assumed full employment. Presumably he would have criticized Friedman for having assumed Ricardo's conclusion in order to conclude Ricardo's assumption.[14] Accepting either proposition on faith will make the other seem plausible. As we saw in the previous section, virtually all those problems with which older theories of central banking sought to cope would simply disappear if intertemporal activities were to be perfectly co-ordinated at all times. That stabilization policy might be as ineffective as it is 'inappropriate'[15] in such a world does not come as a surprise.

Yet the particular case of intertemporal lack of co-ordination that preoccupied Keynes does not seem of much relevance currently. Excessive household saving,[16] or lack of government spending, or bearish speculation have not been the plagues of recent years. It is helpful, instead, to focus on the financial behaviour implied by Keynes's $S > I$ analysis. In his case, the marginal efficiency of investment was declining, but bear speculation on the exchanges prevented the real long-term rate of interest from declining at the same pace. The speculators would move their funds down towards the short and liquid end of the term structure. At the end of the chain of substitutions would emerge an excess demand for (outside) money. If there is no accommodating increase in the supply of outside money, income would then have to fall.

We recognize this attempt to build up liquidity from a number of other situations that are also associated with intertemporal disequilibrium and with unemployment. Perhaps the worst such situation occurs when an entire banking system is scrambling back from the brink of disaster. In this case, a third type of effective demand failure, not drawn from the *General Theory*, may result: prospective future revenues, contingent on present capital investment, will not translate into the effective demand for present resources required to realize that investment. Growth declines when it cannot be financed.

Other examples that should be of concern to central bankers are not hard to find. When capital inflows to Mexico or Argentina reverse, for example, interest rates in the domestic market move up relative to the prospective return to capital and, as the supply of short-term capital drains abroad, a liquidity crunch develops that is associated with a sharp rise in unemployment.[17] When big bubbles in real estate collapse in Japan or Sweden, leaving banks and other lenders in a morass of non-performing loans, all-around attempts to ensure solvency and restore liquidity to balance sheets plunge the economies into recession. The rise in unemployment, which in some of these cases has been abrupt, large and persistent, should not be interpreted as a shift of NAIRU (brought on by increasing 'inflexibility' in the respective labour markets). Like the present South East Asian crises, these are the kind of credit-fuelled booms and busts that traditionally were the responsibility of central banks to prevent or to moderate – or else to clean up afterwards.

Belief in the wrong part of the half-truth has consequences. In particular, it leaves no alternative explanation for European unemployment than that, for reasons seldom given, the natural rate must have shifted up into double digits, and that various specifically European labour-market inflexibilities keeps it there. And it is also taken to mean that macroeconomic policies in general, or monetary policy in particular, cannot do anything about it.[18] Hard-nosed realism is fine, but can we be sure that this is indeed realism?

5 Monetary regimes

For monetary policy to be at all effective in regulating real aggregate demand, it must have some leverage over real interest rates (and perhaps other credit or financial market conditions). The question then becomes: under what conditions will the central bank have 'real' powers? When is monetary policy not equivalent to some sort of trivial currency reform that multiplies nominal values by some constant?

A second question also arises. Clearly, monetary policy aimed at real interest rates and credit conditions, with the ultimate targets being real aggregate demand and employment, must be adaptive, governed by assessments of current conditions. Can central banks be given the discretion to pursue such policies without creating the kind of 'random walk monetary standard'[19] that was suffered around the early 1980s?

The distinction between inside and outside money used to be a simple bookkeeping matter. Money issued directly or indirectly against someone's debt, such that it would be extinguished on the repayment of that debt, was inside money. Money not created against debt – but injected into the system by deficit spending, or, according to time-honoured classroom examples, by 'helicopter drops' or as gifts by the 'tooth fairy' – was outside money. Additions to outside money create a pure real balance effect: the price level must rise to bring perceived and realizable wealth into line and thus re-equilibrate the system. The credit transactions that result in inside money being created are offsetting moves by borrower and lender along their respective intertemporal budget constraints. If they take place at equilibrium real interest rates, the excess demand for present goods and thus the price level should be unaffected.

Intertemporal general equilibrium theory has made the inside–outside distinction, on the one hand, conceptually clearer, and on the other, operationally all but impossible. Gurley and Shaw (1960), who introduced the distinction, brought it to bear simply on the private sector's consolidated balance sheet in the current period. Thus, for example, borrowed reserves were inside money, but the rest of the monetary base was regarded unambiguously as outside. The 'fiscalist' IGE approach to monetary theory[20] makes clear that, in principle, the entire future course of government deficits and surpluses is relevant to the determination of whether an open market operation, for example, should have the real balance effect of an outside money injection or a real liquidity effect. Money that is issued to finance a government deficit today but is foreseen to be retired through a corresponding surplus tomorrow does not give rise to a real balance effect since it does not alter the calculation of the private sector's net worth evaluated at current nominal prices. So it is not inflationary. But in the meantime it eases credit conditions.

An econometrician could handle the Gurley–Shaw concepts. But what is to be done with the conceptually correct intertemporal ones? To make them operational, one would have to predict the entire future time-path of taxes and expenditure. If fiscal policy evolves adaptively as a sequence of short-horizon political compromises, this is not an enviable task.

Consider, then, the problem of some ordinary transactor. For concreteness, let us suppose a seller for whom it would be rational to vary the price he sets in proportion to changes in outside money. If he fails to raise prices when outside money is increased, he will incur losses. But the consequences of mistaking changes in inside money for changes in outside money would be just as bad. Keying on Friedman's M2, for instance, would not have been a strategy with much survival value for most of the twentieth century.

Thus agents face a signal extraction problem: namely, how to distinguish outside from inside money changes. Under certain regimes, they can do so with a high degree of confidence. If a person has lived under conditions of high inflation for years, for instance, it is rational to act on the understanding that the money printed to cover today's deficit is not going to be offset by future surpluses. But under other circumstances, the signal extraction can be exceedingly difficult. It may be, for instance, that the very slow adjustment of nominal interest rates to the US inflation of the 1970s and the equally lengthy period that it took for them to come back down to 'normal' in the 1980s, reflect in part the time it takes the market first to learn and then again to unlearn changes in the fiscal-monetary regime.

It is instructive to examine alternative monetary regimes from the perspective of this particular signal extraction problem. How difficult or easy is it, under a given regime, to determine whether credit obtained today will have to be paid back in money of roughly the same purchasing power or in 'debased coin'? Is the banking system's nominal lending 'real' or based on growth in outside money?

Since the late 1800s, the Western monetary system has evolved from one relying on commodity convertibility to one depending on state control of the quantity of fiat base money. It is with the quantity control system that the problem of ensuring a predictable nominal scale has become so acute that, time and again, rigid rules of one kind or another are proposed that would deprive the monetary authorities of the discretionary ability to pursue stabilization policy.

Convertible systems have problems of their own. The classical gold standard was not all that predictable: the value of gold was subject to new discoveries; to new techniques of extraction; to the decisions by countries to abandon silver or bimetalism for gold; and to the pyramiding of bank reserves and other technical progress in the payment mechanism. Its most important defect was probably its endogenous tendency to evolve into steadily more attenuated and politicized forms – ending in the present system. In any case, there is no reason to wish to have the 'barbarous relic' back – and no point in trying.

But fixed rate convertible systems had one crucial property that would be worth imitating: namely, their built-in mean reversion to the trend of the price level. Monetary policy under convertibility is Bank Rate policy. If the central bank in such a regime tries too hard to keep constant the growth-rate of some inside money aggregate, it will make the banking system 'inelastic' and thus interfere with recovery from recession or with the occasional acceleration of growth that is the appropriate system response to new Schumpeterian opportunities.[21]

Alternatively, it may go too far in stabilizing interest rates in order to accommodate the 'needs of trade', in which case its policy will amplify the fluctuations in activity levels and prices caused by the real business cycle. But since it cannot create outside money, its reserve position will prevent it from erring too far on the upside. More importantly, if it does err, it is forced to restore its depleted reserves before it can do so again. It is this need to manage reserves that will cause the mean-reversion of nominal prices to the trend set by the supply and demand for whatever serves as the outside money of the system.

In such a system, agents know that the rate of inflation is not going to develop as a random walk and, consequently, they will not extrapolate current changes in the price level. Price level expectations will tend to be inelastic, to use the old Hicksian term. Current money supply figures will have little or no information content for price setters.[22] Under such regimes, monetary policy stimuli reduce market interest rates, rather than raise them, and movements of the interest rate are seen as mainly real rate movements, although they may have a partial Fisher premium component as well.

For a central bank to have some, even if limited, leverage over real magnitudes, it is crucial that the general expectation of this mean reversion tendency be the rational expectation. Belief in it may be the only credibility that central banks need. But it is then preferable that it reflects, as far as possible, a 'built-in' institutional property of the regime, rather than the personal reputation of (say) a Volcker, a Greenspan – or a Duisenberg.

6 Transmission mechanisms

Monetary policy transmission is seldom analyzed as regime contingent. Most of the literature reads as if in pursuit of a 'general' theory. Yet the prevailing view among monetary economists of how transmission works and how 'effective' it may be has changed repeatedly over time. In retrospect, it seems obvious that these permutations of transmission theory have been largely driven – with some time-lag – by successive regime changes in the economic system under study (Leijonhufvud (1990)).

In the 1940s and 1950s, transmission was widely believed to be 'ineffective'. There were two versions of this ineffectiveness doctrine. One reflected the experience of the American Great Depression, whereas the other revealed the dawning realization in Europe of the constraints that fixed exchange rates impose on the monetary policy of non-key-currency countries.

6.1 Ineffective transmission 1

The American view was that high interest elasticities of money demand prevented increases in the money supply from depressing 'the' rate of interest significantly and that, besides, the interest-elasticities of investment and the other major spending categories were very low. Monetary policy was ineffective because each link in the main transmission chain was weak and unreliable.[23] A secondary transmission route, the real balance effect, was recognized 'in theory', but seen as having hardly any relevance 'in practice'.

Textbooks of the 1950s and early 1960s taught this view of the matter as 'Keynesian economics'. In the standard exposition, M, usually defined without regard to the inside/outside distinction, was independent of endogenous variables and unilaterally determined by the authorities. Whether M could be controlled was not a focal issue.

6.2 Ineffective transmission 2

The European view was more pessimistic about the ability of the monetary authorities to control M by open market operations and discount policy. In the 1950s, many European countries tried to escape the discipline of their external fixed-rate convertibility by exchange controls, and similarly tried to give their internal monetary policy more bite by various and sundry measures of credit rationing and capital market controls. In Britain, still trying to play the role of a major reserve currency country, the Radcliffe Report of 1959 did not so much dispute controllability as argue that quantity-control of any particular aggregate was pointless in view of the many alternative sources of liquidity in a financially highly developed economy.[24]

By the early 1960s, Tobin, Modigliani and other leading Keynesians had already moved away from these ineffectiveness doctrines. But the most effective challenge came from the monetarist side. The monetarist position has often met with the criticism that explicit monetarist theory did not explain why or how monetary impulses were supposed to be transmitted so strongly and so reliably. The secret to the effectiveness of monetarist transmission, so the quip went, was hidden from unfriendly inspection in a 'black box'.[25] This criticism seems a bit unfair, as one can count at least four distinct monetarist theories of the transmission mechanism.

6.3 Early monetarist-late Keynesian transmission

The first is the account from the early 1960s by Friedman and Schwartz. The main channel is the chain of substitution effects rippling through financial markets, finally to reach and affect the demand prices of producible assets. At this time, Friedman and Schwartz differed from Tobin or Modigliani, if at all, only in being more optimistic about the strength of each link in the causal chain from monetary impulse to real activity response.

6.4 Brunner and Meltzer transmission

Brunner (1970, 1971) sharpened the issue by stressing the difference between two interpretations of the term 'the interest rate' in this context. According to Brunner, Keynesians thought of interest as 'borrowing cost' and tended to believe, therefore, that firms financing investment out of retained earnings would not respond to monetary policy. Brunner and Meltzer (see, for example, Meltzer (1995)), on the other hand, consistently stressed the concept of the interest rate as the (often implicit) relationship between the rental value and asset value of all types of assets, real as well as financial. A decline of 'the' interest rate, for instance, raises the demand price of assets relative to their (imputed) rentals.

To Brunner and Meltzer, monetary policy was more effective than Keynesian theory would indicate, because these relative price effects would reach into every nook and cranny of the economy and raise the demand prices of all kinds of reproducible durables. Note that it is so 'effective', in this account, because it is so all-pervasively non-neutral in the short run.

6.5 The Friedman reformulation

Towards the end of the 1960s, a significant shift took place in the position of Friedman and other Chicago monetarists. The central new postulate was that the real rate of interest was determined by real determinants which change only slowly and basically independently of monetary impulses. The immediate objective was to provide an alternative to the standard 'real' explanation of Gibson's Paradox (which at the time was considered to be 'Keynesian'). But the postulate that the market real rate of interest could be taken as always approximating the natural rate also produced, as we have seen, the lemma of the NAIRU doctrine and the immensely successful attack on the stability of the Phillips curve.

The third monetarist version of the transmission mechanism is another by-product of this Friedman reformulation. Here, the liquidity effect on interest rates is weak and evanescent. The central bank has no significant influence on real rates of interest. Thus, the relative price mechanism is fading out of the picture. The emphasis is shifted, instead, to market anticipations of the growth in nominal income or of rising prices as the present incentive to increased nominal expenditures.

6.6 Rational expectations monetarism

The fourth monetarist transmission theory one meets, of course, is in the work of Lucas (1972, 1975). The theory is in direct line of descent from the Friedman reformulation. In this version, there is no systematic liquidity effect, or indeed any other real effect, except in so far as economic agents are temporarily misinformed. Transmission is entirely via rational expectations. The credible announcement that the money stock is about to be increased will suffice to raise prices and increase nominal spending (just as the credible announcement that it won't is sufficient for monetary stability). When monetary policy is anticipated, it is nominally effective immediately and without fail. And in so far as distribution effects can be ignored, it is neutral and without real effects also in the shortest run.

These four monetarist transmission stories are not successive clarifications of the same doctrine. To Brunner and Meltzer, an increase in high-powered money is effective in raising aggregate demand because it is so pervasively non-neutral. To Lucas, it is instantly effective, although neutral, but effectiveness is then simply a matter of nominal scale.

Clearly, 'money' in Friedman's reformulated model as well as in Lucas' model is outside money or, rather, it is assumed that the M-aggregate is always proportional to the stock of outside money. In the context of the monetary history of the USA, these models are helpful in understanding the inflationary regime of the 1970s. This was a decade of outside-money inflation – as opposed to credit-driven inflation – with government deficits partly financed by the inflation tax. This was also the period when the markets would respond to easier monetary policies by raising interest rates, thus exhibiting the Fisher effect predicted by these models.

That regime, fortunately, did not last. Today, it is again the prospect of tighter, and not easier, monetary policy that will put the markets in fear of capital losses. We are back in a world where the short-run relationship between money and interest rates is the 'old' inverse one, and where monetary transmission appears to work rather after the manner of Tobin,

Modigliani, Brunner and Meltzer, and the early Friedman. The recent literature does not, on the whole, see this as the result of the monetary regime coming again to resemble the regime that these earlier writers took for granted. Instead, it starts from the state of the art as established by Lucas in the 1970s and seeks to recover non-neutrality by adding more or less acceptable imperfections to the intertemporal general equilibrium structure. There are two strands to this transmission literature, neither of which makes much of the distinction between inside and outside money.

6.7 Liquidity effects

By modifying the paradigmatic IGE model to include binding cash-in-advance constraints and transactions costs in the trade also of securities, it can be shown that monetary injections may via distribution effects cause interest rates to deviate temporarily from fundamentals. The distribution effects are of the kind that used to be termed Cantillon effects; that is, it matters who gets the new cash first. Lucas (1990) has also been particularly influential here. Fuerst (1992) and Christiano and Eichenbaum (1992) have developed this line further.

6.8 Credit channel effects

A large and growing literature focuses on transmission effects that do not work directly through the demand prices for assets. Part of it has a strong 'Keynesian' flavour, striving for non-neoclassical results by stressing non-price 'rationing' in credit rather than in labour markets. But in general this literature bases the non-neutrality of monetary policy on the imperfect substitutability of securities and bank loans. The bank loan market is seen as being characterized by informational asymmetries between borrowers and lenders, giving rise to an external finance premium for bank-dependent borrowers. Monetary policy affects bank-financed activity through its effects on this premium transmitted via the 'balance sheet' and the 'bank-lending' channels (Bernanke and Blinder (1992), Bernanke and Gertler (1995) and, for a more sceptical view, Meltzer (1995)).[26]

In the present context, I want to stress the importance of the prevailing regime rather than that of particular channels in understanding transmission. As far as I am aware, we do not have clear evidence showing whether the speed and effectiveness of monetary transmission differs significantly, for example, between countries in which bank credit channels predominate and those in which the main impulses propagate across financial markets. The view advocated here is perhaps most closely akin to that of Brunner and Meltzer, who in some of their later work (for example, 1993) argued that the real effects of monetary policy stemmed from the inability of agents to distinguish between permanent and transitory components of monetary policy. The full adjustment of money prices occurs only gradually, as the uncertainty about the permanence of nominal shocks dissolves. In the meantime, policy is seen to have non-neutral effects. Their point is similar to the signal-extraction argument of the previous section, where the problem of agents was to distinguish between changes in outside and changes in inside money in an intertemporal context. Here, the uncertainty to be resolved concerns the extent to which the government will follow a policy that balances the budget over time and thus avoid the issue of outside money. An injection of money that is 'permanent' in the sense that it will never be retired is, by that token, 'outside' and represents an inflation tax levy. It will eventually prove neutral in its effects. Monetary operations that do obey the governmental intertemporal budget constraint (such as central bank re-discounting, for example) are 'inside' and also 'transitory' in the sense that they will be offset over time. In this mean-reverting context, central banks have some power to influence output and employment. The problem is finding an institutional arrangement such that this power can, at least occasionally, be used in a manner that will do more good than harm.

7 A rule with some discretion

Suppose then, at least for the sake of argument, that it is possible for a central bank to have some influence on the real rate of interest and on the liquidity position of the private sector (also in real terms). Such powers would give it some limited ability to affect output and employment in the short run, and therefore potentially to moderate the cycle. The question would remain whether it should be allowed to exercise these powers. The arguments against it are familiar. Countercyclical monetary policy would have to be adaptive and discretionary.[27] Given 'long and variable lags', it is likely to be ill-timed on occasion. And concern over reputation and credibility is not a reliable check to the tendency for successive discretionary actions to end up as an inflationary Random Walk Monetary Standard in the long run.

With unlimited discretion, we want a rule to provide nominal stability; given a framework of nominal stability, we want discretion. Combining the two is the trick. It is possible to devise monetary regimes that combine stability and relatively good predictability of nominal values over the long run with the limited exercise of discretionary policy in the short run. The gold standard was such a regime and, for the non-key-currency countries, so was Bretton Woods – as long as the key-currency country behaved itself. True, the discretion that Bretton Woods allowed resulted in much derided 'stop-and-go' policies. But a look back at the growth and unemployment figures of the stop-and-go era from today's vantage point does not make it appear particularly dreadful.

As an example of a regime with the desired characteristics that would not depend solely on the reputation for conservatism of central bankers, let me revive an old proposal[28] for a 'one-sided growth path rule'. The proposal is intended to apply to a key currency, such as the euro.

In this regime, a ceiling is legislated for the monetary base that the central bank could have in existence at any one time. This ceiling on the base should be made to rise (like a Friedman rule) at x per cent per year, x being computed (approximately) as the difference between some long-run average for the growth rate of real output and the trend in the velocity of base money. The intercept of the rule; that is, the initial legal maximum when the legislation goes into effect, should be set some 10–20 per cent above the actual base at that date.

The monetary base, as discussed above, is not the theoretically true 'nominal scalar' of an economy. But the measure of outside nominal assets that determines the nominal scale in an IGE model is not operational in practice. However, the base ceiling might also be supplemented by a ceiling on the central bank's holdings of government securities, as was written into the constitutions of many of the new central banks created after the First World War. Such a supplemental restriction should prevent the inconsistency between the operational rule and the theoretically perfect rule resulting in practical problems of consequence.

This rule leaves some room for discretion. It also leaves open the choice of short-term policies and operating procedures.[29] As long as the central bank finds itself well below the ceiling, it can expand or contract, and can execute either policy by targeting a money aggregate, an interest rate, or an inflation rate. But while the authorities would retain short-term discretion as long as they stayed below the ceiling, the risk that monetary policy might evolve as a long sequence of predominantly inflationary moves would have been eliminated.

A central bank operating under a base ceiling law would have to treat the difference between the maximum legal and the actual base as if it were its foreign exchange reserves and the bank were operating in a fixed exchange rate system. It could pursue an expansionary policy (or step in as lender of last resort) only as long as it had excess reserves. If, in trying to help the economy out of one recession, it were to go so far as to hit the ceiling, it would have to plan on a prolonged period of expanding at less than the permissible Friedmanite rate in order to accumulate the ammunition to help it out of another.

In this regime, the price level should exhibit the reversion to trend property which, in my view, is the crucial fulcrum that provides the central bank some leverage over real, as opposed to merely nominal, magnitudes. The longer-term nominal expectations of the public should come to approximate the expectations that are rational under a gold standard – with the added benefit that agents do not have to worry about the vagaries of world gold production and the like.

One obvious problem with this proposal is that the current pace of financial innovation is such that the future demand for base money is hardly predictable very many years into the future. I would approach this problem by making price-level stabilization over the longer term the basic and overriding responsibility of the central bank. This provision should be seen as stating the basic intent of the monetary constitution and would serve as the escape clause under which changes in the growth rate rule could be made. If, for instance, the initially-chosen growth rate turns out in a few years of dwindling base money demand to be quite inflationary, it could be adjusted downward[30] for this reason – but for this reason only. This author would feel more comfortable with a European Central Bank operating under a rule of this sort than with one bound by a zero or low-and-constant inflation rule.

8 Conclusion

Up to a not very distant past, the theory and the practice of central banking were based on the belief that central banks could exert considerable influence on the real interest rate and the real volume of credit. Furthermore, it was believed that the private sector might from time to time develop endogenous cumulative expansions or contractions of credit that would take real activity above or below the equilibrium employment level. The central bank's powers to regulate the price and availability of credit could then be useful as a tool to help 'stabilize' activity.

In recent years, these beliefs are hardly ever voiced. Instead, a widespread consensus has emerged, which holds that the only useful thing that monetary policy can accomplish is nominal stability. Either a great many of the heretofore distinguished figures of our monetary past were sadly deluded – or perhaps the world has changed even more than meets the eye?

Two closely related monetarist hypotheses have played a crucial part in this change in the collective system of beliefs. One is the 'vertical Phillips curve' and the other the invariance of the real rate of interest to monetary policy. But labour market flexibility and the absence of (unanticipated) nominal policy shocks are not sufficient conditions to guarantee strong stability of (un)employment at its natural rate. Failures of intertemporal co-ordination – too high or too low a level of real interest – may keep employment persistently below or above the natural rate.[31] Moreover, within a monetary regime that will more-or-less guarantee mean-reversion to trend of the price level, the monetary authorities will have some useful powers to influence real interest rates and credit conditions.

A third issue, also most often associated with monetarism, remains, namely, rules versus discretion. But regimes can be constructed that leave some room for discretion within a rule-bound framework. This chapter gives one example of this that draws its inspiration from by now rather old monetary history. I have little doubt that better proposals more suited to modern times can be designed.

Notes

1 Sargent and Wallace (1981); Sargent (1987, chs 5 and 7).
2 Compare, for example, Heymann, Kaufman and Sanguinetti (Chapter 6 in this volume).
3 An effective demand failure 'of the third kind' which may be of more contemporary relevance will be proposed below.
4 If textbook Keynesianism dealt with the money stock 'as if' it were outside money, the post-Keynesian literature tended to the other extreme, concentrating on inside money to the virtual neglect of outside money.
5 Most of it stemming from Barro and Gordon (1983a and 1983b). For an expression of utter disbelief in this model, see Leijonhufvud (1986).
6 Reserve requirements may perhaps be left on the books as long as the monetary authorities do not move to block their *de facto* avoidance through reserve management by 'sweeps'. I am indebted to John Duffy for this point.
7 Compare Black (1970), Fama (1980), Greenfield and Yeager (1983) and Woodford (1995, 1996).
8 But see the dissents (from very different perspectives) of Galbraith and of Rogerson in the 1997 *Journal of Economic Literature* Symposium.
9 'Catching up', in this context, may involve not only learning to anticipate but also overcoming frictions, such as Taylor-type staggering of wage agreements.
10 We are concerned here with degrees of wage flexibility of the sort that realistic supply-siders might hope to bring about with their sundry flexibility proposals, so Pigou-effect fantasies may be disregarded.
11 And if the central bank can affect the real (and not just the nominal) rate of interest, *it can do something about it.*

12 The IGE may not be unique, of course, in which case the 'natural rate of (real) interest' may not be unique either. Here, however, I am concerned with the consequences of deviations from IGE pricing in general.
13 Yet the intertemporal equilibrium assumption seems never to be brought up in the debates over unemployment theory. It is not mentioned, for instance, in any of the assessments of the natural rate doctrine in the 1997 *Journal of Economic Perspectives* Symposium (compare the papers by Stiglitz; Gordon; Staiger; Blanchard and Katz; Rogerson; and Galbraith). In Hoon and Phelps (1992), the real interest rate does affect employment, but by a channel very different from that in the Wicksellian tradition.
14 Compare Leijonhufvud (1981), pp. 188ff.
15 'In practice I view stabilization policies as largely inappropriate for reasons that have been offered by everyone from Milton Friedman to Robert Lucas' (Charles Plosser interviewed in Snowdon, Vane and Wynarczyk (1994, p. 282)).
16 Japan might be the exception.
17 See, again, Heymann, Kaufmann and Sanguinetti (Chapter 6 in this volume).
18 Compare the paper by Fitoussi and the comment by Streissler (Chapter 7 in this volume).
19 Compare, for example, Leijonhufvud (1984, 1985).
20 Compare esp. Wallace (1981), Sargent (1987), Woodford (1995, 1996).
21 My apprehension is that a constant inflation rate target may do the same (see below).
22 Prior to the heyday of monetarism, most countries neither published nor compiled money stock figures. Under convertibility, knowledge of the aggregate stock of banking system liabilities is of no particular value to either governmental or private-sector decision-makers. Note also that the intense interest in the weekly money supply figures, that the markets evidenced in the early 1980s, has by now completely abated.
23 The most extreme version of this ineffectiveness doctrine was summarized in the 'pushing on a string' metaphor often satirized by Karl Brunner. Is it perhaps gaining renewed popularity within the Bank of Japan these days?
24 Even as the Radcliffe Report has largely been forgotten, this particular view has been carried forward as 'Goodhart's Law' – a law that, once anathema to monetarists, should fit well in the context of modern IGE monetary theory.
25 A quip still remembered, as in the oblique reference in the title of Bernanke and Gertler (1995).
26 The above review of transmission theories is not complete. In particular, it omits the *exchange rate channel* which is, of course, of critical importance for countries on flexible rates that do not harmonize their monetary policies with their major trading partners; compare, for example, Taylor (1995) and Obstfeld and Rogoff (1995).
27 Most recently, the discussion of alternative monetary regimes has favoured giving central banks independence (to insulate them from their respective Treasuries) but to dictate that they pursue a target of constant low inflation. Are inflation targets good enough? Would an inflation target policy have prevented the stock market and real estate bubbles in Japan, for instance? Or, suppose a recovery of real activity from double-digit unemployment requires *some* rise in the price level. A zero inflation target, intended as a non-contingent neutral

regime, would then turn out to be a perverse, feedback-governed strategy making the central bank take action against each incipient recovery.

28 Compare, for example, Leijonhufvud (1984).

29 The proposal is in some respects analogous to Peel's Bank Act of 1844. That Act divided the Bank of England into an Issue Department and a Banking Department. The Issue Department operated on a rule (although, of course, this was a gold standard and not a Friedman growth-rate rule). It issued Bank of England notes as a simple linear function of its gold holdings: note issue = fiduciary issue + gold in vault. The Banking Department could then engage in discretionary stabilization policy with the note issue as the base for the entire monetary system. The total amount of Issue Department note liabilities set the ceiling on feasible Banking Department expansionary ambitions at any one time. Obviously, the system had the disadvantage that external and internal drains of gold might combine to bring the ceiling crashing down.

30 But if the demand for base money goes to zero? Well, then we would have to think again! In principle, an equilibrium with a finite price level will still exist (Woodford (1995)) but keeping the public sector on its 'Ricardian' intertemporal budget constraint may not suffice for stability if asset price/credit bubbles take the private sector into 'non-Ricardian' territory.

31 Such a deviation of employment from the natural rate may persist for quite some time without producing a deflation (or inflation) enough to trigger corrective monetary action by a central bank cueing on a constant low inflation target. Consider, for example, the course of the price-level in Japan over several years before as well as after the collapse of the stock market and real estate booms.

References

Barro, Robert J. and David B. Gordon (1983a) 'A Positive Theory of Monetary Policy in a Natural Rate Model' in Barro, Robert J. (ed.), *Macroeconomic Policy* (Cambridge, Mass.: Harvard University Press), pp. 29–51.

Barro, Robert J. and David B. Gordon (1983b) 'Rules, Discretion and Reputation in a Model of Monetary Policy' in Barro, Robert J. (ed.), *Macroecomic Policy* (Cambridge, Mass.: Harvard University Press), pp. 52–76.

Bernanke, Ben S. and Alan S. Blinder (1992) 'The Federal Funds Rate and the Channels of Monetary Transmission', *American Economic Review*, vol. 82, no. 4, pp. 901–24.

Bernanke, Ben S. and Mark Gertler (1995) 'Inside the Black Box: The Credit Channel of Monetary Policy Transmission', *Journal of Economic Perspectives*, vol. 9, no. 4, pp. 27–48.

Bernanke, Ben S. and Frederic S. Mishkin (1997) 'Inflation Targeting: A New Framework for Monetary Policy?' National Bureau of Economic Research Working Paper No. 5893, January.

Black, Fischer (1970) 'Banking and Interest Rates in a World without Money', *Journal of Bank Research*, Autumn, pp. 9–20.

Blanchard, Olivier and Lawrence F. Katz (1997) 'What We Know and Do Not Know About the Natural Rate of Unemployment', *Journal of Economic Perspectives*, vol. 11, no. 1, pp. 51–72.

Brunner, Karl (1970) 'The "Monetarist Revolution" in Monetary Theory', *Weltwirtschaftliches Archiv*, vol. 105, pp. 1–30.

Brunner, Karl (1971) 'A Survey of Selected Issues in Monetary Theory', *Schweizerische Zeitschrift für Volkswirtschaft und Statistik*, vol. 186, pp. 1–129.
Brunner, Karl and Allan H. Meltzer (1993) *Money and the Economy: Issues in Monetary Analysis* (Raffaele Mattioli Lectures) (Cambridge University Press).
Christiano, Lawrence J. and Martin Eichenbaum (1992) 'Liquidity Effects and the Monetary Transmission Mechanism', *American Economic Review*, vol. 82, no. 2, pp. 346–53.
Fama, Eugene (1980) 'Banking in a Theory of Finance', *Journal of Monetary Economics*, vol. 6, no. 1, pp. 39–57.
Friedman, Milton (1956) 'The Quantity Theory of Money: A Restatement', in Milton, M. (ed.), *Studies on the Quantity Theory of Money* (University of Chicago Press), pp. 3–21.
Friedman, Milton (1968) 'The Role of Monetary Policy', *American Economic Review*, vol. 58, no.1, March, pp. 1–17.
Friedman, Milton and Anna J. Schwartz (1963) 'Money and Business Cycles', *Review of Economics and Statistics*, Supplement, vol. 45, February, pp. 32–64.
Fuerst, Timothy S. (1992) 'Liquidity, Loanable Funds, and Real Activity', *Journal of Monetary Economics*, vol. 29, no. 1, pp. 3–24.
Galbraith, James K. (1997) 'Time to Ditch the NAIRU', *Journal of Economic Perspectives*, vol. 11, no. 1, pp. 93–108.
Gordon, Robert J. (1997) 'The Time-Varying NAIRU and its Implications for Economic Policy', *Journal of Economic Perspectives*, vol. 11, no. 1, pp. 11–32.
Greenfield, R. L. and Leland B. Yeager (1983) 'A *laissez faire* Approach to Monetary Stability', *Journal of Money, Credit and Banking*, vol. 15, no. 3, pp. 302–15.
Gurley, John and Edward S. Shaw (1960), *Money in a Theory of Finance* (Washington, DC: Brookings Institution).
Heymann, Daniel and Axel Leijonhufvud (1995) *High Inflation* (Oxford University Press).
Hoon, Hian Teck and Edmund S. Phelps (1992) 'Macroeconomic Shocks in a Dynamized Model of the Natural Rate of Unemployment', *American Economic Review*, vol. 82, no. 4, pp. 889–900.
Leijonhufvud, Axel (1981) 'The Wicksell Connection', in Leijonhufvud, A. (ed.), *Information and Coordination: Essays in Macroeconomic Theory* (New York: Oxford University Press), pp. 131–202.
Leijonhufvud, Axel (1984) 'Inflation and Economic Performance', in Siegel, Barry N. (ed.), *Money in Crisis* (Cambridge, Mass.: Ballinger), pp. 19–36.
Leijonhufvud, Axel (1985) 'Constitutional Constraints on the Monetary Powers of Government', in Dorn, James A. and Anna J. Schwartz, *The Search for Stable Money: Essays on Monetary Reform* (University of Chicago Press), pp. 129–43.
Leijonhufvud, Axel (1986) 'Rules with Some Discretion: Comment on Barro', in Campbell, C. D. and W. R. Dougan (eds), *Alternative Monetary Regimes* (Baltimore, Md: Johns Hopkins University Press), pp. 38–43.
Leijonhufvud, Axel (1990) 'Monetary Policy and the Business Cycle under "Loose" Convertibility', *Greek Economic Review*, Supplement: The Monetary Economics of John Hicks', vol. 12, pp. 133–51.
Leijonhufvud, Axel (1997) 'The Wicksellian Heritage', *Economic Notes*, vol. 26, no. 1, pp. 1–10.
Leijonhufvud, Axel (1998) 'Mr. Keynes and the Moderns', in Pasinetti, Luigi and Bertram Schefold (eds), *The Impact of Keynes on Twentieth Century Economics*

(Cheltenham: Edward Elgar), pp. 16–35; also in the *European Journal of the History of Economic Thought*, vol. 5, no. 1 (1998), pp. 169–88.

Lucas, Robert E., Jr (1972) 'Expectations and the Neutrality of Money', *Journal of Economic Theory*, vol. 4, pp. 103–24.

Lucas, Robert E., Jr (1975) 'An Equilibrium Model of the Business Cycle', *Journal of Political Economy*, vol. 83, pp. 1113–44.

Lucas, Robert E., Jr (1990) 'Liquidity and Interest Rates', *Journal of Economic Theory*, vol. 50, no. 2, pp. 237–64.

Meltzer, Allan H. (1995) 'Monetary, Credit (and Other) Transmission Processes: A Monetarist Perspective', *Journal of Economic Perspectives*, vol. 9, no. 4, pp. 49–72.

Mishkin, Frederic S. (1995) 'Symposium on the Monetary Transmission Mechanism', *Journal of Economic Perspectives*, vol. 9, no. 4, pp. 3–10.

Obstfeld, Maurice and Kenneth Rogoff (1995) 'The Mirage of Fixed Exchange Rates', *Journal of Economic Perspectives*, vol. 9, no. 4, pp. 73–96.

Rogerson, Richard (1997) 'Theory Ahead of Language in the Economics of Unemployment', *Journal of Economic Perspectives*, vol. 11, no. 1, pp. 73–92.

Sargent, Thomas J. (1987) *Dynamic Macroeconomic Theory* (Cambridge, Mass.: Harvard University Press).

Sargent, Thomas J. and Neil Wallace (1981) 'Some Unpleasant Monetarist Arithmetic', *Federal Reserve Bank of Minneapolis Quarterly Review*, vol. 5, no. 3, pp. 15–31.

Snowdon, Brian, Howard Vane and Peter Wynarczyk (1994) *A Modern Guide to Macroeconomics: An Introduction to Competing Schools of Thought* (Aldershot: Edward Elgar).

Staiger, Douglas, James H. Stock and Mark W. Watson (1997) 'The NAIRU, Unemployment and Monetary Policy', *Journal of Economic Perspectives*, vol. 11, no. 1, pp. 33–49.

Stiglitz, Joseph (1997) 'Reflections on the Natural Rate Hypothesis', *Journal of Economic Perspectives*, vol. 11, no. 1, Winter, pp. 3–10.

Taylor, John B. (1995) 'The Monetary Transmission Mechanism: An Empirical Framework', *Journal of Economic Perspectives*, vol. 9, no. 4, pp. 11–26.

Vaz, Daniel (1998) *Four Banking Crises: Their Causes and Consequences*, PhD dissertation, University of California at Los Angeles.

Wallace, Neil (1981) 'A Modigliani–Miller Theorem for Open Market Operations', *American Economic Review*, vol. 71, no. 3, pp. 267–74.

Wicksell, Knut (1898) *Geldzins und Güterpreise: Eine Studie über die den Tauschwert des Geldes Bestimmenden Ursachen* (Jena: Gustav Fisher Verlag).

Woodford, Michael (1995) 'Price Level Determinacy without Control of a Monetary Aggregate', National Bureau of Economic Research Working Paper No. 5204, August.

Woodford, Michael (1996) 'Control of the Public Debt: A Requirement for Price Stability?', National Bureau of Economic Research Working Paper No. 5684, July.

Comment

Jacques Mélitz
University of Strathclyde, Glasgow, UK and Centre de Recherche en Economie et Statistique, Paris, France

Rapid progress in a field means faster depreciation of intellectual capital, but rapid forgetting does not necessarily mean progress. While being a keen observer of the current literature on monetary economics, Leijonhufvud has a long memory, and the most stimulating part of his chapter lies in the even contest in his rendering of the state of thought about monetary policy between the fashionable and the out-of-date. The chapter shows us that present thinking fits into a larger, and not always shallower, reservoir of ideas. Some of the statements of historical affiliations are also challenging. Thus is the Miller–Modigliani theorem of irrelevance of corporate financial decisions portrayed as an extension of the occasional, earlier principle of the irrelevance of inside money; and the injection of rational expectations into monetary economics is considered largely as an outgrowth of the older inquiry into the relationship between money and the natural rate of interest, and the associated concern about issues of intertemporal equilibrium (for example, by von Mises, Hayek and Keynes). I do not try to summarize this rich opus, but in the usual manner of commentators, focus on a couple of mild differences of opinion.

Changes in nominal money bear 'relative yield' or 'liquidity' effects. But only those parts of the changes that remain after consolidation of the aggregate balance sheet of the private sector also bear a 'wealth effect'. The part with a wealth effect is known as 'outside' money. The rest is 'inside' money. Leijonhufvud wants professional reasoning about money always to be explicit about the distinction between inside and outside money. No one can quarrel with a demand for clarity. But the importance that Leijonhufvud attaches to the distinction between inside and outside money goes far beyond matters of formal rigour to practical issues of the effects of monetary policy (independently of considerations of 'liquidity traps'). Thus does the section on 'monetary regimes' open up with an extensive discussion of inside and outside money. We even read there of a 'signal extraction' problem for the ordinary household in separating the two. As often when the issue of inside and outside money looms large, 'outside' money has pride of place. In line, Leijonhufvud defines his monetary rule for anchoring the price level – once he gets down to this practical matter – in terms of the growth rate of 'base' money, or a close cousin of 'outside' money (though the two may differ greatly and do so in the continental-European types of monetary systems which have now been enshrined in the choice of blueprint for the EMU).

Yet I would have preferred more support for all the fuss about inside and outside money in the context of policy. Is not the essential consideration the stability of the empirical relationship between monetary instruments and the end-targets of monetary policy? Does not the information-value of different money measures as intermediate targets constitute an empirical issue? If broad measures of money display more stability than narrow ones, is it not right for the monetary authorities to assume an Olympian disregard for the size of the monetary base and a strict Wicksellian attention to the profitability of bank credit expansion? So what if financial innovation drives the demand for currency to zero and interest must therefore be paid on bank reserves in order to preserve an aggregate demand for the 'monetary base'? This would simply mean the disappearance of seigniorage. Does this not pose a problem for fiscal policy rather than monetary policy? Are we not generally prone to worry about the impact of government financing on monetary policy, and might we therefore not even rejoice at the prospect of an end to seigniorage?

My only other qualm regarding Leijonhufvud's stimulating discussion relates to the lesser emphasis than I would have preferred on the international dimension and exchange rates. At an early point in the paper, Leijonhufvud properly points out that 'for small open economies the room for independent macroeconomic policies is all but non-existent'. Nevertheless, his whole section on 'transmission mechanisms' refers strictly to US evidence and shows no particular concern for the wide differences in the sequences of events tripped off by changes in monetary policy in the USA and most other places. In this respect, it is interesting to contemplate another of the papers at the Trento conference with a long historical sweep: Mundell (2001). For Mundell, the essential monetary action occurs at the world level: there is a world monetary order, within which there are centre countries (a very few of them leaders and the rest followers), and were each country (roughly 200 of them) to adopt an independent monetary policy, the result could be chaos. Perhaps Leijonhufvud would agree. If so, he might then reason that his monetary policy rule would translate into the acceptance of fixed exchange rates in well over a hundred – nearly two hundred? – of the national cases. But we can only guess.

Reference

Mundell, Robert (2001) 'Money and the Sovereignty of the State', in Leijonhufvud, Axel (ed.), *Monetary Theory and Policy Experience* (London: Palgrave), ch. 9.

Part I

Intertemporal General Equilibrium

2
Intertemporal General Equilibrium and Monetary Theory*

Jacques H. Drèze and Heracles M. Polemarchakis
CORE, Université Catholique de Louvain, Belgium

1 Preview

1.1 Conclusions

Theory is often at odds with the thinking and practice of monetary authorities. A confrontation of this situation is timely. General equilibrium theory serves to check the consistency of models and to bring out some of their properties. Surprisingly, an enquiry into monetary theory from the perspective of general equilibrium leads to conclusions that resemble views expressed recently by specialists in monetary theory and policy, and suggests an approach to policy resembling that practised by monetary authorities. Also, it delineates theoretical issues more sharply than do less abstract formulations.

Conclusions, not original, though their emergence from a general equilibrium model is perhaps new, are that:

(i) monetary policy is defined by a choice of instruments and a state-contingent rule for adjusting these instruments as information is revealed;
(ii) the rule is bound to remain largely implicit, but greater transparency should help;
(iii) interest rates or, alternatively, money supplies are suitable instruments for the control of expected inflation, but not of the variability of inflation; and
(iv) the real process of nominal price formation restricts, in an insufficiently understood manner, the ability of monetary policy to control nominal variables.

* This chapter presents results of the Belgian Programme on Interuniversity Poles of Attraction initiated by the Belgian State, Prime Minister's Office, Science Policy Programming. The scientific responsibility is assumed by its authors. The Commission of the European Communities provided additional support through the Human Capital and Mobility grant ERBCHRXCT940458.

Effectiveness of monetary policy is synonymous with departures from monetary neutrality. Although neutrality is a theoretical possibility, it is associated with extreme assumptions and of little relevance.

The theory of monetary policy is concerned with the identification of significant departures from neutrality which have clearcut implications. Such departures include:

(i) the negative wealth effect of higher nominal interest rates, when Ricardian equivalence is only partial, as it is bound to be under an incomplete market structure; and
(ii) the partial translation of nominal interest rates into real rates, associated with nominal stickiness of prices and wages.

The extension of the formal analysis to incomplete asset markets and non-Walrasian equilibria should add to this list.

These conclusions are extrapolative of theoretical results.

1.2 Organisation

The theoretical work by Drèze and Polemarchakis (2000, 1999) underlying this chapter consists in formulating an intertemporal general equilibrium model with money; spelling out reasonable assumptions that guarantee the existence of competitive equilibria; and characterizing these equilibria, with particular attention to nominal indeterminacy and to neutrality. The presentation here is largely expository and partly speculative. Section 2 records concisely the essentials of the model of general equilibrium with time and uncertainty; Section 3 extends the model to monetary economies and states an existence result proved in Drèze and Polemarchakis (2000); Section 4 presents a basic result on nominal indeterminacy and draws implications for the definition of monetary policy; Section 5 discusses, somewhat heuristically, significant departures from neutrality; and Section 6 illustrates the contents of the third, fourth and fifth sections with examples. Conclusions are outlined above.

2 Intertemporal general equilibrium

2.1 An abstract model

The Arrow–Debreu (1954) model of general competitive equilibrium is structured on:

(i) commodities, $l \in \mathcal{L} = \{1,\ldots,L\}$; bundles of commodities are $x = (\ldots, x_l, \ldots)$;
(ii) firms, $j \in \mathcal{J} = \{1,\ldots,J\}$; each firm is described by Y^j, a set of feasible production plans, y^j and

(iii) individuals or households, $i \in \mathcal{I} = \{1,\ldots,I\}$; each individual is described by $\mathcal{Z}^i$, a set of feasible net trades in commodities, z^i, including prestations of labour; R^i, a preference ordering on $\mathcal{Z}^i$; and θ^i, the endowment of shares in firms.

An *allocation* is an array $a = (\ldots, y^j,\ldots, z^i,\ldots)$, of production plans for firms and net trades for individuals; it is *feasible* when:

$$\sum_{i \in \mathcal{I}} z^i - \sum_{j \in \mathcal{J}} y^j = 0$$

Market decentralization is structured on prices of commodities, $p = (\ldots,p_l,\ldots)$, and the budget constraints of individuals:

$$pz \leq \sum_{j \in \mathcal{J}} \theta^{i,j} v^j$$

where $v^j = py^j$ are the profits or market values of firms.

A feasible allocation and a price vector define a *market allocation* when the net trade of every individual satisfies the budget constraint.

A market allocation is a *competitive equilibrium allocation* and the associated prices are *competitive equilibrium prices* if:

(i) the net trade of every individual is maximal for his/her preference relation subject to the budget constraint; and
(ii) the profit of every firm is maximal.

The structure is general and lends itself to other equilibrium concepts, such as equilibria with imperfectly competitive markets, game-theoretic equilibria, co-operative or non-cooperative, equilibria with quantity constraints or equilibria with incomplete markets.

2.2 Time and uncertainty

The relevance of the model of general equilibrium is substantially enhanced by the observation in Arrow (1953) and Debreu (1959, 1960) that a commodity can be defined, not only by its physical characteristics, including a time and place of delivery, but also by the 'state of the world' prevailing at delivery.

The primitives of an economy, the list and characteristics of commodities, firms and households evolve over time under the influence of exogenous circumstances: the physical environment, discoveries and technological advances, population or culture. One may conceive of a description of such circumstances exhaustive enough that, for any date,

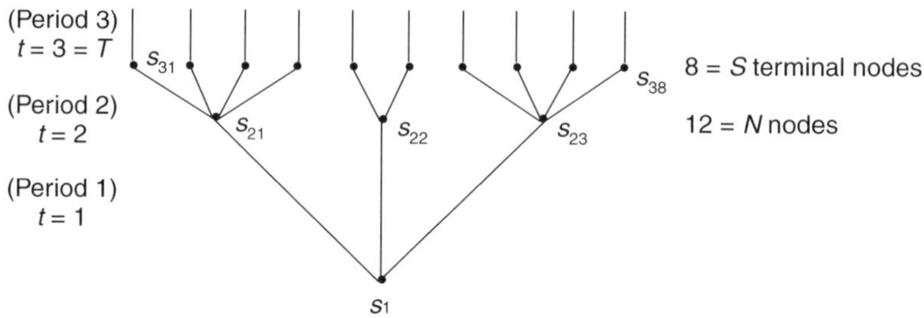

Figure 2.1 An event tree

primitives are defined uniquely up to that date, though contingently on developments over the remaining future. Applied to a terminal date, such a description defines a 'state of the world'; applied to an intermediate date, it defines a subset of the states, an 'event'; over a finite horizon, a 'tree' describes the sequential resolution of uncertainty, technically, a filtration of the set of states (see Figure 2.1).

Although the very idea of a finite tree is problematic, for practical purposes it is justified by the discreteness of measurements and the irrelevance at a date of branchings in a very distant future.

Dates are $t \in \mathcal{T} = \{1,\ldots,T\}$.

A finite tree, $\mathcal{F}$, contains nodes or date-events $n \in \mathcal{N} = \{1,\ldots,N\}$, of which S are terminal nodes or states of the world; evidently,

$$1 \leq S \leq N, 1 \leq T \leq N$$

Events at date t are $s_t \in \mathcal{S}_t$, with $\mathcal{S}_1$ a singleton and $\mathcal{S}_T$ of cardinaliy S.

One identifies commodities and, hence, prices by the pair of subscripts (l, s_t), where l refers to physical characteristics and s_t to the date-event contingently on which delivery takes place; x_{l,s_t} is a quantity of the physical commodity l at date t, contingent on the event s_t. The index of commodities runs over $\mathcal{L} \times \mathcal{N}$.

In market economies, the price p_{l,s_t} is the price of the contract traded at date 1 that gives right to one unit of commodity l at date t if, and only if, the event s_t obtains; $\sum_{s_t \in \mathcal{S}_t} p_{l_{s_t}}$ is the price of an unconditional promise to deliver one unit of commodity l at date t.

This framework is sufficiently general to encompass as special cases most models or situations. This does not negate the technical advantages that may result from treating time as continuous, possibly open-ended, or from relying on continuous random variables to describe some contingencies, or from analysing aggregative or representative individual models.

2.3 Incomplate markets

Events and event trees are a useful conceptual abstraction that help to clarify a number of issues in the economics of uncertainty. The specification that requires that markets clear at some initial date for delivery of any physical commodity contingent on any date-event has made the well-developed theory of general equilibrium directly applicable to uncertain environments. But it is difficult to conceive of such a complete market structure as a realistic possibility. Reasons for scepticism are that:

(i) to clear all markets at some initial date requires trading then by as-yet-unborn individuals;
(ii) to enter a complete description of states of the world is informationally and computationally forbidding; and
(iii) to transact on that many markets would be too costly for individuals as well as for organized exchanges.

A more realistic specification recognises that markets are incomplete. Individuals and firms trade on a limited set of markets, knowing that additional markets – spot markets, but also markets for assets, futures or options – will open at future dates. Trading is thus of necessity based on expectations about the prices that will prevail on these additional markets, when they open. Strong assumptions on the sequential structure of markets and on the expectations of individuals are required to obtain competitive equilibria, following Radner (1972), as 'equilibria of prices, plans and price expectations'.

3 Money in general equilibrium

3.1 Modelling options

Modelling options are guided by the desire to capture as simply as possible the essential roles and institutional features of money.

Fiat money produced at no cost by banks serves as a medium of transaction. Banks lend money to households and firms against a promise of reimbursement with interest or, equivalently, in exchange for interest-bearing bonds. All initial holdings of money are the counterpart of debts to banks.[1] In the vocabulary of monetary economics, this is a model of 'inside money'. It is the model appropriate for economies with properly functioning central banks that only issue money in exchange for offsetting nominal claims. There is no default and loan contracts are met. Interest earned by banks accrues to shareholders as dividends.[2]

Banks also accept deposits and pay depositors the same rate of interest that they charge on loans; equivalently, there are interest-bearing nominal assets, including savings accounts, which dominate money as a store of value. The only reason for holding non-interest-bearing money is its usefulness as a means of payment and the cost or inconvenience of withdrawals or deposits at banks. This is also, for most, the only reason for holding non-interest-bearing money.[3] It is a convincing reason and there is no need to look for another.[4]

The demand for money at given commodity prices and interest rates results from the preference-maximizing choices of individuals and the profit-maximizing choices of firms.

An important modelling choice concerns the treatment of time. In line with the standard model of general equilibrium, there is a finite number of dates or elementary periods. Formally, a date is a point in time. For purposes of interpretation, the length of a time period is more naturally thought of as non-trivial, but rather short. In particular, within each period, (i) no new information accrues; (ii) prices and rates of interest are constant; (iii) the precise timing of transactions and the resulting profile over time of consumption and production do not affect preferences or production possibilities, while it does affect money balances and interest accounting; and (iv) banks accommodate variations in money demand.[5]

A realistic, detailed treatment of the transaction technology and of its implications for preferences and production possibilities should allow for non-convexities. The simplest example, the impossibility of trading without at least one transaction with the bank, introduces a non-convexity as does, more generally, the integer nature of the number of financial transactions. Disregarding the integer condition on financial transactions is neither more nor less serious than disregarding the integer condition on the purchase of most physical commodities. There, the usual disregard for these non-convexities is justified by the argument that they are eliminated by aggregation over a large number of transactions, none of which affects the aggregate significantly. The same applies here.

3.2 Model and notation

There is one currency, with no specification of a place where the currency is held or used; but there is the distinction between date-events: on a tree with N nodes, there are, effectively, N distinct currencies.

The notation is that of the second section, above. Prices of commodities are nominal. Nominal interest rates are $r = (\ldots, r_{s_t}, \ldots)$. In the tradition of general equilibrium, prices are expressed as date 1 values, in units of money at the single event associated with date 1. This convention applies also to prices of balances held at other date-events, and to interest rates. For interest rates, the convention means that r_{s_t} is the value at date 1 of the interest due for a unit loan at date t contingent on s_t and reimbursed at date $t + 1$. Given the other components of the price system, r_{s_t} stands in one-to-one correspondence with the spot one-period nominal rate. These conventions simplify accounting drastically. Spot prices and interest rates at s_t are $\tilde{p}_{s_t}$ and $\tilde{r}_{s_t}$ respectively.

Balances held by individuals or firms are $m = (\ldots, m_{s_t}, \ldots) \geq 0$. The usefulness of balances for transactions is captured in two ways: through generalizations of the consumption sets of individuals and/or through generalizations of the preferences of individuals.

It is easiest to introduce these generalizations through standard examples. A net trade in commodities, z, can be expressed as the sum of a non-negative part, z^+, where $z^+_{l,s_t} = \max\{z_{l,s_t}, 0\}$ and a non-positive part, z^-, where $z^-_{l,s_t} = \min\{z_{l,s_t}, 0\}$. The cash-in-advance model in Clower (1967) imposes the constraint that:

$$m_{s_t} \geq \tilde{p}_{s_t} z^+_{s_t}$$

where m_{s_t} are interpreted as beginning-of-period money holdings. More generally, the exchange set correspondence, $\Phi^i(p,r)$, allows for more complex constraints involving nominal interest rates as well as prices.

Alternatively, the inventory model of Baumol (1952) and Tobin (1956) can be formulated in terms of a transaction cost consisting in time spent on 'trips to the bank'. During the period corresponding to the date-event s_t, the required number of trips is determined by the ratio:

$$\frac{\tilde{p}_{s_t} z^+_{s_t}}{m_{s_t}}$$

where m_{s_t} is now interpreted as average money holdings within the period. For instance, with a constant rate of expenditure, the number of trips is equal to $2\tilde{p}_{s_t} z_{s_t^+} m_{s_t}$. It is then natural to enter that ratio as an argument of the preference ordering, $R^i(z, m, p, r)$, which, as a consequence, is defined conditionally on prices and, more generally, on interest rates as well.

By analogy, the liquidity services of cash balances to firms are captured by generalising their production sets into a production correspondence

$\Psi^j(p, r)$, which defines, conditionally on prices and rates of interest, the production plans, y, and balances n, which are feasible; in line with the convention of measuring outputs positively and inputs negatively, $n \leq 0$.

The profits of the firm are:

$$v^j(y, n, p, r) = py + rn$$

which it maximizes.

The bank, denoted by the index $j = J + 1$, extends loans $M \geq 0$, on which it collects interest in the amount $v^{J+1}(M, r) = rM$, paid out as dividends.

The budget constraint of an individual, a single constraint under a complete asset markets, takes the elementary form:

$$pz^i + rm^i \leq \sum_{j \epsilon J} \theta^{i,j} v^j(y, n, p, r) + \theta^{i,J+1} v^{J+1}(M, r)$$

The interest accounting is implicit. In a deterministic world, all transactions on commodities are entered at values discounted to period 1. This is equivalent to settling them sequentially on the spot through credits and debits with the bank, and letting the bank pay or collect interest on the account's balance. The equivalence results from the assumption that the interest rate is the same for positive and negative balances. Similarly, profit shares may indifferently be collected initially at present value or period by period, as dividends credited to the bank account. There is, however, an exception to this accounting, namely cash balances on which no interest is earned. Accordingly, the interest forgone on cash balances must be added to the expenditures or deducted from the receipts.

The link between the overall budget constraint as written above and the spot accounting identities at individual nodes is readily illustrated for the case where $T = 2$. It is then economical to index the initial node, the date-event at date 1, as 0 and the different states of the world, date-events at date 2, as $s \in S = \{1, \ldots, S\}$. Also, it helps to denote by $d^j = (d^j_0, \ldots, d^j_s)$ the net dividends paid by firm j across the nodes of the event-tree. The spot price at 0 of a contingent claim to commodity l in state $s, p_{l,s}$, may be expressed as the product of the spot price, q_s, of a contingent claim to one unit of money in state s and the spot price $\tilde{p}_{l,s}$ there. One writes f_s for the net purchases at 0 of nominal claims contingent on state s. Commodity prices and interest rates are constant within periods. Interest on initial or average balances is due at end of period, when dividends are also paid. The accounting identities, in beginning-of-period values, are then:

$$p_0 z_0^i + \frac{\tilde{r}_0}{1+\tilde{r}_0} m_0^i + \Sigma_{s\in\mathcal{S}} q_s f_s^i =$$

$$\frac{1}{1+\tilde{r}_0}\{\Sigma_{j\in\mathcal{J}}\, \theta^{i,j} d_0^j + \theta^{i,J+1}\tilde{r}_0 M_0\},$$

$$\tilde{p}_s z_s^i + \frac{\tilde{r}}{1+\tilde{r}_s} m_s^i =$$

$$f_s^i + \frac{1}{1+\tilde{r}_s}\{\Sigma_{j\in\mathcal{J}}\theta^{i,j} d_s^j + \tilde{r}_s M_s\}, \quad s\in\mathcal{S}$$

If one multiplies the budget constraint at $s \in \mathcal{S}$ by q_s, adds it to the budget constraint at 0 and does so for all $s \in S$, the terms in f_s^i cancel out, yielding:

$$p_0 z_0^i + \Sigma_{s\in\mathcal{S}} q_s \tilde{p}_s z_s^i + \frac{\tilde{r}_0}{1+\tilde{r}_0} m_0^i + \Sigma_{s\in\mathcal{S}} q_s \frac{\tilde{r}_s}{1+\tilde{r}_s} m_s^j =$$

$$\Sigma_{j\in\mathcal{J}}\theta^{i,j}\Big(\frac{1}{1+\tilde{r}_0} d_0^j + \Sigma_{s\in\mathcal{S}} q_s \frac{1}{1+\tilde{r}_s} d_s^j\Big) + \theta^{i,J+1}\Big(\frac{\tilde{r}_0}{1+\tilde{r}_0} M_0 + \Sigma_{s\in\mathcal{S}} q_s \frac{\tilde{r}_s}{1+\tilde{r}_s} M_s\Big)$$

With $q_s\tilde{p}_s = p_s$, $\tilde{r}_0/(1+\tilde{r}_0) = r_0$, $q_s\, \tilde{r}_s/(1+\tilde{r}_s) = r_s$, $v^j = d^j{}_0/(1+\tilde{r}_0) + \Sigma_{s\in\mathcal{S}}\, q_s d^i{}_s/(1+\tilde{r}_s)$, and $v^{J+1} = \tilde{r}_0 M_0/(1+\tilde{r}_0) + \Sigma_{s\in\mathcal{S}} q_s \tilde{r}_s\, M_s/(1+\tilde{r}_s)$, the last expression takes the simpler form written above, where $p = (p_0,\ldots,p_s,\ldots), z^i = (z_0^i,\ldots,z_0^i,\ldots)$, and so on, as in the second section above.

The equilibrium conditions must be augmented to require clearing of the market for balances:

$$\sum_{i\in\mathcal{I}} m^i - \sum_{j\in\mathcal{J}} n^j \le M$$

3.3 Monetary equilibrium

A monetary economy is defined by.

(i) an event tree, $\mathcal{F}$, extending over dates $t \in \mathcal{T} = \{1,\ldots,T\}$, with nodes, date-events $s_t = n \in \mathcal{N} = \{1,\ldots,N\}$ of which $s = s_T \in \{1,\ldots,S\}$, terminal;
(ii) primary commodities, $l \in \mathcal{L} = \{1,\ldots,L\}$;
(iii) contingent commodities, associated with the L primary commodities and the N date-events, $(l,s_t) \in \mathcal{L} \times N$;
(iv) prices of the contingent commodities, $p = (\ldots,p_{l,s_t},\ldots)$ as of date 1;
(v) a single currency, issued by a bank, indexed $J+1$, charging or paying interest on account balances; the currency is not interest-bearing;
(vi) interest rates, $r = (\ldots,r_{s_t},\ldots)$, one for each date-event, expressed as values of date 1;
(vii) firms, $j \in \{1,\ldots,J\}$; each firm is defined by its production correspondence $\Psi^j(p, r)$;

(viii) individuals or households, $i \in \mathcal{I} = \{1, \ldots, I\}$; each individual is defined by a triple, (Φ^i, R_i, e^i), where $\Phi^i(p, r)$ is the exchange set correspondence, R_i is a preference ordering on the graph of Φ^i, and e^i is the endowment of state-contingent commodities.

A private ownership monetary economy is defined by a monetary economy and an ownership matrix $\Theta = (\theta^{i,j})$, $i = 1, \ldots, I$, $j = 1, \ldots, J, J+1$, where $\theta^{i,j}$ is the share of firm j, if $j \leq J$, or of the bank, if $j = J + 1$, owned by individual i.

The aggregate balances issued by the bank are M, an N-vector. At interest rates r, bank profits are rM.

The budget set of individual i is:

$$B^i(p, r, y, M) = \{(x, m) \epsilon \Phi^i(p, r) : \\ px + rm \leq pe^i + \sum_{j \epsilon J} \theta^{i,j}(py^j + rn^j) + \theta^{i,J+1} rM\}$$

A competitive equilibrium is defined by an allocation, $(\ldots,(x^i,m^i),\ldots,(y^j,n^j),\ldots)$, a price vector, p, a vector of interest rates, r, and aggregate balances, M, such that:

(i) for every individual, (x^i,m^i) belongs to $B^i(p,r,y,M)$ and is R_i-maximal;
(ii) for every firm, (y^j,n^j) belongs to $\Psi^j(p,r)$ and $py^j + rn^j \geq py + rn$, for all $(y,n) \in \Psi^j(p,r)$;
(iii) $\Sigma_{i \in \mathcal{I}} x^i \leq \Sigma_{j \in \mathcal{J}} y^j + \Sigma_{i \in \mathcal{I}} e^i$;
(iv) $\Sigma_{i \in \mathcal{I}} m^i - \Sigma_{j \in \mathcal{J}} n^j \leq M$.

Proposition 1 *Under standard assumptions, competitive equilibria exist, for all* $\bar{r} \geq 0$, *all general price levels* $\Sigma_{l,s_t} pl,_{s_t} = \bar{c} > 0$, *and some associated* M.

One assumption is not standard: in order to allow for homogeneity of degree zero, of the exchange set correspondence and the preference ordering, in prices of commodities and money balances, it is logically required, and it is analytically possible, to weaken the standard continuity assumption when both $z^+_{s_t}$ and m_{s_t} vanish.

4 Nominal indeterminacy and monetary policy

4.1 Nominal indeterminacy

The complication introduced by money in general equilibrium analysis is increased nominal indeterminacy. The 'degrees of nominal indeterminacy' (d.o.n.i.) are the dimension of a set of nominal variables that may be specified exogenously, while maintaining the existence of a competitve equilibrium. In the Arrow–Debreu model, there is a single d.o.n.i., the overall price level. It is indeed easy to give examples of economies that admit a unique competitive equilibrium in quantities and relative prices. In contrast, Proposition 1 reveals that monetary economies with N date-events admit at least $N + 1$ d.o.n.i. – N nominal interest rates and one overall price level. A more precise statement is possible.

> **Proposition 2** *Competitive equilibria for a monetary economy on an event-tree with N date-events, of which S terminal, display N + S degrees of nominal indeterminacy. A similar property holds on each subtree, conditionally on any initial date-event and compatible terminal date.*[6]

At each date-event, three nominal variables must be set: a short-run, within-period, nominal interest rate; a price level; and money balances. Given two of these, the third follows through money demand by firms and individuals, at equilibrium. This leaves two free nominal variables per node.

When $N = S = 1$, which corresponds to one period under certainty, $2 = N + S$ variables are indeed free. For instance, the price level could be inherited, with the interest rate or money supply set by the bank.

Nominal interest rates carry real effects – up to a negligible set of primitives – because (i) higher rates lead agents to economise on money balances, at real costs; (ii) higher rates widen the wedge between effective buying prices, which include liquidity costs, and selling prices; and (iii) higher rates entail redistributive effects between borrowers, lenders and bank shareholders. On the other hand, because preferences and constraints are assumed to be homogeneous of degree zero in nominal prices and money balances, there is absence of money illusion, and the price level and the associated supply of inside money have no real implications. This last property is lost when nominal claims and liabilities appear in the initial endowments.

When $N > S = 1$, which corresponds to multiple periods certainty, the two nominal variables per period are constrained by $N - 1$ no-arbitrage conditions, the 'Fisher conditions'. At each non-terminal node, the nominal short rate, $\tilde{r}_t$, the real short rate, $\tilde{\rho}_t$ and the one-period prospective inflation rate, $\tilde{\varphi}_t$, must satisfy, at equilibrium, the relation $1 + \tilde{r}_t = (1 + \tilde{\rho}_t)(1 + \tilde{\varphi}_t)$, often approximated by the statement that the real rate is equal to the nominal rate minus inflation. There remain $2N - (N - 1) = N + 1 = N + S$ degrees of nominal indeterminacy. If all nominal rates are set by the bank, all inflation rates are determined, at equilibrium; but the overall price level remains free. If all price levels are determined, through a process of nominal price formation, initialised, the terminal interest rate, $\tilde{r}_T$ is free. For a long horizon, $\tilde{r}_T$ is of little consequence to initial decisions, whereas the overall price level has immediate import. There is an inescapable asymmetry between the forward-looking implications of interest rates for inflation, and the backward-looking implications of inflation for interest rates.

When $N > S > 1$, which corresponds to multiple periods under uncertainty, there are $2N$ nominal variables to be determined, and $N - S$ non-terminal nodes. At each of these, a no-arbitrage condition links the short nominal rate to the present value, at prices for contingent nominal claims, of real rates and inflation rates one period hence. This property is conveniently illustrated on the standard two-period, single physical commodity model where $N = S + 1 > 2$, $L = 1$. Nominal, *spot* prices of the commodity are $\tilde{p} = (p_0, \tilde{p}_1, \ldots, \tilde{p}_s, \ldots, \tilde{p}_S)$, and, $q = (q_1, \ldots, q_S)$ are the nominal prices at 0 of claims to one unit of money contingent on states $s = 1, \ldots, S$. The nominal rate $\tilde{r}_0$ and the vector q are related by $\sum_{s \in S} q_s = (1 + \tilde{r}_0)^{-1}$: one unit of money in each state can be acquired either by buying S unit claims at prices q_s, or by buying a one-period nominal bond at price $(1 + \tilde{r}_0)^{-1}$. This is the single no-arbitrage condition. It leaves free both the second period nominal rates $\tilde{r}_s$ and the second period relative prices $\tilde{p}_s / \sum_{s \in S} \tilde{p}_s$, with associated relative prices for contingent claims, $q_s / \sum_{s \in S} q_s$. In particular, if a competitive equilibrium specifies the interest rates $\tilde{r} = (\tilde{r}_0, \tilde{r}_1, \ldots, \tilde{r}_S)$ and spot prices $(\tilde{p}, q)$, the same physical allocation would also be sustained by $(\tilde{r}, \tilde{p}', q')$, where $p'_0 = p_0$, $\tilde{p}'_s = \lambda_s \tilde{p}_s$, $q'_s = \lambda_s^{-1} q_s$, for each s, and $\lambda = (\lambda_1, \ldots, \lambda_S) >> 0$ satisfies $\Sigma_{s \in S} \lambda_s^{-1} q_s = (1 + \tilde{r}_0)^{-1}$. One concise way to capture that property is to note that, at equilibria consistent with given nominal rates of interest, expected inflation is well-defined, but the variability of inflation is unrestricted.[7]

Similarly, if the money supply at each node were fixed, but interest rates adjusted flexibly to clear the money market, there would remain S degrees of price level indeterminacy. With p_0 inherited from the past, r_0 would follow from (p_0, M_0) through money demand. Once again, expected inflation would be determined by a no-arbitrage condition. But the variability of price levels and of the associated $\tilde{r}'_s$ s would be unrestricted.

The twin property just exhibited for the two-period, one-commodity model is fully general and worth stating as a corollary to Proposition 2:

Corollary 1 *In a monetary economy on an event-tree with N date-events, of which S terminal, competitive equilibria at given nominal interest rates* $\bar{r}$

or, alternatively, at given money supplies $\bar{M}$ display S degrees of nominal indeterminacy, corresponding to the price levels at the terminal nodes. Looking at inflation rates between any non-terminal node and its successors, expected inflation rates, suitably defined, are well-defined, but the variability of inflation is unrestricted.

This corollary has important implications for monetary policy. The *S* d.o.n.i.s associated with the price levels have no real consequences, in the formulation with complete markets and no nominal claims in the initial endowments.[8]

4.2 Monetary policy

Monetary policy removes the degrees of nominal indeterminacy

'*Comprehensive*' monetary policy removes all *N* + *S* degrees of indeterminacy.

A monetary policy is a choice of instruments, at most *N* + *S*, and a pre-announced, state-contingent rule for setting these instruments on the basis of sequential information about the resolution of uncertainty. It is neither a fixed, state-independent rule, nor a purely discretionary policy. If the policy is announced and followed, there are no 'surprises': adjustments in the level of the instruments may be regarded as 'anticipated', though in a contingent sense. Changes in the rule, on the other hand, may be labelled unanticipated.[9]

Four aspects of these definitions will be discussed. Current trends in monetary thinking set the stage.

Regarding choice of instruments, the trend is to privilege nominal short rates. This seems to reflect, at least in part, growing reservations about the meaningfulness of controlling the money supply, in a world of money-market accounts and credit card transactions. Simultaneously, the targeting of monetary aggregates is losing ground to inflation targeting. Central bank independence is increasingly seen as being necessary, and perhaps also sufficient, for an efficient conduct of monetary policy, namely one that contains inflation. Regarding the cost of inflation, levels and variability both matter, and are seen as being positively correlated.

4.2.1 Interest policies and comprehensiveness

In an event-tree with *N* date-events, of which *S* terminal, there are *N* + *S* degrees of nominal indeterminacy, but only *N* short nominal rates, one per node. A monetary policy relying on nominal short rates as instruments is not comprehensive. As stated in Corollary 1, competitive equilibria associated with such a policy have at each node well-defined expected rates of inflation, compatible with the announced interest rates, but the variability of inflation is unrestricted. As a consequence, the long-run realised inflation, or even the conditional expected inflation given a future date-event, are uncontrolled.

These considerations suggest that *nominal rates do not provide suitable instruments for inflation targeting, and, in particular, for containing the variability of inflation, at equilibrium.*

Our incursions into the monetary literature have not led to any discussion of this difficulty; and discussions with better-read colleagues and informed practitioners have not dispelled the mystery. This raises the following:

> **Question** *Is the inability of interest policies to control inflation variability, at equilibrium, recognised by monetary theory? If so, why is it not in the foreground of the discussions on inflation targeting through interest policies? If not, is it because the models of monetary theory hide the fact, or lead to different conclusions? Is it because the control of inflation variability is deemed to follow from the control of expected inflation? Or is it because monetary theory is concerned with out-of-equilibrium situations?*

4.2.2 Additional instruments

What instruments, other than nominal short rates, could be used to implement a comprehensive monetary policy? If the price level were treated as adjusting passively to a comprehensive monetary policy, at equilibrium, then control of the money supply would remain desirable *as a complement, not a substitute,* to interest policies. The fact that there are $N + S < 2N$ d.o.n.i.s reveals that the two sets of instruments should be used in a coordinated manner. That is, contingent money growth at $t + 1$ must be compatible with the expected inflation associated with the nominal rate at t. Subject to that constraint, a state-independent, though time-dependent, growth of the money supply would deserve consideration as a 'rough' approach to containing inflation variability at equilibrium.[10]

In the framework of complete asset markets, an interesting alternative set of instruments is provided by open-market operations on contingent nominal claims, or 'Arrow securities', after Arrow (1953). Indeed, in a monetary economy, complete markets mean markets for both real and nominal state-contingent claims. Given the real allocation, hence the real rates, the price at node s_t of a unit nominal claim contingent on any successor event s_{t+1} is subject to a no-arbitrage condition, akin to a 'contingent Fisher condition', yielding the inflation factor $1 + \tilde{\varphi}_{st+1}$ as the ratio of the price of a real contingent claim to the price of a nominal contingent claim. Given the real price, controlling the nominal price means controlling the state-contingent inflation, at equilibrium. With options markets and derivative pricing, that unexplored avenue is not outlandish. The sobering fact is that markets for options are developing mostly for price-contingent options, with mixed success for options contingent on economic indicators, as the fate of the Chicago exchange for options on the CPI and the absence of macromarkets[11] indicate, and with no markets in sight for options contingent on exogenous events.

4.2.3 Autonomous inflationary pressures

The root of the inflation problem, also as seen by policy analysts, is that the price level does not adjust passively to a comprehensive monetary policy, but is instead subject to autonomous impulses. Prices are set by agents, firms and unions, or emerge on organized markets, for oil or agricultural crops. Some degrees of nominal indeterminacy are *de facto* lifted by the process of nominal price formation. Hence they are not available to conduct a comprehensive monetary policy.

In order to assess realistically the prospects for controlling nominal variables through monetary policy, it is imperative to understand the process of nominal price formation. Current understanding is far from adequate.[12] Example 6.2 (see pp. 53) illustrates the extent to which nominal price formation curtails the scope of monetary policies. It introduces as a property of nominal price formation the stipulation that nominal prices of individual commodities are non-decreasing over time. The nominal interest rate has a uniquely determined floor. If the bank sets a lower rate, it forces the economy out of competitive equilibrium; if it sets a higher rate, it induces unnecessary excess inflation.

When the price level does not respond passively to a comprehensive monetary policy, a number of intriguing questions arises. First, one would like to know whether the process of nominal price formation claims fewer or more than S d.o.n.i.s. If fewer, one could still think about interest rate policies as part of a definition of equilibrium; if more, one should consider such policies outright as calling for out-of-equilibrium analysis, unless the range of admissible policies be suitably curtailed. Second, should one think about out-of-equilibrium situations as arising within a non-tâtonnement process of adjustment towards equilibrium; or as successive elements in a sequence of short-run equilibria; or possibly as situations of persistent disequilibrium? There is clearly room for alternative, perhaps partly complementary, approaches to out-of-equilibrium analysis of monetary policy, with qualitatively different implications.

The qualitative differences are suggestively illustrated by a simple remark. Staggered contracts are supposed to define a sequence of short-run equilibria, constrained by the rigidity of the prices which are not currently up for revision, but were previously set under rational expectations. Positive inflation implies continuously changing relative prices, and the dispersion of prices is a source of misallocation.[13] In contrast, along an adjustment process, prices move to correct disequilibria, which, incidentally, is more convincing than moving according to a fixed or random sequence; speedier price adjustments, possibly accompanied by higher inflation, if there is asymmetry between upward and downward flexibility, entail less misallocation.[14] It is, thus, important to understand the process of nominal price formation.

An intriguing question about the process of nominal price formation is whether states of the world can be defined so exhaustively that nominal price levels are uniquely determined, given the state. This would call for introducing such qualitative considerations as union militancy or oil cartel effectiveness in the definition of the states, along with crop sizes, indirect tax rates and the like. That question arises in non-monetary general equilibrium theory as well.[15] The monetary context is somewhat more complex, because of the nominal indeterminacies. One should rather expect the nominal price level to be fully determined, given the state and the preannounced monetary policy. But this also calls for a very extensive concept of states, implying grossly incomplete markets. The situation is more problematic than it appears at first, because of the uncertainty about the very process of nominal price formation; should the alternative theories, and learning about their plausibility, also appear in the definition of the states?

4.2.4 *Transparency*

Explicit, state-contingent monetary policy is not easy. The difficulty is the same for a central bank as for private agents drawing state-contingent contracts. In practice, one would expect the rule to be defined with reference to a few economic indicators, such as inflation rates, unemployment rates, capacity utilization rates, and so on. These are not primitive exogenous events, like a political decision about EMU or the outcome of an election, as the logic underlying event-trees requires.

It is possible that sophisticated central bankers do in fact follow a state-contingent rule, but choose to keep the rule implicit. They prefer to evaluate the state of the economy on the basis of all the evidence in their possession and draw conclusions, without tying themselves down to an explicit rule involving a limited set of indicators. A formal discussion of the relative merits of these two approaches lies beyond the scope of this chapter. Yet, advocates of transparency as a virtue in the conduct of monetary policy would plead for a gradual shift of emphasis towards more explicit disclosure of the indicators used by central bankers, and of their influence on the adjustments of instruments.

5 Non-neutrality

5.1 Liquidity costs

Nominal rates of interest almost always carry real effects, when money balances do not earn interest. In the simplest possible framework, an Edgeworth box extended to monetary exchange, as in Example 6.1 (p. 51) money demand results from a cash-in-advance constraint. The bank sets the rate of interest, and the price level via money supply. Alternatively, the price level, which is inconsequential, is exogenous, and the bank accommodates money demand.

Higher rates of interest restrict trade and, up to redistributive aspects which favour the shareholders of the bank, they lower utility. This is the general argument, following Vickrey (1959) and Friedman (1968), that it is inefficient to economise on costless balances.

This particular departure from neutrality is not very significant, in a world of electronic and plastic money, where demand deposits or money-market accounts pay interest.[16] But the cost is largely independent of nominal rates; rather, it is due to the difference between two rates: the rate on demand deposits versus the rate on savings deposits. In any case, the cost is small compared to the real cost of credit card transactions.

With reference to current debates on monetary policy, real effects associated with monetary transactions are not in the foreground. The concern lies with the impact of monetary policy on inflation and activity levels. Monetary theory deals with the identification of such an impact, or absence thereof, and with the transmission channels along which they operate.

The theory of competitive equilibria in economies with complete markets is ill-suited for that task. Incomplete asset markets and non-Walrasian equilibria must be brought in. There are good independent reasons for doing so in any case. But it is technically more demanding. It is necessary to rely on examples to illustrate the possibility of fitting empirically relevant departures from neutrality into intertemporal general equilibrium theory, suitably broadened.

5.2 Wealth effects

A significant source of effectiveness of monetary policy lies in the wealth effects of interest rates when there is outstanding public debt and 'Ricardian equivalence' is only partial; meaning that the households do not match increases in public debt by increases in private savings to service the debt , and retire it at maturity. The empirical record[17] suggests indeed a match by private savings well below 100 per cent. The econometric work on the transmission mechanism,[18] similarly points to the effect on consumer wealth, hence on savings, as the main transmission channel from nominal interest rates to consumer spending. For the general equilibrium theorist, incomplete Ricardian equivalence and incomplete markets go hand-in-hand. The fact that many households involved in market clearing at future dates, when debt will be retired, are not participating in transactions today is one reason for the nonexistence of long-term contingent or futures markets. The suggestion that they may be represented by dynastic ancestors is well taken, but the representation is only partial, and the practical impossibility of borrowing today on the strength of future earnings of descendants puts many households at corner solutions. Hence the partial equivalence.

This significant component of the thinking of policy analysts and monetary authorities is easily embodied in formal models of intertemporal general equilibrium; Example 6.3 (on p. 54) illustrates this point.

5.3 Nominal rigidities

Nominal wage and price stickiness is another major source of monetary policy effectiveness. This is natural, since downward nominal rigidities of wages and prices, the more relevant case, individually breed involuntary unemployment and excess capacities. Excess supply of labour or goods generates income effects which reduce aggregate spending, thereby reducing the need for price increases on other goods. Policy analysts seem to agree that in the short run, contractionary monetary policies are effective in curbing inflation through reduced activity. A suitably flexible general equilibrium model allows for that feature. The real challenge to general equilibrium theorists is to model the price formation process, allowing for quantity-constrained allocations during the adjustment process, which now interacts with the monetary policy.

Models with many goods – but no auctioneer – are needed to develop relevant theories of price formation and inflation. When some prices – oil or wages of high-skilled employees, for example – rise for exogenous reasons – a cartel, an energy tax, or skill-biased technological progress, say

– there is no mechanism whereby the myriad of prices for goods and services not directly affected by this development should fall by the amount required to keep the price level constant.

An incomplete asset market, especially in economies with production and asymmetric information, provides additional and distinct, if related, arguments for the effectiveness of monetary policy; interestingly, some formalize earlier arguments and rely solely on the role of money as a unit of account.

Assets serve to transfer revenue across dates and realizations of uncertainty; a transfer of revenue is attainable if it is the payoff of a portfolio of marketed assets; the allocation of resources at equilibrium depends essentially on the attainable transfers of revenue. When the asset market is complete, all transfers of revenue are attainable; when the asset market is incomplete, policies that alter the span of the payoffs of marketed assets affect the allocation of resources at equilibrium. If assets are real or indexed, changes in the price level across dates or realizations of uncertainty fail to alter the span of the payoff of marketed assets and are neutral. If assets are nominal, changes in the price level, the reciprocal of the purchasing power of units of account, alter the span of the payoffs of marketed assets and have real effects.[19]

A limitation of several previous results is the fact that they establish the existence of real effects of price level variability; they typically also demonstrate the suboptimality of state-independent rates of inflation, but fail to characterize in operational terms second-best efficient state profiles of inflation.[20]

6 Examples

6.1 Liquidity costs

Money provides liquidity, and balances are issued by a bank that accomodates demand and pays out its profit as dividend to shareholders. There exists a continuum of competitive equilibria indexed by the rate of interest. Up to redistributive effects, competitive allocations are Pareto ranked, and a vanishing rate of interest yields a Pareto optimal allocation.[21]

There is one time period and no uncertainty – the indices of dates and date-events or states of the world are unnecessary.

Commodities are $l \in \mathcal{L} = \{1, 2\}$.

A bundle of commodities is $z = (z_1, z_2)$, and prices of commodities are $p = (p_1, p_2)$.

There is one medium of exchange, and balances are m.
A monetary authority controls the rate of interest, r, and the supply of balances, M.
There is no production.
Individuals are $i \in \mathcal{I} = \{1, 2\}$.

The exchange set correspondence of each individual is defined by $\Phi^i(p, r) = \{(z, m) : pz^+ \leq m\}$: a cash-in-advance constraint is operative. The preference correspondence of individual 1 is represented by the utility function $u^1(z) = \ln(1 + z_1) + \ln z_2$, and of individual 2 by the utility function $u^2(z) = \ln z_1 + \ln(1 + z_2)$; the $(z_j)'$ s are net trades summing, at equilibrium, to zero for each commodity. Equivalently, individuals 1 and 2 have identical preferences represented by logarithmic utility functions over consumption and endowments (1, 0) and (0, 1) respectively. The share of individual 1 in the bank is $\theta^1 \geq 0$, and that of individual 2 is $\theta^2 = 1 - \theta^1 \geq 0$.

At rate of interest $\bar{r}$, competitive equilibrium prices of commodities are:

$$p_1 = \bar{M}\frac{2 + 2\bar{x} + \theta^1\bar{r}^2}{2 + \bar{r}}$$

$$p_2 = \bar{M}\frac{2 + 2\bar{r} + \theta^2\bar{r}^2}{2 + \bar{r}}$$

The net trade of commodities of individual 1 is:

$$z_1^1 = \frac{(1 + \bar{r})(1 + \theta^1\bar{r})}{2 + 2\bar{r} + \theta^1\bar{r}^2} - 1$$

$$z_2^1 = \frac{1 + \theta^1\bar{r}}{2 + 2\bar{r} + \theta^2\bar{r}^2}$$

and the utility of either individual at equilibrium is:

$$u^i = \ln(1 + \bar{r}) + 2\ln(1 + \theta^i\bar{r}) - \ln(2 + 2\bar{r} + \theta^1\bar{r}^2) - \ln(2 + 2\bar{r} + \theta^2\bar{r}^2)$$

There is a continuum of distinct equilibrium allocations indexed by the nominal rate of interest, $\bar{r}$.

For $\theta^1 = \theta^2 = 1/2$, the competitive equilibrium allocation associated with $\bar{r}$ is Pareto superior to that associated with $\bar{r}' > \bar{r}$; and the competitive equilibrium allocation associated with $\bar{r} = 0$ is Pareto superior to all others. But this is not necessarily the case when $\theta^1 \neq \theta^2$; in general, transfers of revenue may be required to compensate individuals for the loss in dividend income from their shares in banks.

6.2 Nominal rigidities

Price rigidities affect equilibrium nominal interest rates.

Dates or time periods are $t \in \{1, 2\}$. There is no uncertainty – the indices of date-events or states of the world are unnecessary.
Commodities are $l \in \mathcal{L} = \{1, 2\}$.
A bundle of commodities is $z = (z_{1,1}, z_{2,1}, z_{1,2}, z_{2,2})$, and spot prices of commodities are $\tilde{p} = (\tilde{p}_{1,1}, \tilde{p}_{2,1}, \tilde{p}_{1,2}, \tilde{p}_{2,2})$.
Transactions do not require the use of a medium of exchange and there is no bank and no balances.
There is no production.
Individuals are $i \in \mathcal{I} = \{1, 2\}$.

The exchange set and the preferences of individuals are invariant with respect to the prices of commodities and the interest rate; the exchange set coincides with the set of net trades that yield strictly positive consumption. The preferences of individual 1 are represented by the utility function $u^1(z^1) = \ln((1/2) + z^2_{1,1} + \ln z^1_{2,1} + \ln(1 + z^2_{1,2}) + \ln z^1_{2,2}$, and of individual 2 by the utility function $u^2(z^2) = \ln z^2_{1,1} + \ln((1/2) + z^2_{2,1}) + \ln z^2_{1,2} + \ln(1 + z^2_{2,2})$; the (z_l)'s are net trades summing, at equilibrium, to zero for each commodity. Equivalently, individuals 1 and 2 have identical preferences represented by intertemporal logarithmic utility functions over consumption and endowments (1/2, 0, 1, 0) and (0, 1/2, 0, 1) respectively.

Nominal spot prices are downward rigid, with:

$$\tilde{p}_{1,1} \geq 1, \tilde{p}_{2,1} \geq 1$$

and

$$\tilde{p}_{1,2} \geq \tilde{p}_{1,1}, \tilde{p}_{2,2} \geq \tilde{p}_{2,1}$$

Equilibrium obtains at:

$$x^i_{l,1} = \frac{1}{4}, x^i_{l,2} = \frac{1}{2}, \quad l \epsilon \mathcal{L}, i \epsilon I$$

provided that:

$$\tilde{p}_{l,1} = \frac{2\tilde{p}_{l,2}}{1+r}, \quad l \epsilon \mathcal{L}$$

Thus, $\tilde{p}_{l,2} \geq \tilde{p}_{l,1}$ requires $r \geq 1$.

For $r < 1$, only equilibria with quantity constraints exist.

6.3 Wealth effects

Interest rates have wealth effects when Ricardian equivalence fails, because of staggered generations.

Dates or periods are $t \in \mathcal{T} = \{1, 2\}$; there is no uncertainty – the indices of date-events or states of the world are unnecessary.
Commodities are $\{n, c\}$, labour and a produced consumption good, respectively.
A bundle of commodities is $z = (n_1, c_1, n_2, c_2)$ and spot prices of commodities are spot wages, $\tilde{w}_t$, and $\tilde{p}_t$, spot prices for the consumption good: $\tilde{p} = (\tilde{w}_1, \tilde{p}_1, \tilde{w}_2, \tilde{p}_2)$; the overall price level is defined by $\tilde{w}_1 = 1$, probably inherited.
Transactions do not require the use of a medium of exchange and there is no bank and no balances. However, individuals have, possibly, non-zero initial holdings of 'inside' money or purchasing power.
There is a single firm. Variables without superscript refer to the firm's activity.
The production set of the firm is invariant with respect to prices and the rate of interest. The production set of the firm is $Y = \{y : c_1 = \theta(-n_1)^{1/2}, n_1 \leq 0, \theta > 0, c_2 = -n_2, n_2 \leq 0\}$.
Equilibrium requires $\tilde{w}_2 = \tilde{p}_2$.
At each date, labour is employed as input in order to produce the consumption good, as output. There is no storage.
Individuals are $i \in \mathcal{I} = \{1, 2, 3\}$.

The exchange set and the preferences of individuals are invariant with respect to the prices of commodities and the interest rate; the exchange set coincides with the set of net trades that yield non-negative consumption. The demographic structure of the economy corresponds to a 'slice' from an economy with overlapping generations.

Individual 1 lives through period 1; his/her preferences are represented by the utility function $u^1(z^1) = c_1^1$; the individual has no endowment in commodities; but s/he is endowed with a bond promising d units of money or purchasing power at the beginning of period 2, with value $d/(1 + r)$ at period 1; s/he consumes $c_1^1 = d/(1 + r)p_1$, in period 1.

Individual 2 lives through periods 1 and 2; his/her preferences are represented by the utility function $u^2(z^2) = c_1^2 c_2^2(2 + n_1^2)$; equivalently, the individual is endowed with $\bar{n}_1^2 = 2$ units of labour in period 1; in addition, the individual is endowed with the ownership of the firm. Consequently, the budget constraint of the individual is:

$$\tilde{w}_1 n_1^2 + \tilde{p}_1 c_1^2 + \frac{\tilde{p}_2 c_2^2}{1+r} \leq v$$

where v are the profits of the firm; $v = \tilde{p}_1 \theta(-n)^{1/2} + n_1$ is maximal at:

$$-n_1 = (\frac{\theta \tilde{p}_1}{2})^2,\ c_1 = \frac{\theta^2 \tilde{p}_1}{2},\ v = \frac{\theta^2 \tilde{p}_1^2}{4}$$

Utility maximization by individual 2 implies that:

$$\tilde{p}_1 c_1^2 = \frac{\tilde{p}_2 c_2^2}{1+r} = 2 + n_1^2$$

The budget constraint imposes that:

$$2\tilde{p}_1 c_1^2 = -n_1^2 + v = -n_1^2 + \frac{\theta^2 \tilde{p}_1^2}{4}$$

Individual 3 lives through period 2; his/her preferences are represented by the utility function $u^3(z^3) = c_2^3$; the individual is endowed with labour at date 2, $\bar{n}_2^3 = 1$, which s/he supplies inelastically: $n_2^3 = -1$; in addition, s/he is subject to a levy of d, in order to retire the bond; s/he consumes $c_2^3 = (\tilde{w}_2 - d)/\tilde{p}_2$, in period 2.

With the good not storable, equilibrium at date 1 requires that:

$$c_1 = c_1^1 + c_1^2 \text{ with } -n_1 = -n_1^2 = (\frac{\theta \tilde{p}_1}{2})^2,\ c_1^2 = \frac{\theta^2 \tilde{p}_1}{4}$$

Hence,

$$c_1 = \frac{\theta^2 \tilde{p}_1}{2} = \frac{d}{(1+r)\tilde{p}_1} + \frac{\theta^2 \tilde{p}_1}{4},\ \tilde{p}_1 = \frac{2}{\theta}(\frac{d}{1+r})^{1/2}$$

so that

$$c_1 = \theta(\frac{d}{1+r})^{1/2},\ -n_1 = \frac{d}{1+r} = \tilde{p}_1 c_1^2 = v$$

This equilibrium has the property that $\tilde{p}_1$, c_1 and $|n_1|$ are decreasing in r: there is an input–inflation trade-off.

Also, $\tilde{p}_2 c_2 = (1 + r)\ \tilde{p}_1 c_1^2 = d$.

Equilibrium at date 2 requires that $c_2 = -n_2 = -n_2^3 - d/\tilde{p}_2 + d/\tilde{p}_2 = -n_2^3$: it obtains as an identity. The price $\tilde{p}_2$ is indeterminate, but affects the allocation of output between individuals 2 and 3. A unique $\tilde{p}_2$ is easily obtained, for instance by changing the preferences of individual 2, so that $u^2(z^2) = c_1^2(b + c^2{}_2)\ (2 + n_1^2)$.

Remark

If the productivity parameter, θ, which is known at the beginning of period 1, is stochastic, as is the case in real business-cycle models, the interest rate, r, can be chosen, as a function of θ:

(i) to stabilize the price of the consumption good, $\tilde{p}_1$, which calls for $1 + r \propto \theta^{-2}$;
(ii) to stabilize output, c_1, which calls for $1 + r \propto \theta^2$; or
(iii) to stabilize employment, $-n_1$, which calls for constant r.

Naturally, one cannot stabilize 3 variables with a single instrument.

Notes

1 Initial debts place implicit restrictions on price levels if survival of debtors is to be guaranteed. That complication is eschewed in Drèze and Polemarchakis (2000) by assuming zero initial holdings of nominal claims or liabilities. Note 8, below, elaborates on this.
2 This distinguishes the formulation from that of Dubey and Geanakoplos (1992), and accounts for the indeterminacy of interest rates.
3 It was pointed out by Jean-Michel Grandmont that non-interest-bearing money could be regarded as a form of price rigidity, which tilts the scale against neutrality. The remark is well taken, but the specification remains empirically relevant; also, all markets, including the markets for balances, do clear.
4 It is natural that some authors – among others, Ostroy and Starr (1974) and more recently Kiyotaki and Wright (1989) – have looked upstream of simple market institutions in order to explain why most transactions take the form of exchanges of goods for money. Here, this commonplace observation is a factual starting point.
5 For specific purposes of financial analysis, such as cash management, detailed attention is paid to the day-to-day profile of money demand and overnight interest rates; Hellwig (1992). At the same time, it is legitimate to disregard these aspects when investigating the theoretical foundations of monetary policy. It is, after all, an intrinsic feature of fiat money that its supply can be adjusted from day to day at no real cost, and it is a property of a well-functioning banking system that it accommodates smoothly short-run variations in money demand.
6 The precise meaning of 'similar' is explained in Note 8 below.
7 Technically, the expectation is defined, not with respect to the probabilities of future states, which may differ across individuals, but with respect to the prices q_s for unit nominal claims contingent on the states. This expectation is well defined because $(\Sigma_{s \in \mathcal{S}} q_s (\tilde{p}_s - p_0)/p_0)/\Sigma_{s \in \mathcal{S}} q_s = (\Sigma_{s \in \mathcal{S}} q'_s\, (\tilde{p}'_s - p_0)/p_0)/\Sigma_{s \in \mathcal{S}} q'_s$. The variability of inflation is unrestricted, because the vectors $(\ldots, \tilde{p}_s/\Sigma_{s \in \mathcal{S}}\, \tilde{p}_s, \ldots)$ and $(\ldots, \tilde{p}'_s/\Sigma_{s \in \mathcal{S}}\, \tilde{p}'_s) = (\ldots, \lambda_s\, \tilde{p}_s/\Sigma_{s \in \mathcal{S}}\, \lambda_s \tilde{p}_s, \ldots)$ are variation-free, up to the constraint $\Sigma_{s \in \mathcal{S}}\, \lambda_s^{-1} q_s = (1 + r_0)^{-1}$.

8 When Proposition 1 is applied to the subtree starting at some node s_t, $t > 1$, a competitive equilibrium defined over the entire tree starting at s_1 typically entails non-zero nominal claims or liabilities at s_t. The indeterminacy of nominal variables over the subtree follows from the indeterminacy over the entire tree, but is accompanied by variations in the nominal claims and liabilities at s_t matching the variations in the price level there. Survival of consumers is not an issue, because the nominal liabilities at s_t are part of a feasible allocation over the entire tree.

9 Interestingly, Eichenbaum (1997), also quoting Chari, Christiano and Eichenbaum (1996), advocates an 'institutional innovation', whereby monetary policy would take the form of a commitment to one-period-ahead, state-contingent policy actions.

10 The approach is 'rough' because different states and events may entail (i) different growth rates of real output; or (ii) different levels of nominal interest rates; in addition to (iii) different inflationary pressures. Differences (i) and (ii) entail differences in money demand that could be matched by adjustment of money supply at unchanged price levels.

11 Shiller (1993).

12 Several simple models have been proposed; for instance, staggered contracts by Taylor (1980) and Calvo (1983), or menu-costs by Mankiw (1985) and Blanchard and Kiyotaki (1987).

13 As in Goodfriend and King (1997).

14 As in Drèze (1993b).

15 Drèze (1993a).

16 Feldstein (1996) estimates liquidity cost at 0.01 per cent of GDP per percentage point of nominal interest. This estimate is consistent with the inventory-theoretic equality between interest forgone on balances and the value of real resources devoted to economize on balances. Lucas, in Chapter 4 in this volume, obtains slightly higher values, which are, however, sensitive to modelling assumptions at very low levels of inflation, or of interest differentials.

17 For example, Tobin (1980).

18 For example, the FMP model – Modigliani (1971).

19 This argument was developed by Detemple, Gottardi and Polemarchakis (1993) and Magill and Quinzii (1992), exploiting the argument of Balasko and Cass (1989), Cass (1985) and Geanakoplos and Mas-Colell (1989) for the indeterminacy of competitive equilibrium allocations when assets are nominal and the asset market is incomplete.

20 The most constructive result in this vein, due to Magill and Quinzii (1996), establishes that adding a price-level variability within exogenous real events can only do harm; this is a plausible, useful result – but it does not have a bearing on the issue of improving risk-sharing through suitably characterized second-best state-profiles of inflation rates. Another constructive result is that, in an economy with risky assets and a defaultless nominal bond, where the CAPM assumptions on endowments and preferences are satisfied, state-independent inflation is efficient.

21 Drèze and Polemarchakis (1999).

References

Arrow, K. J. (1953) 'Le rôle des valeurs boursières pour la répartition la meilleure des Risques', *Econométrie*, vol. 11, pp. 41–8, (Paris: Edition du CNRS).

Arrow, K. J. and G. Debreu (1954) 'The Existence of Equilibria for a Competitive Economy', *Econometrica*, vol. 22, pp. 265–90.

Balasko, Y. and D. Cass (1989) 'The Structure of Financial Equilibrium, I: Exogenous Yields and Unrestricted Participation', *Econometrica*, vol. 57, pp. 135–62.

Baumol, W. J. (1952) 'The Transactions Demand for Cash: an Inventory Theoretic Approach', *Quarterly Journal of Economics*, vol. 66, pp. 545–56.

Blanchard, O. J. and N. Kiyotaki (1987) 'Monopolistic Competition and the Effects of Aggregate Demand', *American Economic Review*, vol. 77, pp. 647–66.

Calvo, G. (1983) 'Staggered Prices in a Utility-maximizing framework', *Journal of Monetary Economics*, vol. 12, pp. 383–98.

Cass, D. (1985) 'On the "Number" of Equilibrium Allocations with Financial Markets', Working Paper No. 8500, CARESS, University of Pennsylvania, Philadelphia.

Chari, V. V., L. J. Christiano and M. Eichenbaum (1996) 'Expectation Traps and Discretion', NBER Working Paper No. 5541.

Clower, R. (1967) 'A Reconsideration of the Microfoundations of Monetary Theory', *Western Economic Journal*, vol. 6, pp. 1–8.

Debreu, G. (1959) *Theory of Value* (New York: John Wiley).

Debreu, G. (1960) 'Une économie de l'incertain', *Economie Appliquée*, vol. 13, pp. 111–16.

Detemple, J., P. Gottardi and H. M. Polemarchakis (1993) 'The Relevance of Financial Policy', *European Economic Review*, vol. 39, pp. 1133–54.

Drèze, J. H. (1993a) 'The Formulation of Uncertainty: Prices and States', Discussion paper 9347, CORE, Université Catholique de Louvain, Louvain-la-Neuve.

Drèze, J. H. (1993b) *Money and Uncertainty* (Rome: Edizioni del Elefante).

Drèze, J. H. and H. M. Polemarchakis (2000) 'Monetary Equilibria', Discussion paper 2000–44, CORE, Université Catholique de Louvain, Louvain-la-Neuve.

Drèze, J. H. and H. M. Polemarchakis (1999) 'Money and Monetary Policy in General Equilibrium', in Gérard-Varet, L.-A., A. P. Kirman and M. Ruggiero (eds), *Economics, the Next Ten Years* (Oxford University Press).

Dubey, P. and J. D. Geanakoplos (1992) 'The Value of Money in a Finite Horizon Economy: a Role for Banks', in Dasgupta, P. S., D. Gale, O. D. Hart and E. Maskin (eds), *Economic Analysis of Markets and Games, Essays in Honor of Frank Hahn* (Cambridge, Mass.: MIT Press).

Eichenbaum, M. (1997) 'Some Thoughts on Practical Stabilization Policy', *American Economic Review*, vol. 87, pp. 236–9.

Feldstein, M. (1996) 'The Costs and Benefits of Going from Low Inflation to Price stability', Discussion Paper No. 5469 (Cambridge, Mass.: NBER).

Friedman, M. (1969) 'The Optimum Quantity of Money', in Friedman, M., *The Optimum Quantity of Money and Other Essays* (Chicago: Aldine).

Geanakoplos, J. D. and A. Mas-Colell (1989) 'Real Indeterminacy with Financial Assets', *Journal of Economic Theory*, vol. 47, pp. 22–38.

Goodfriend, M. and R. C. King (1997) 'The New Neoclassical Synthesis and the Role of Monetary Policy', Mimeo, University of Virginia, Charlottesville.

Hellwig, M. (1992) 'The Challenges of Monetary Theory', *European Economic Review*, vol. 37, pp. 215–42.

Kiyotaki, N. and R. Wright (1989) 'On Money as a Medium of Exchange', *Journal of Political Economy*, vol. 97, pp. 927–54.
Magill, M. J. P. and M. Quinzii (1992) 'Real Effects of Money with Nominal Assets', *Journal of Mathematical Economics*, vol. 21, pp. 301–42.
Magill, M. J. P. and M. Quinzii (1996) *Theory of Incomplete Markets* (Cambridge, Mass.: MIT Press).
Mankiw, G. (1985) 'Small Menu costs and Large Business Cycles: a Macroeconomic Model of Monopoly', *Quarterly Journal of Economics*, vol. 100, pp. 529–39.
Modigliani, F. (1971) 'Monetary Policy and Consumption: Linkages via Interest Rates and Wealth Effects in the FMP Model', in Federal Reserve Bank of Boston, *Consumer Spending and Monetary Policy: The Linkages* (Boston, Mass.).
Ostroy, J. M. and R. M. Starr (1974) 'Money and the Decentralization of Exchange', *Econometrica*, vol. 42, pp. 1093–113.
Patinkin, D. (1965) *Money, Interest and Price*, 2nd edn (New York: Harper and Row).
Radner, R. (1972) 'Existence of Equilibrium of Plan, Prices and Price Expectations', *Econometrica*, vol. 40, pp. 289–303.
Shiller, R. J. (1993) *Macro Markets: Creating Institutions for Managing Society's Largest Risks* (Oxford: Clarendon Press).
Taylor, J. B. (1980) 'Aggregate Dynamics and Staggered Contracts', *Journal of Political Economy*, vol. 88, pp. 1–24.
Tobin, J. (1956) 'The Interest-elasticity of Transactions Demand for Cash', *Review of Economics and Statistics*, vol. 38, pp. 241–47.
Tobin, J. (1980) *Asset Accumulation and Economic Activity* (Oxford: Basil Blackwell).
Vickrey, W. (1959) 'The Optimum Trend of Prices', *Southern Economic Journal*, vol. 25, pp. 315–16.

Comment

Jean-Michel Grandmont
Centre de Recherche en Economie et Statistique, Paris, France

This chapter is a welcome attempt to reformulate and extend the standard Arrow–Debreu general equilibrium model, to make it fitting to the study of monetary issues, with the hope that this endeavour will stimulate a useful exchange with specialists of monetary theory and policy.

The basic framework is relatively standard. The economy evolves finitely over many discrete time periods, $t = 1,\ldots,T$. At each date $t > 1$, there are (possibly random) shocks that affect the 'fundamentals' of the economy (endowments, technology, tastes). The heuristic Arrow–Debreu representation (which is also used by game theorists, with a different interpretation) of the dynamics of the system, is a 'tree', as shown in Figure 2.2. Each 'node' (a 'date-event') of the tree stands for a date, and the

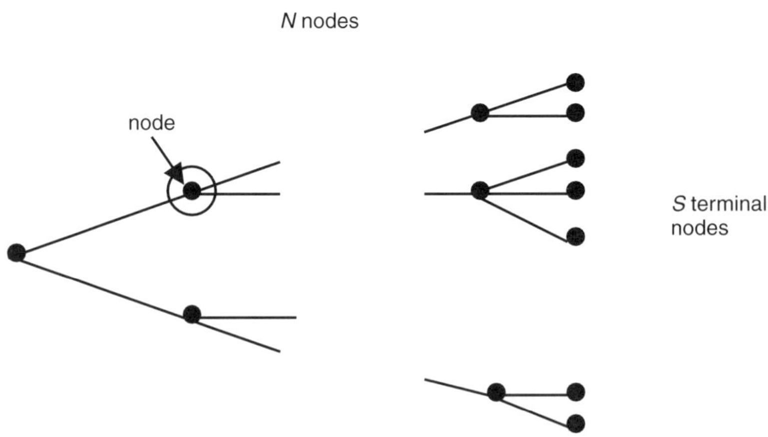

Figure 2.2

history of shocks to the fundamentals up to (and including) that date. In the authors' notation, the tree involves N nodes, including S terminal nodes ('states of the world') at the final date T. This representation is technically useful as it allows the redefinition of commodities, not only by their physical characteristics (and location), but also by the circumstances; that is, the node at which they are available. When markets are complete, as is assumed by the authors, this trick permits the reduction of the economy to a static one, which is technically convenient when studying existence of a competitive equilibrium and its efficiency.

I shall at times refer to another equivalent heuristic representation, that may be more easily interpretable by the numerous students who have analyzed monetary issues over the years, in perhaps more specific frameworks (representative agents, aggregative macroeconomic models, with or without explicit microeconomic choice theoretic foundations), but have nevertheless imposed on their models the discipline of the equilibrium approach. There (Figure 2.3), the economy evolves along the one-dimensional time variable (the horizontal axis). Considering the economy at some date, conditionally on the history of shocks up to that date, is equivalent to considering the corresponding node in the Arrow–Debreu tree.

Trade takes place sequentially over time. The money considered here is of the 'inside' variety: at each date, the amount of money in circulation is the exact counterpart of the total debt owed by borrowers. It is further supposed that the interest rates paid on money balances in banking accounts, and charged to borrowers, are equal. Money also plays an explicit role in exchange, that is, modelled through a transactions constraint (a general form of, say, Clower's cash-in-advance constraint) and/or generalized preferences or technologies (a general form of 'money in the utility or production function'). Markets are competitive, complete (there are enough financial assets to enable agents to insure themselves against all possible contingencies), and anticipations are rational. A significant feature of the model is that money used in transactions does not bear interest. A variation of the nominal interest rate at some date (node) will then have typically real effects, since it modifies the spread between the interest rates paid on money balances deposited in the banking system, and on money (for example, cash) used in the transactions process (that is, zero): these are, in effect, two different assets.

The main focus of the chapter is to assess the possibility of influencing equilibrium through monetary policy. The authors adopt a not-entirely-unheard-of definition of a 'monetary policy': it is a choice of instruments (interest rate, money supply), together with a 'state-contingent rule' specifying the values of these instruments as a function of the information available to the monetary authorities. Now, if equilibrium were unique there would be no possibility of monetary policy influencing equilibrium, except in purely nominal terms. So any study of this issue necessarily goes through an analysis of the dimension of indeterminacy of equilibrium. The authors indeed show a result that, in their own words, 'lies at the core of [their] thinking about monetary policy': the set of equilibria can be indexed by $N + S$ nominal magnitudes. This means that, if monetary authorities set (to fix ideas) the nominal interest rate at each node of the Arrow–Debreu tree in Figure 2.2, there remain S nominal variables to be set, which we may take for the purpose of this discussion as the price 'levels' at each of the S terminal nodes of the tree. One of these degrees of indeterminacy is purely nominal (one can always multiply prices at every node in the tree by a common positive number without changing equilibrium real magnitudes when there are no initial assets at the first date $t = 1$). The remaining $S - 1$ degrees of indeterminacy are typically real, since they involve the *relative* price levels between the S terminal nodes. To sum up: even when monetary authorities can control nominal interest rates at each node of the tree, the relative terminal price levels are indeterminate.

The authors draw a provocative conclusion from this analysis: 'one cannot hope to control variability of inflation through nominal interest rates alone, at equilibrium'. It may be worth reflecting a little on the assumptions underlying this conclusion, as it appears to be slightly at variance with the conclusions reached by numerous monetary policy analysts, using admitted more specific models but adopting a similar equilibrium methodology, who have studied over the years how monetary policy rules could affect not only the levels of output, inflation, but also their variability.

It seems to me that the authors, considering that monetary authorities can set an instrument (in this discussion, the nominal interest rate) at each *node* of the Arrow–Debreu tree in Figure 2.2, implicitly assumed that the only information available to the monetary authorities, at that node, is the history of real shocks affecting the fundamentals up to that date. While this formulation of a 'state contingent policy rule' appears natural in an orthodox Arrow–Debreu framework, where the definition of a state typically involves only exogenous events, it seems to restrict unduly the information upon which monetary authorities can act. Most monetary students, using more or less explicitly the equivalent but more flexible framework underlying Figure 2.3, would also incorporate in the information set of the monetary authorities the sequence of current and past

Figure 2.3

prices, and nominal interest rates. If the authors investigate the influence of monetary policy rules (for example, the choice of nominal interest rates) based upon the full information available to monetary authorities (including current and past equilibrium prices and interest rates), they might find that monetary policy has more scope in their model. Implementing this programme under various assumptions about the information available to the monetary authorities (for instance, one might assume that they cannot condition their choice of instruments on the *current* price system, or in the specific language of students of monetary issues, the policy rule is 'predetermined'), would be an interesting project. It would allow, in particular, to compare the findings obtained in this integrated general Arrow–Debreu framework, with the results of the numerous studies of the same issues that appear in the monetary literature.

When there is indeterminacy of equilibrium, one may argue that the model is incomplete, because it lacks a theory of price formation that might alleviate the indeterminacy. The point is well taken, and goes well beyond the present model. It is also not entirely unheard of: there is a voluminous literature on equilibrium selection in macroeconomic models with rational expectations (as well as in game theory!). On the other hand, the point does not appear to me to undermine the analysis of monetary policy effectiveness: if a properly designed policy based on appropriate information does, under rational expectations, remove part or all of the indeterminacy, this fact stands no matter what is 'the process of price formation', if expectations are rational. The only way to impair the ability of monetary policy to select from among indeterminate equilibria in the present model, would be (to me) to impose nominal 'rigidities' that are independent of the agents' expectations about monetary policy. I have nothing against a weakening of the axiom of rational expectations, but it would seem that the analysis of this issue would call for a somewhat different model. And I do not think I have to remind anybody of the conceptual difficulties involved in an 'independent' nominal price-formation process that would be subject to the so-called 'Lucas critique'.

The authors remark that state-contingent rules used by monetary authorities are largely implicit, and advocate that certain key elements of these rules be made more explicit. The argument may be relevant in practice (it goes back at least to Friedman): one of the most important practical roles of monetary policy may indeed be to stabilize the environment of the economy, so that agents can form 'better' expectations, and one way to implement this may be to have preannounced monetary policy rules. Yet the argument seems to negate one of the basic tenets of the Arrow–Debreu model, namely rational expectations, so that, again, analysis of this issue may call for a somewhat different model. Also, study of this point might benefit from the voluminous related literature on the 'rule versus discretion' debate, credibility, and so on.

Finally, the authors note that the most relevant sources of the effectiveness (non-neutrality) of monetary policy are likely to be related to features that are as yet absent from the Arrow–Debreu framework studied in the present chapter (the authors acknowledge that the mechanism though which monetary policy is effective in their chapter (that is, the interest forgone for cash balances used in transactions) may not be empirically significant), namely incomplete markets (and incomplete information) and non-Walrasian (imperfect competition) equilibrium. These features are indeed likely to be important, and they have not been ignored by macroeconomic or monetary policy analysts. I am thinking in particular of efficiency wages models (and their consequence: involuntary unemployment), credit rationing under incomplete information, models of search, and so on. As noted by the authors, a great unsolved difficulty is that no one knows what the nature of a firm and its objectives are under incomplete markets (not to speak of imperfect competition!). I would like to add that, as I have argued elsewhere for efficiency wages, incomplete markets and/or imperfect competition should only induce 'real' rigidities under the extreme rationality postulates that are often imposed on our models (in particular, rational expectations). Although these models have the interesting feature of involving 'disequilibria' (involuntary unemployment), the channels through which monetary policy may affect real equilibrium magnitudes in such models, are unlikely to differ significantly from those of market-clearing models with variable labour supplies (for example, unemployment will be 'classical'). The hypothetical (and often empirically questioned) presence of 'nominal' price rigidities, and 'why money influences output', are still theoretical puzzles, and the explanations proposed in the literature (menu costs, nominal rigidities associated with real rigidities under near rationality, and so on) are not fully convincing.

I suggest adding to the authors' 'short list' of the channels for monetary policy effectiveness, violations of the 'sacred cow' in economic theory; that is, of the rational expectations hypothesis, which does not seem to fare well in empirical tests. After all, perhaps the main rationale for the design of our economic institutions and policies, may be that private agents, *as well as policymakers*, have some difficulties in predicting the future, quite independently of incomplete markets, imperfect competition, or nominal 'rigidities'. As noted above, the argument is old (Friedman), and appears to favour *simple* monetary rules such as a constant rate of growth of the money supply. As far as I know, the argument has still to be put within a consistent and satisfactory equilibrium framework.

One can only applaud the efforts of two such distinguished theorists in bringing abstract general Arrow–Debreu theory to bear upon monetary policy issues. However, the difficulties of the task should not be underestimated.

Comment

Juan Urrutia
Universidad Carlos III, Madrid, Spain

1 Are Drèze and Polemarchakis up to their ambition?

The paper of J. Drèze and H. Polemarchakis (DP henceforth) is a piece of research on money and monetary policy that tries implicitly to come as close as possible to being simultaneously theoretically and empirically interesting, to use the authors' own language. My first task as a discussant is therefore to ascertain how close the authors come to this desideratum. I will not comment on the technical third part of the chapter (except to say that, although complicated, it is not insurmountable). Instead I shall concentrate on the conceptual difficulty of the chapter, which is by no means small. And I also feel obliged to finish with some very general comment about monetary activism.

The paper is 'interesting' and fresh. Its interest springs from several sources. To begin with, the obvious must be restated. In spite of all neutrality theorems, the practice of monetary authorities (and the thinking behind this practice) is sometimes reputed to be the cause of stable growth and sometimes said to be the detonator of several well-detected, monetary-engineered recessions. No wonder, then, that these practices pose a challenge: they need to be understood. The title of the IEA conference ('Monetary Theory as a Basis for Monetary Policy') patently uncovers this need.

However, to understand something means to ground it in well-known theory. The second source of interest of the DP chapter is that they do not try to ground the thinking and practices of monetary authorities in any more or less fancy monetary theory, but rather on the value theory of money. More precisely, they use the Arrow–Debreu model of general equilibrium in its contingent and temporal interpretation, and with money grafted into it. Recall that this model with T dates can be understood as a tree with S final nodes and N total nodes, and that each branch can be conceived as a state of nature reflecting a (partial) history of stochastic shocks. Within this well-known benchmark they introduce a bank and 'inside' money needed for transaction purposes. Then they fix the vector of short-term interest rates and the vector of short-run price levels, going on to prove the existance of equilibrium and that the degree of nominal indeterminateness is precisely $N + S$.

Any monetary policy that does not try to do more than to determine $N + S$ nominal variables is thus admissible and can be studied in this framework. The authors do this by submitting several possible situations to close scrutiny. The extrapolative way in which they do this, going beyond the limits imposed by naked modelling, is the last source of interest of their chapter and certainly makes for its freshness.

Let us move to the theoretical aspect of this commentary. Is the DP paper wanting theoretically? By this I do not refer to fine technical mathematical points but rather to the use of some features one might have thought had been superseded, and to research strategy in general.

Except in the case of one example, concerned with overlapping generations, the horizon of the model (T) is finite. The conventional reader might forgive this slip, first because the main purpose of the authors is not to endow money with positive value but rather to speculate on monetary policy, and second because, in this context, to observe what happens as T gets larger is a conventional exercise. The more alert reader can even conjecture that the cash-in-advance constraint à la Clower may eliminate the backward induction problem that Hahn pointed to in the late 1960s. But this in itself is not enough. The real cause of the positive value of money is that the money is of the 'inside' type, and as such is issued by the bank against offsetting interest-bearing debt.

Nor do the authors admit the possibility of bankruptcies or the choice of a transaction technology. The former would have posed imposing technical problems and the latter would have not added much to the purpose of the chapter. As previously mentioned, this purpose is not to understand the use of money as a medium of exchange, but rather to make sense of those practices of monetary authorities that can be construed as stylized facts.

One should never judge a piece of research according to what the authors have not done. However, this is precisely what I intend to do now. My only excuse is that this will allow me to identify what their research strategy *cannot* accomplish. An 'old fashioned' theoretician would have introduced a parametrized state-contingent monetary rule in the model, thus abiding by the authors' main result, together with all the fancy features it could accommodate. Then he would have tried to: (i) find conditions that guarantee the existence of an equilibrium in which the vectors of short-run interest rates and price levels are determined; (ii) find conditions under which the equilibrium set is finite; and (iii) perform exercises of comparative statics, changing the parameters of the monetary rule. Had DP done this, they might have confronted technical difficulties in the proof of existence. Is continuity of the generalized consumption correspondence guaranteed under any admissible monetary rule? Is the production correspondence continuous when bankruptcies are allowed? Is convexity not a problem when a detailed transaction technology is admitted? These technical matters are not, however, my main concern here.

What I want to stress is that while it might have been difficult to discuss some of the stylized facts under this alternative set-up, other issues, which I deem to be at least as interesting as those discussed in the chapter, could have been addressed thoroughly. Let me briefly mention two that are conspicuous by their absence. Take first the question of time inconsistency of the policy (and the related issues of reputation and credibility). It could be studied fruitfully in the presence of a specific rule, the parameters of which might be difficult to discover, even under rational expectations and rational learning especially when other rigidities are involved. The second question is not unrelated to the first. It has to do with the fact that the state contingent rule is often implicit. The authors mention the possible analogy to implicit contracts but fail to draw this out, probably because the selected framework is not attuned to the task. In the alternative set-up I am discussing, the literature on optimal contracts could have been brought to bear, and something like the *simplicity* of the rule could have been discussed. The optimal rule could be too complicated and difficult – if not impossible – to discover.

I finally come to what might be called the empirical part of the chapter. I really think that, despite my previous comments, the DP chapter ought to be judged according to how well it accommodates the following list of stylized empirical facts or beliefs:

(i) central banks use some kind of rule: for instance, the so-called Taylor rule which, incidentally, shows that they think they can influence activity;
(ii) central banks believe that manipulation of short-run interest rates has real effects on activity;
(iii) central banks believe that, in the short-term, reducing activity curbs inflation;

(iv) central banks try to avoid inflationary spirals by raising short-term interest rates when inflation expectations are booming; and
(v) central banks try to reduce the volatility of the rate of inflation.

Note that this list – if correct – shows that central banks assume first, that there is an autonomous, independent process of nominal price determination, and second, that monetary interventions have real effects. Do these assumptions and consequent practices make any sense? That is, can they be understood as emerging from a well-defined model of a monetary economy? The chapter seems to support an affirmative answer, but in a way that may cloud clear understanding. The line of reasoning seems to be as follows (including my comments in square brackets):

(i) Monetary policy is a state-contingent (implicit) rule that is used to eliminate nominal indeterminacy. [However, in the model there is not only nominal indeterminacy but also real indeterminacy because of the cash in advance constraint. Therefore, *in the model* a selection of a monetary regime might imply a selection of a particular allocation of resources which in general cannot be Pareto-ranked against its alternatives.]
(ii) Before using monetary policy to eliminate nominal indeterminacy one has to make sure that it has not already been eliminated by some undefined, autonomous process of nominal price determination. [Anything resembling the fiscal theory of price-level determination could be an example of this autonomous process, but one might also take any rigidity that propels an autonomous dynamic of, for example, price levels. Nothing like this exists *within the model*.]
(iii) If there is some space for a monetary policy, one has to decide which instruments can and ought to be used. [The model fixes no problem at this point since it has enough instruments.]
(iv) Before using the available instruments, though, it should be ascertained whether their use may have real effects. [The authors stress that real effects are to be expected in the presence of the assumed autonomous process of nominal price determination. But, as I mentioned above, the model does not eliminate real effects of the selected monetary regime.]
(v) And, of course, the monetary regime should be selected according to the efficiency of the resulting allocation of resources, taking into account the presence of rigidities. [This, of course, cannot always be done.]

If my rendering of their line of reasoning is correct, and my comments not too far-fetched, it follows that DP cannot hope to go through the whole line of reasoning *within their model*. They know that, and they depart from it as often as they see fit, to convey some of their extrapolative ideas. They are in fact very good at finding suggestive examples where a certain well-selected rigidity ends up by making sense of a particular feature of monetary policy. Let me single out for consideration just three of the examples they offer, corresponding to the second, third and fifth 'stylized facts' of my above-mentioned list:

(i) Incomplete markets make the Ricardian equivalence only partial, and in such a world changes in nominal interest rates have real effects, providing there is debt outstanding. (Partial Ricardian equivalence produces the same effects under the same circumstances even with complete markets but it is difficult to understand why equivalence should then be only partial.)
(ii) In a world of disequilibrium, increases in short-term nominal interest rates reduce activity and also inflation. It should be mentioned, however, that this result has nothing to do with the fixed-price type of analysis but rather with considerations of interactions among adjustments in different markets or sectors of the economy.
(iii) In a world of incomplete markets (that is, a model with a set of asset markets that do not span the whole commodity space), it can be shown that the reduction of inflation variability may make sense in terms of risk-sharing in the case of a simple example. No such strong statement has been proved in general.

If, as stated, the chapter has to be judged according to its performance in this empirical aspect, one is liable to say that while it goes a certain way towards closing the gap between monetary theory and monetary policy, the end of this endeavour is not close at hand. A rather harsh summary might sound like this: monetary policy as we know it *plus* something or other is not incompatible with a theory of monetary general equilibrium. Is 'empirically pat' a good expression for summarizing my summary?

In spite of my misgivings, I wish to record that the DP paper comes as close as possible to being simultaneously theoretically and empirically interesting.

The fancy features I miss are not very relevant to the authors' aim, and the alternative model I have suggested is only meant to be constructive and of some use in the deployment of their research strategy.

As stated, I want to close with a very general comment on monetary intervention. Something in the research strategy and the writing of the authors makes the reader believe that they do not have much faith in neutrality theorems applying in the real world. After all, the real effects of monetary policy stem from rigidities proper to the real world. We do not know, however, which particular rigidity is at work in each case and, even worse, we cannot guarantee that, without rigidities, changes in monetary policy will not have real effects. Do not these two details tilt towards non-intervention?

3

The Fiscal Theory of Money as an Unorthodox Financial Theory of the Firm

*Ramon Marimon**
European University Institute, Florence, Italy and Universitat Pompeu Fabra, Barcelona, Spain

1 Introduction

There are three issues in which everyday macroeconomic life and economic theory seem to be quite apart. The first is the zeal with which governments in Europe and elsewhere pursue fiscal discipline as almost a precondition for price stability. One would think that governments were trying to implement a well-established theorem in monetary theory, but while the need to co-ordinate fiscal and monetary policies is a well-understood principle,[1] such a theorem has been missing.

The second issue is the fact that, in many rational expectations monetary equilibrium models, the price level is indeterminate: a fact that the quantity theory had long ago unveiled. In contrast, everyday discussions regarding exchange rate (or other asset prices) movements seem to take prices as being determined.

The third issue is that, while in order to avoid indeterminacy problems, many economists, notably Friedman (1959), have advocated monetary policies that target the supply of money, increasingly central banks have been following endogenous monetary policies – for example, by targeting nominal interest rates, raising again the problem of price determinacy.

In this context, the fiscal theory of money (Sims (1994, 1995); Woodford (1995, 1996)) seems to be the missing theory for which many

* I must thank, and blame, Axel Leijonhufvud for insisting that I write a paper on the *Fiscal Theory of Money*, and for being patient about it. I also want to thank Seppo Honkapohja for his discussion of the paper, Larry Jones who made me aware of the problems with a theory that does not respect Walras's Law, and Giorgia Giovannetti for her comments. The original paper upon which this chapter is based was written while visiting the Elba Center for Economic Research and I thank the staff for their hospitality and patience.

had been looking. It is a theory that provides a rationale to the above three 'common views'. The main elements of the theory are not new. For example, real balance effects had already been accounted for by Fisher (1911) and Wicksell (1936) and, in particular, in Patinkin's seminal work (Patinkin, 1965). Similarly, properly specified models have always taken into account the government's budget, although Christ (1979) had to insist on the importance of taking into account the consolidated budget of the government. What is new in the fiscal theory of money is that the implications of a government's budget accounting and of possible wealth effects are fully worked out in the context of rational expectations models with no special distortions. That is, in models where one would have expected that Ricardian equivalence results would have washed out real balance effects. The results on price determination are in striking contrast to standard quantity theory prescriptions.

The fiscal theory of money is based on an important feature that makes governments different from other agents – say, for example, households: namely, the government's monopoly of a nominal asset: that is, money. But, in this important respect, governments are not different from other agents that issue nominal assets – and in particular, firms. As a way to expose, and assess, the central elements of the fiscal theory, I develop it and present it in the context of an equilibrium model with firms that use a mix of debt and equity as outside financing. The corresponding fiscal financial theory of the firm also appears in marked contrast with standard asset price theory. In the context of the firm, however, it appears to be very transparent how the theory, as a theory of price determination, relies on letting agents (firms, in our case) make plans that violate their 'no default' constraints. This allows for real balance effects (real financial assets effects) based on a peculiar failure of the Modigliani–Miller theorem: fully rational and unconstrained agents do not take debt and equity financing as being equivalent, since (unless prices adjust) they may fail to satisfy standard – 'no default' – transversality constraints.

I present the model in Section 2. In Section 3, I develop some of the implications of the theory and discuss its relationship with asset price theory. In Section 4 I discuss in what sense the fiscal theory determines prices when firms' policies are endogenous. In particular, I show how the indeterminacy problem is related to a problem of policy misspecification. Section 5 concludes.

2 A model with representative agents and firms

In this section I develop a modified version of the Lucas's (1978) model of asset prices. There is a representative firm and a representative consumer.

The firm can use as a source of outside financing a mix of debt and equity. Markets are complete, and agents, being fully rational, only have to satisfy their present value constraints. Financial decisions of the firm are not subject to any distortion, such as taxes, or to legal restrictions on the issuing of new debt or equity. Asset demands are well-defined, since I assume that the consumer, as a proud owner, derives utility from his/her ownership of the firm. I do not discuss whether this is a reasonable assumption (it may well be). Nevertheless, it should be clear from the outset that one can consider an economy without 'preferences for ownership' as a limiting case of the economies studied here (as Woodford's (1998a) 'cashless economies' are limiting cases of monetary economies). I also simplify the analysis by considering a deterministic model.

2.1 Households

Households are represented by an infinitely-living consumer who receives an exogenous stream of income $\{y_t\}$ as well as initial stock of the firm s_0. If the initial total outstanding stock is S_0, its resulting share of the firm is $\theta_0 = s_0/S_0$. In this representative agent economy $\theta_0 = 1$. At any point in time – say, t – the consumer receives from the firm a dividend d_t per unit of stock (which, unless otherwise stated, and consistent with common and legal practice, I assume to be non-negative). S/he can sell his/her stock, $s_t = \theta_t S_t$, and purchase a new one, $s_{t+1} = \theta_{t+1} S_{t+1}$, at the current stock price of q_t (in units of consumption). S/he can also purchase or sell (real) debt issued by the firm, b_{t+1}, which has a (real) return – between periods t and $t+1$ – of R_{t+1}. Therefore, the consumer's problem is:

$$\max \sum_{t=0}^{\infty} \beta^t [u(c_t) + v(\theta_{t+1})]$$

s.t

$$q_t\theta_{t+1}S_{t+1} + b_{t+1} \leq y_t - c_t + (q_t + d_t)\theta_t S_t + R_t b_t$$
$$\text{and} \lim_{T\to\infty} R_{0,T}^{-1}(b_{T+1} + q_T\theta_{T+1}S_{T+1}) = 0$$

where $R_{t,t} \equiv 1$; $R_{t,T} \equiv R_{t+1} \times \ldots \times R_T$. It is assumed that u and v satisfy standard monotonicity, strict concavity and differentiability properties. Furthermore, $v'(1) > 0$ and $\lim_{c\to 0} u'(c) = \infty$.

Whenever the consumer buys stock, s_{t+1}, it must be that:

$$\frac{v'(\theta_{t+1})}{v'(c_t)} = q_t\left\{1 - \frac{q_{t+1} + d_{t+1}}{q_t}\frac{1}{R_{t+1}}\right\} S_{t+1}$$
$$\equiv qt\left(1 - \frac{R^s_{t+1}}{R_{t+1}}\right) S_{t+1} \equiv q_t \Delta_{t+1} S_{t+1} \tag{3.1}$$

where R^s_{t+1} is the return on a unit of stock held from period t to period $t+1$. The consumer also satisfies the standard Euler equation:

$$u'(c_t = \beta R_{t+1} u'(c_{t+1}) \tag{3.2}$$

The two conditions in Equations (1) and (2), together with the consumer's budget constraint, characterize the consumer optimal consumption and portfolio decisions.

The intertemporal budget constraint, together with the transversality condition (the present value of his/her 'terminal' portfolio must be zero), are equivalent to his/her present value budget constraint. To see this, let $V_t \equiv (q_t + d_t)\theta_t S_t + R_t b_t$; that is, the value of the household portfolio – of the firm's equity and debt – at the beginning of period t after the stock market has cleared. Then, the value of the portfolio has the following law of motion:

$$V_{t+1} = R_{t+1}[V_t + y_t - c_t - q_t \Delta_{t+1} \theta_{t+1} S_{t+1}]$$

which results in:

$$V_0 + \sum_{t=0}^{T} R_{0,t}^{-1}(y_t - c_t - q_t \Delta_{t+1} \theta_{t+1} S_{t+1}) = R_{0,T+1}^{-1} V_{T+1}$$

or, even more conveniently, in:

$$\begin{aligned} V_0 + (y_0 - c_0) + \sum_{t=1}^{T} R_{0,t}^{-1}(y_t + d_t \theta_t S_t + (q_t - q_{t-1} R_t)\theta_t S_t - c_t) \\ = R_{0,T}^{-1}(b_{T+1} + q_T \theta_{T+1} S_{T+1}) \end{aligned} \tag{3.3}$$

and, by the transversality condition, the consumer's present value budget constraint is satisfied:

$$V_0 + (y_0 - c_0) + \sum_{t=1}^{\infty} R_{0,t}^{-1}(y_t + d_t \theta_t S_t + (q_t - q_{t-1} R_t)\theta_t S_t - c_t) = 0$$

Notice how the consumer's income is composed of external income, y_t, dividends, $d_t \theta_t S_t$, and capital gains, $(q_t - q_{t-1} R_t)\theta_t S_t$, derived from his/her portfolio of stock.

2.2 Firms

I shall not focus on firms' objectives or investment decisions, but instead on their financial plans (one can easily embed the current analysis in a more explicit model with profit-maximizing firms). Therefore, the description of a firm is very simple: associated with an investment policy $\{i_t\}$ there is a stream of profits $\{\pi_t\}$. In addition to its investment policy, the firm must decide a dividend policy $\{D_t\}$, $D_t = d_t S_t$, a stock policy $\{S_t\}$ and a debt policy $\{b_t\}$. Although different units within a firm may decide these policies, such decisions cannot be made independently, since together they must satisfy the firm's budget constraint. The firm's intertemporal budget constraint is:

$$q_t S_{t+1} + b_{t+1} + \pi_t \geq i_t + q_t S_t + D_t + R_t b_t \tag{3.4}$$

Such a constraint, of course, does not prevent the firm from running a Ponzi scheme. A minimal requirement is that the present value of its 'terminal' liabilities must be zero. If the outstanding liabilities in period t are $W_t \equiv (q_t + d_t)\, S_t + R_t\, b_t$ (that is W_t *is the value of the firm*), and I define $z_t \equiv \pi_t - i_t$ (that is, the 'primary surplus' of the firm in period t) then Equation (3.4) can be written as:

$$W_{t+1} \geq R_{t+1}[W_t - z_t - q_t \Delta_{t+1} S_{t+1}] \tag{3.5}$$

which, without loss of generality, can be assumed to be satisfied as equality; that is:

$$W_t = R_{t,T}^{-1} W_T + \sum_{n=t}^{T-1} R_{t,n}^{-1}[z_n + g_n \Delta_{n+1} S_{n+1}]$$

Then the requirement that the present value of its 'terminal' liabilities be zero is

$$\lim_{T\to\infty} R_{0,T}^{-1} W_T = 0 \tag{3.6}$$

which guarantees that the current liabilities (the current value of the firm) are equal to the present value of its net revenues. That is,

$$(q_t + d_t)S_t + b_t R_t = \sum_{n=t}^{\infty} R_{t,n}^{-1}[z_n + q_n \Delta_{n+1} S_{n+1} \tag{3.7}$$

Since the firm can raise rents by expanding its stock, it is convenient to express its outstanding liabilities in terms of the price of the stock. That is, let $\omega_t \equiv \frac{W_t}{q_t}$, then its liabilities evolve according to:

$$\omega_{t+1} = I_{t+1}\left[\omega_t - \frac{1}{q_t}(z_t + q_t \Delta_{t+1} S_{t+1})\right] \tag{3.8}$$

where $I_{t+1} \equiv R_{t+1}\frac{q_t}{q_{t+1}}$. Notice that if I_{t+1} is given, then, and only then, ω_{t+1} is predetermined, before the stock market operates, in period $t + 1$.

In summary, the firm's present value constraint in period t, (Equation (3.7)), can be expressed as:

$$q_t \omega_t = \sum_{n=t}^{\infty} R_{t,n}^{-1}[z_n + q_n \Delta_{n+1} S_{n+1}] \tag{3.9}$$

2.3 Equilibria

We can now define rational expectations equilibria for this economy. We shall take as given the endowment sequence, $\{y_t\}_{t=0}^{\infty}$, and the initial conditions: $S_0 > 0$, $\theta_0 = 1$ and b_0 (unless stated otherwise, $b_0 = 0$ is assumed). Then a rational expectations equilibrium is a price system, of positive sequences, $(\{R_t\}_{t=1}^{\infty}, \{q_t\}_{t=0}^{\infty})$, an allocation $(\{\pi_t\}_{t=0}^{\infty}, \{i_t\}_{t=0}^{\infty}, \{c_t\}_{t=0}^{\infty})$, and debt–equity $(\{b_t\}_{t=1}^{\infty}, \{S_t\}_{t=1}^{\infty})$ and divided $\{d_t\}_{t=0}^{\infty}$ policies such that: (i) it satisfies the resource feasibility constraint: $c_t = y_t + \pi_t - i_t \equiv y_t + z_t$, for all $t \geq 0$; (ii) given the price system, the consumer's optimisation problem is satisfied with $\theta_t = 1$, for all $t > 0$; and (iii) the firm's investment, debt–equity and dividend policies are consistent with the price system and satisfy the firm's budget constraint (Equation (3.7) at $t = 0$; (alternatively, Equation (3.4), for all $t \geq 0$ and Equation (3.6a)).

If the feasibility constraint in Equations (3.2) and (3.1) is substituted, it can be seen that rational expectations equilibria must satisfy, for $t \geq 0$:

$$R_{t+1} = \beta^{-1}\frac{u'(y_t + z_t)}{u'(y_{t+1} + z_{t+1})} \tag{3.10}$$

and

$$f(y_t + z_t) \equiv \frac{u'(1)}{u'(y_t + z_t)} = q_t \Delta_{t+1} S_{t+1} \tag{3.11}$$

which can also be written as:

$$f(y_t + z_t) = q_t S_{t+1}(1 - I_{t+1}^{-1}) - d_{t+1} S_{t+1} R_{t+1}^{-1} \tag{3.12}$$

More precisely, Equations (3.10) and (3.11), together with the transversality conditions on portfolios and liabilities, *characterize rational expectations equilibria*.

For further reference, notice that one can substitute Equations (3.10) and (3.11) into the firm's budget constraint (Equation (3.9)) to obtain:

$$q_t \omega_t = \sum_{n=t}^{\infty} \left(\beta^{n-t} \frac{u'(y_n + z_n}{u'(y_t + z_t)} \right) [z_n + f(y_n + z_n)] \tag{3.13}$$

3 The contrast between the fiscal financial theory and the asset price theory

Our simple financial model of the firm illustrates a theorem on the *irrelevance of dividend and stock policies*. It does not consider the possible neutrality of the debt-equity mix (as in the Modigliani–Miller theorem), but rather the possible independence of asset prices from dividend and stock policies. It is a simple translation of the theorem of the irrelevance of 'quantitative guided' money supply policies (Woodford (1995)); Sims (1994) shows similar irrelevance results.

3.1 The fiscal theory irrelevance proposition

In the economy under study, once the real output sequences ($\{y_t\}$, $\{z_t\}$) are defined (resulting in the right-hand side of Equation (3.13) being positive: $y_t \geq 0$, $z_t \geq 0$, $y_t + z_t > 0$), then interest rates, $\{R_{t+1}\}$, and 'real' liabilities $\{q_t w_t\}$ are determined. If, without loss of generality, the initial conditions are given by: $S_0 = 1$, $b_0 = 0$, then:

$$q_0 \omega_0 = q_0 + d_0 \tag{3.14}$$

Now, for arbitrary non-negative sequences ($\{S_t\}_{t=0}^{\infty}$, $\{D_t\}_{t=1}^{\infty}$), (with $\{D_t\}_{t=1}^{\infty}$ satisfying the minimal restriction that the resulting sequence of prices is non-negative), Equation (3.14) together with Equation (3.13) determines q_0, and Equation (3.12), I_1. Equation (3.8), defining the evolution of the firm's liabilities, determines w_1. By iterating this process forward, one can generate a unique path that, as can easily be seen, defines a *rational expectations equilibrium*.

This irrelevance results seems a paradox at first sight. On the one hand, given initial liabilities w_0 (alternatively, given the initial dividends, d_0), the price of the stock q_0 – determined by Equation (3.13) – is given by the present value of the firm's net profits, which seems to be what financial theory should say. On the other hand, one seems free to choose the stock and, in particular, the dividend policies almost independently of the firm's profits, while the asset price theory argues that the price of the stock must reflect the present value of the stream of dividends!

3.2 Asset pricing computations

To unveil the mystery, it is helpful to see a particular example. Let $y_t = y > 0$, and $z_t = z > 0$, for $t \geq 1$, $z_0 = 0$ and $y_0 = y + z$. Given the initial conditions, $S_0 = 1$ and $b_0 = 0$, let the equity and dividend polices be defined as: $S_t = 1$, $t > 0$, and $d_0 = 0$ and, for $t > 0$, $d_t = d$; satisfying $0 \leq d \leq z$.

Notice that, in this case, the equilibrium Equations (3.10) and (3.11) (for $t \geq 0$) reduce to:

$$R_{t+1} = \beta^{-1}$$
$$q_t = f(y + z) + \beta(q_{t+1} + d) \tag{3.15}$$

while the firm's present value constraints (Equation (3.13) take the form:

$$\begin{aligned} q_0 w_0 &= [f(y+z) + \beta z]/(1-\beta) \\ &\equiv q(z) \end{aligned} \tag{3.16}$$

and, for $t > 0$:

$$\begin{aligned} q_t w_t &= [f(y+z) + z]/(1-\beta) \\ &= q(z) + z \end{aligned} \tag{3.17}$$

According to the standard asset price theory (for example, Lucas (1978)) one must compute asset prices using the forward iteration of Equation (3.15); that is:

$$q_t = [f(y+z) + \beta d]/(1-\beta d]/(1-\beta) + \lim_{n\to\infty} \beta^n q_n$$

and, imposing the transversality condition,

$$\lim_{n\to\infty} \beta^n q_n = 0 \tag{3.18}$$

resulting in:

$$q_t = q(d)$$

However, given $d_0 = 0$, unless $d = z$, the transversality condition cannot be satisfied. Otherwise, since $w_0 = 1$, a dividend plan that does not satisfy the budget constraint in Equation (3.16) could be implemented. It follows that *asset prices are uniquely determined*: $q_t = q(z)$.

According to the fiscal financial theory of the firm Equation (3.16) determines q_0, and therefore, as with the asset price calculation, $q_0 = q(z)$. But, for $t > 0$, determining q_t through Equation (3.17), together with the evolution of the firm's liabilities (Equation (3.8)) may result in a difference sequence of prices. To see this, notice that, with $S_t = 1$ and $R_{t+1} = \beta^{-1}$, Equation (3.8) can be written as:[2]

$$q_{t+1} = q_{t+1}\omega_{t+1} - d_{t+1} + \beta^{-1}(-q_t)(-q_t\omega_t + q_t + z_t)$$

therefore, in our example, it follows that, for $t > 0$:

$$q_t = q(z) + (z-d) + \beta^{-(t-1)}\frac{1-\beta^{(t-1)}}{1-\beta}(z-d) \tag{3.19}$$

That is, unless $d = z$, $\lim_{n\to\infty} \beta^n q_n = (z-d)\beta/(1-\beta) > 0$. The explosive path of stock prices reflects the fact that the dividend policy is a policy of permanent undistributed profits. The firm satisfies the present value budget constraint (in any period) with identity, reflecting the fact that all the rents are properly accounted for. In other words, according to the fiscal financial theory of the firm there is no problem in that the 'dividend unit' has made a wrong dividend policy: 'the market will discipline the firm'. There is a unique price sequence, consistent with such dividend policy, that satisfies the difference equation (Equation (3.15)), resulting in positive prices, and satisfying the budget constraint. The price sequence obtained above that, instead of taking Equation (3.18) as the terminal condition, takes Equation (3.13) as the initial condition determining q_0.

3.3 Has the fiscal theory solved the firm's default problem?

The (weak) requirement has been imposed that the firm's policies should satisfy the *no Ponzi scheme constraint* (Equation (3.6)), $\lim_{T\to\infty} R_{0,T}^{-1} W_T = 0$. Since $W_t \equiv (q_t + d_t)S_t + R_t b_t$, a policy fails to satisfy $\lim_{T\to\infty} R_{0,T}^{-1} (q_T + d_T) S_T = 0$ if, and only if, it fails to satisfy $\lim_{T\to\infty} R_{0,T}^{-1} R_T b_T = 0$. That is, there is another side to the asset price miscalculation and this is a debt policy miscalculation.

To see how orthodox debt policies can change the price determination results, notice that from Equation (3.4) is obtained that the firm's debts satisfy:

$$\begin{aligned} b_t &= R_t^{-1}[b_{t+1} - (D_t - z_t) + q_t(S_{t+1} - S_t)] \\ &= R_{t,T}^{-1} b_{T+1} + \sum_{n=t}^{T} R_{t-1,n}^{-1}[-(D_n - z_n) + q_n(S_{n+1} - S_n)] \end{aligned} \tag{3.20}$$

Therefore, under the 'no default constraint':

$$\lim_{T\to\infty} R_{0,T}^{-1} b_{T+1} = 0 \tag{3.21}$$

the current (real) debt liabilities are equal to the present value of the undistributed profits, and of the *seigniorage* rents from expanding its stock. That is:

$$b_t = \sum_{n=t}^{\infty} R_{t-1,n}^{-1}[-(D_n - z_n) + q_n(S_{n+1} - S_n)] \tag{3.22}$$

that is,

$$b_t = R_t^{-1}\left[-(qt + d_t)S_t + \sum_{n=t}^{\infty} R_{t,n}^{-1}[z_n + q_n \Delta_{n+1} S_{n+1}]\right]$$

Recall, however, that the firm's present budget constraint, at t (Equation (3.7)), is:

$$(q_t + d_t)S_t + b_t R_t = \sum_{n=t}^{\infty} R_{t,n}^{-1}[z_n + q_n \Delta_{n+1} S_{n+1}]$$

and therefore it is automatically satisfied, under the *no default constraint*, (Equation (3.21)). In other words, the equilibrium identity:

$$b_t = R_t^{-1}[-(q_t + d_t)S_t + q_t \omega_t] \tag{3.23}$$

is already satisfied and can not be used to determine q_t, given d_t.

In the above example, $b_0 = 0$ is predetermined, and, for $t > 0$, Equation (3.20) results in:

$$b_t = \beta^{-(t-2)} \frac{1 - \beta^{(t-1)}}{1 - \beta}(d - z) \tag{3.24}$$

In other words, by not distributing all profits, the firm becomes a net creditor, even in the long run. It is also clear that, given $d_0 = 0$, the only dividend policy that is stationary from period one (that is, $d_t = d, t > 0$) and satisfies Equation (3.21) is $d_t = z$, resulting in $b_t = 0$.

One can argue that the firm's policies do not have to be constrained by Equation (3.21), as long as they are constrained by Equation (3.6) *and* consumers are constrained by a *no default constraint* of the form $\lim_{T\to\infty} R_{0,T}^{-1} R_T b_T = 0$. Of course, in our economy, if the representative consumer has to satisfy this additional constraint, in making his/her consumption and portfolio decisions, then the present value of the 'undistributed profits' must be zero *in equilibrium*. There are, however, two problems with this argument. First, it is not clear why consumers should have different borrowing constraints than firms (notice that symmetric terminal conditions have been imposed on consumers and firms). Second, with many – say, J – firms, it is not enough to impose a *no default constraint* of the form: $\lim_{T\to\infty} R_{0,T}^{-1} R_T \sum_{j=1}^{J} b_T^i = 0$, since, obviously, this condition does not imply that, for every j, $\lim_{T\to\infty} R_{0,T}^{-1} R_T b_T^i = 0$. It is enough to consider the case in which firms can hold (debt and equity) portfolios from other firms to see that, unless the later – stricter – condition is required, *asset price miscalculations* may prevail in equilibrium.[3]

In summary, there is a sense in which there is no debt default problem. As long as a firm's financial policy guarantees that its value is positive (that is, the right-hand side of Equation (3.13) is positive and the resulting stock prices are positive), it should be free to borrow or lend and to define fairly arbitrary dividend policies. After all, in such a rational expectations world, stock prices will adjust to reflect the *true value* of the firm (that is, $q_t w_t$). For example, if the value of the firm becomes non-positive, this will be reflected in a stock price collapse. It is in this sense that the stock market provides enough information regarding the financial viability of the firm's policies and there is no need for additional debt constraints.

3.4 The unorthodox failure of the Modigliani–Miller theorem

Associated with the *unorthodox* policies (that is, policies that are designed to satisfy Equation (3.6), but not necessarily Equation (3.21)) there is a *peculiar failure of the Modigliani–Miller theorem.* Households cannot perceive the value of the firm as being independent of the debt–equity mix. To see this, we can go back to our previous example (with $y_t = y > 0$, and $z_t = z > 0$, for $t \geq 1$, $z_0 = 0$ and $y_0 = y + z$; initial conditions $S_0 = 1$ and $b_0 = 0$ and a constant stock policy $S_t = 1$, $t > 0$). Suppose that $d_0 = 0$ and, for $t \geq 1$, $d_t = d < z$. As we have seen, if stockholders were to compute prices according to their stream of dividends (that is, according to asset price computations), then they would make plans according to $q_t = q(d)$. However, at these prices, the firm's present value constraint (Equation (3.23)) is satisfied with equality only if the firm is financing a positive amount of debt; in particular, $b_t = (\frac{\beta}{1-\beta})\ (z - d)$. That is, the undistributed benefits should count as liabilities held by consumers. In other words, as in a Modigliani–Miller world, the household would properly count the firm's debt as expected payments, being indifferent between the corresponding portfolio $((q_t + d_t), b_t) = ((q(d) + d), (\frac{\beta}{1-\beta})\ (z - d))$ and the portfolio $((q_t + d_t), b_t) = ((q(z) + z), 0)$. But, as we have seen, with the (d_0, d) dividend policy equilibrium prices are given by Equation (3.19) with the corresponding level of the firm's debt – more precisely, credit – given by Equation (3.24). Something must be wrong with the household's asset pricing computation to account for the fact that the corresponding portfolio cannot be part of an equilibrium.

The mechanism that detects this 'violation' is the real balance effect, which can easily be illustrated in our context. With a predetermined level of debt, given by Equation (3.24), with $(q(d) + d)$ the household, who owns all the firm's liabilities, perceives that its wealth is lower – say, than with q_t given by Equation (3.19) – and, therefore its demands (not just of the stock) are too low. There will be excess supply of goods at prices $q(d)$, implying that they cannot be equilibrium prices. Only the forward sequence $\{q_t\}$, given by Equation (3.19) satisfies equilibrium restrictions for the dividend policy (d_0, d), given the initial liabilities $b_0 = 0$ and the exogenous process of firm's surpluses (z_0, z).

Notice that for the real balance effect to work, in this context, it is crucial that the household does not perceive, as a Modigliani–Miller believer would, that the value of the firm is independent of the debt–equity mix. Otherwise, faced with a dividend stream *d*, it would compute asset prices *q*(*d*) as if taking for granted that the firm has the appropriate debt policy in order to satisfy the firm's present value budget; the same reasoning it would follow if faced with dividends *z* resulting in prices *q*(*z*). In other words, the real balance effect can only undertake its function of detecting that *q*(*d*) are not equilibrium prices if the household does not believe that there is the corresponding change of debt policy associated with a change in dividend policy which would leave constant the value of the firm and its portfolio. It cannot have Modigliani–Miller beliefs even if it lives in a world without frictions or distortions, in a world where there is no reason not to be a Modigliani–Miller believer, other than the fact that firms are no longer constrained to satisfy the *no default constraint* (Equation (3.21)).

In summary, the failure of the Modigliani–Miller theorem is not associated with any of the standard market or firm's financing distortions, which are known to invalidate the theorem's result. It is simply that firm's debt policies can be designed without accounting for the 'no default constraint'. Therefore, paraphrasing Woodford,[4] we shall call a regime where Equation (3.22) is satisfied, regardless of the evolution of $\{q_t\}$ (and of $\{R_t\}$, which the firm takes as given) a Modigliani–Miller policy regime. In such a regime, different debt–equity policies cannot change the value of the firm and the household can maintain Modigliani–Miller beliefs in making its consumption and portfolio choices.

4 Has the fiscal theory solved the indeterminacy problem?

The demands for assets depend on the expected returns and not on their current dividends (or past returns), unless they convey information about future returns. In our model – as in most dynamic equilibrium models – the demands for assets as such only depend on expected returns. That is, if in period *t*, $\hat{R}^s_{t+1}$ is the expected return on a unit of stock, the demand (Equation (3.1)) is given by:

$$\frac{v'(\theta_{t+1})}{u'(c_t)} = q_t\left(1 - \frac{\hat{R}^s_{t+1}}{R_{t+1}}\right)S_{t+1}$$

and in equilibrium it must be that:

$$f(y_t + z_t) \equiv \frac{v'(1)}{u'(y_t + z_t)} = q_t\left(1 - \frac{\hat{R}^s_{t+1}}{R_{t+1}}\right)S_{t+1}$$

and, in this context, rational expectations simply requires that $\hat{R}^s_{t+1} = R^s_{t+1}$. Nevertheless, rational expectation restrictions may leave the initial price of the stock (or any period price if taken as initial) undetermined. To see this in our model, fix, as before, $z_0 = 0$, $z_t = z$, $t \geq 1$, $b_0 = 0$ and $S_0 = 1$. Now suppose that the firm follows a stock policy aimed at achieving certain asset return R^{s*} ($R^{s*} < \beta^{-1}$). Since $R^s_{t+1} = \frac{q_{t+1}}{q_t} + \frac{d_{t+1}}{q_t}$ there is a manifold of dividend and stock policies that could implement R^{s*}. In particular, let $S_{t+1} = \mu S_t$ and $d_{t+1} = \alpha q_t$, where (μ, α) satisfy: $\frac{1}{\mu} + \alpha = R^{s*}$. Then, using Equation (3.1) we obtain:

$$\frac{q_t}{q_{t-1}}\mu = \frac{q_t S_{t+1}}{q_{t-1} S_t} = \frac{\Delta_t}{\Delta_{t+1}}$$

that is,

$$\mu = \frac{(1-\alpha\beta)/\pi_t - \beta}{(1-\alpha\beta) - \beta\pi_{t+1}} \tag{3.25}$$

Let $\gamma = \beta/(1-\alpha\beta)$, then Equation (3.25) reduces to the following rational expectations equilibrium equation:

$$\pi_t = (\mu + \gamma - \mu\gamma\pi_{t+1})^{-1}; \quad t > 0 \tag{3.26}$$

Since for $t = 0$ Equation (3.11) takes the form:

$$f(y_0 + z_0) = q_0(1 - \frac{q_1 + \alpha q_0}{q_0}\beta)\mu S_0$$

and $S_0 = 1$, $y_0 + z_0 = y + z$, we obtain:

$$q_0 = \frac{1}{\mu}\frac{f(y+z)}{(1-\beta(\alpha+\pi_1))} \tag{3.27}$$

There are two steady state solutions to Equation (3.26): $(1/\mu, 1/\gamma)$ with corresponding rates of return $(R^s_\mu, R^s_\gamma) = R^{s*}, \beta^{-1})$; that is, given our assumption on the targeted rate of return, $R^s_\mu < R^s_\gamma$; that is, $\mu > \gamma$.

The *indeterminacy problem* in this context is that there is a continuum of solutions to Equation (3.26), of equilibrium asset prices, characterised by $\pi_1 > 1/\mu$, (Equation (3.27)) and $\pi \to 1/\gamma$. Does Equation (3.26), together with Equation (3.27), fully characterize the set of rational expectations equilibria?

The answer to the last question depends on how the firm's policies are defined. Notice that, given initial conditions, we have defined a stock policy $S_{t+1} = \mu S_t$ and an endogenous dividend policy $d_{t+1} = \alpha q_t$, for $t \geq 0$. To see that, with these policies, in equilibrium budget constraints are also satisfied, notice that now the firm's liabilities – that is, Equation (3.8) – evolve according to:

$$q_{t+1}\omega_{t+1} = \beta^{-1}[q_t\omega_t - z_t - (q_t(1-\alpha\beta) - q_{t+1}\beta)\mu^{t+1}]$$

and, taking into account that, as before, the firm's present value budget constraints (Equation (3.13)) reduce to: $q_t w_t = q(z) + z$, for $t > 0$, and $q_0\, w_0 = q(z)$, it follows that asset prices evolve according to:

$$q_{t+1} = -\beta^{-1}\left(\frac{1}{\mu}\right)^{t+1} f(y+z) + \frac{1}{\gamma}q_t \tag{3.28}$$

However, Equation (3.28) is automatically satisfied whenever Equations (3.26) and (3.27) are satisfied. Furthermore, since $R^s_\gamma = \beta^{-1}$, the transversality conditions are satisfied. In this sense, the indeterminacy problem remains even when the firm's – and consumer's – budgets are accounted for. But there is a missing piece in our definition of the firm's policies: d_0. That is, our endogenous dividend policy is not completely defined unless dividends in period zero are defined. Period zero dividends must, in turn, satisfy the firm's budget constraint. That is,

$$q_0 + d_0 = q_0\omega_0 = q(z) \tag{3.29}$$

It follows that, given a choice of d_0, there is a unique sequence of equilibrium asset prices satisfying Equations (3.29), (3.26) and (3.27), provided that $\pi_1 \geq 1/\mu$. Alternatively, for any sequence of asset prices satisfying Equations (3.26) and (3.27), with $\pi_1 \geq 1/\mu$, there is a unique initial dividend d_0 satisfying Equation (3.29). It is in this sense that the indeterminacy problem disappears.

For example, by reverting Equation (3.28) we can consider again the asset price computation; that is, for any $T > t$,

$$q_t = \beta^{-1}\left(\frac{1}{\mu}\right)^t f(y+z)\frac{\gamma}{\mu}\frac{1-(\gamma/\mu)^T}{1-(\gamma/\mu)} + \gamma^T q_T$$

and imposing the transversality condition $\lim_{n\to\infty}\gamma^n \mathrm{q}_{n+1} = 0$ (the effective discount factor is γ), results in $\pi_t = 1/\mu$, $t > 0$ and

$$q_0 = \beta^{-1}f(y+z)\frac{\gamma/\mu}{1-(\gamma/\mu)} = \frac{1}{\mu}\frac{f(y+z)}{(1-\beta R^{s*})}$$

In other words, the only initial dividend policy consistent with the target R^{s*}) being achieved is

$$\begin{aligned} d_0 &= q(z) - \frac{1}{\mu}\frac{f(y+z)}{(1-\beta R^{s*})} \\ &= \left[f(y+z)\left(\frac{\mu-\gamma\beta^{-1}}{\mu-\gamma}\right) + \beta z\right](1-\beta)^{-1} \end{aligned}$$

Notice that the requirement $d_0 \geq 0$ restricts R^{s*} not to be to close to β^{-1}.

4.1 It is not just a question of transversality conditions

The previous discussion, and some of the criticisms of the 'fiscal theory of money' relies on the firm not satisfying the 'no-default' constraint, but this, although revealing, is not a crucial feature. A local version of the above determinacy results can still be satisfied when restrictions are imposed on the amount of debt, and therefore the 'no-default' constraint is satisfied (see, for example, Woodford (1998)).

A simple example can, again, be used to illustrate the point. As before, let $z_0 = 0$, $z_t = z$, $t \geq 1$, $b_0 = 0$ and $S_t = 1$, $t \geq 0$. But now consider the possibility of 'over-distributing' dividends. In particular, let $z \leq d \leq z$ $(1 - \beta)^{-1}$. As Equation (3.19) shows, this may result in negative prices. To avoid such a stock collapse, let $T(d)$ be the largest integer t satisfying:

$$(\beta^{-t} - 1)(d - z) \leq z$$

(notice that by assumption $T(d) \geq 1$), and let $d_t = d$, for $t = 1, \ldots, T(d)$ and $d_t = 0$ for $t > T(d)$, then:

$$\begin{aligned} q_{T(d)} &= \bar{q}(z) \equiv f(y+z)/(1-\beta) \\ &= q(z) - \beta z/(1-\beta) \end{aligned}$$

and, iterating on Equation (3.15), we obtain

$$q_0 = (1 - \beta^{T(d)})q(d) + \beta^{T(d)}q(z)$$

that is, the policy of distributing $d \geq z$ for $T(d)$ periods results in asset prices decaying from q_0 to $\bar{q}(z)$ if $d > z$ and in constant prices $q_t = q(z)$ if, and only if, $d = z$. Notice, furthermore, that:

$$\begin{aligned} q_0 &= f(y+z)/(1-\beta) + (1-\beta^{T(d)})\beta d/(1-\beta) \\ &\approx f(y+z)/(1-\beta) + \beta z/(1-\beta) = q(z) \end{aligned}$$

In other words, within the stated bounds, d can be chosen arbitrarily, but if $d_t = d$, for $t = 1, \ldots, T(d)$ and $d_t = 0$ for $t > T(d)$, then $d_0 \approx 0$. Alternatively, one can choose $d_0 > 0$ and (provided that $\beta z > (1 - \beta)d_0$) a d which satisfies $(1 - \beta)z \leq (1 - \beta)d \leq z - (1 - \beta)d_0$, and then define the dividend policy $d_t = d$, for $t = 1, \ldots, T(d,d_0)$ (where $T(d,d_0)$ is the largest integer t such that $\beta(\beta^{-t} - 1)d \leq \beta z - (1 - \beta)d_0)$ and $d_t = 0$ for $t > T(d, d_0)$. In this case, $q_0 \approx q(z) - d_0$ and $q_{T(d,d_0)} = \bar{q}(z)$.

Notice that $b_t = \bar{b}(z) \equiv \beta z/(1 - \beta)$ is the maximum amount of debt consistent with the present value constraint (Equation (3.17)) being satisfied and $q_t = \bar{q}(z)$. That is, the above policies can be stated alternatively in terms of a debt ceiling $\bar{b}(z)$, resulting in a dividend period $T(d)$, such that $b_{T(d)} = \bar{b}(z)$.

The question arises as to whether one can state the dividend policy in the following terms: 'choose $d_0 \geq 0$ and d (satisfying the above restrictions) and let $d_t = d$ for as long as $q_t \geq \bar{q}(z)$ (alternatively, for as long as $b_t \leq \bar{b}(z)$) and $d_t = 0$ thereafter'. Notice that, stated like this, one cannot make an asset price computation since, in principle, the terminal condition for Equation (3.15) is undefined. Nevertheless, a rational expectations path (satisfying the present value budget constraint), results in a uniquely defined dividend period $T(d, d_0)$, consistent with such a dividend policy. For example, as we have seen, $d_0 = 0$ and $d_t = z$ results in $T(d) = \infty$.

In this context, the fiscal theory states that the above loose statement of policy is admissible since, by only considering rational expectations equilibrium paths, such a policy results in a unique dividend period $T(d, d_0)$ and a corresponding sequence of asset prices – satisfying Equation (3.15).

5 Conclusions

I have extended (translated) the fiscal theory of money to the problem of outside financing of a firm through debt and equity. While with this change from governments to firms I have lost some degree of freedom (the ability of governments to affect economies in ways that firms usually cannot), I may have gained in clarity. In fact, since, on the one hand, large firms hold fairly sophisticated portfolios and their revenues far exceed the GDP of some countries, and, on the other, governments neither act in isolation nor have unlimited monopoly power, it is far from clear that governments should be treated differently from other economic agents – in particular, firms.

I have emphasised how the fiscal theory works as a theory of price determination, in contrast with the asset price theory. In particular, I have stressed how a precondition for price determination is that firms are allowed to make plans that do not satisfy their budgets. In such regimes, the Modigliani–Miller theorem fails, since the debt–equity mix should be perceived as affecting the value of the firm. Furthermore, since price determination means that *in equilibrium* budgets are satisfied in spite of the 'unorthodox' policy design, in a way the theory solves the firm's *default problem*. These features, however, more than the strength of the theory, may be showing its weakness. The real balance effects as price determination mechanisms, in which the theory is based, seem more implausible when considered in a more general setting where many economic agents supply nominal financial assets, and households (and firms) hold fairly diversified portfolios. In our model, when households perform asset price calculations resulting in non-equilibrium asset prices, they react with excessively low (or high) demands. Market clearing requires prices given by a firm's present value budget constraints, as the fiscal theory postulates. It is an empirical matter whether such adjustments take place. There is ample evidence that bankruptcy problems result in efficiency losses. As we have seen, with the *right prices* (that is, given by fiscal theory computations), there are no efficiency losses, the market properly prices the – possibly, unreasonable – policies of firms. No need for restrictions on stock policy or other forms of regulation either.

There is ample experimental evidence, and a corresponding learning theory, showing that, when there is an indeterminacy problem, taking into account the learning process can help to predict which equilibria are more likely to occur (see, for example, Marimon and Sunder (1993), and Evans and Honkapohja (1999)). In contrast, as we have seen, the fiscal theory resolves in many contexts, the indeterminacy problem. In our model of the firm this is fairly transparent. The indeterminacy problem is associated with a misspecification of policy; in particular, with a misspecified period zero dividend. Nevertheless, the determinacy result requires that proper present value calculations are made by all agents. In our deterministic context this is already difficult; in a stochastic context, as Hansen *et al.* (1991) have pointed out, it may be close to impossible. Adaptive learning agents may make miscalculations, but the final process may still be well defined even if, corresponding to these miscalculations, the initial price is no longer determined. As existing experimental evidence suggests, it is unlikely that all the equilibrium paths determined by the fiscal theory will arise. This, again, is an empirical matter, but if I had to bet. . . .

Notes

1 See, for example, Sargent and Wallace (1981).

2 Or, equivalently, use the fact that (15) can also be written as

$$q_{t+1} = \beta^{-1} q_t + (z - d) - \beta^{-1}(1 - \beta) q(z)$$

3 Notice that we are not allowing for private agents to make plans resulting in unbounded demands – by rolling over debts, say – which, as Woodford (1998b) recognizes, will result in the non-existence of equilibrium.

4 Woodford (1995, 1996) calls a regime in which government policies satisfy the 'no default constraint', regardless of the evolution of prices, a *Ricardian policy regime*. In such a regime, the Ricardian proposition is satisfied (see Woodford (1995, 1996) for a further discussion of this issue).

References

Aiyagari, Rao and Mark Gertler (1985) 'The Backing of Government Bonds and Monetarism', *Journal of Monetary Economics*, vol. 16, pp. 19–44.

Buiter, Willem (1998) 'The Young Person's Guide to Neutrality, Price Level Indeterminacy, Interest Rate Pegs, and Fiscal Theories of the Price Level', NBER Working Paper No. 6396.

Canzoneri, Matthew B., Robert E. Cumby and Behzad T. Diba (1998) 'Is the Price Level Determined by the Needs of Fiscal Solvency?' NBER Working Paper No. 6471.

Christ, Carl (1979) 'On Fiscal and Monetary Policies and the Government Budget Constraint', *American Economic Review*, vol. 69, pp. 526–38.

Dupor, Bill (1998) 'Exchange Rates and the Fiscal Theory of the Price Level', Mimeo, The Wharton School, University of Pennsylvania, February.

Evans, George W. and Seppo Honkapohja (1999) 'Learning Dynamics', in Taylor J. B. and M. Woodford (eds) *Handbook of Macroeconomics* (Amsterdam: Elsevier).

Fisher, Irving (1911) *The Purchasing Power of Money* (New York: Macmillan).

Friedman, Milton (1959) *A Program for Monetary Stability* (New York: Fordham University Press).

Friedman, Milton (1969) *The Optimum Quantity of Money and Other Essays* (Chicago: Aldine).

Hansen, Lars P., William Roberds and Thomas Sargent (1991) 'Time Series Implications of Present Value Budget Balance and of Martingale Models of Consumption and Taxes', in Hansen, P. and T. Sargent (eds), *Rational Expectations and Econometrics* (Boulder, Co: Westview Press).

Kurz, Mordecai (1996) 'Asset Prices and Rational Beliefs', Fondazione Eni Enrico Mattei, Nota di Lavoro No. 39.96.

Leeper, Eric M. (1991) 'Equilibria Under "Active" and "Passive" Monetary and Fiscal Policies', *Journal of Monetary Economics*, vol. 27, pp. 129–47.

Lucas, Robert E., Jr (1978) 'Asset Prices in an Exchange Economy', *Econometrica*, vol. 46, pp. 1426–45.

Marcet, Albert and Thomas J. Sargent (1989) 'Least Squares Learning and the Dynamics of Hyperinflation', in Barnett, W. A., J. Geweke and K. Shell (eds), *Economic Complexity: Chaos, Sunspots, Bubbles, and Nonlinearity* (Cambridge University Press).

Marimon, Ramon, Juan Pablo Nicolini and Pedro Teles (1997) 'Electronic Money: The End of Inflation?', Working paper, European Forum of the European University Institute.

Marimon, R. and S. Sunder (1993) 'Indeterminacy of Equilibria in a Hyperinflationary World: Experimental Evidence', *Econometrica*, vol. 61, pp. 1073–107.

McCallum, Bennett T. (1998) 'Indeterminacy, Bubbles, and the Fiscal Theory of Price Level Determination', NBER Working Paper No. p. 6456.

Patinkin, Don (1965) *Money, Interest, and Prices,* 2nd edn (New York: Harper Dynamic Macroeconomic Theory (Cambridge, MA: Harvard University Press).

Sargent, Thomas, J. (1996) 'Macroeconomic Theory', Mimeo, University of Chicago.

Sargent, Thomas, J. and Neil Wallace (1981) 'Some Unpleasant Monetarist Arithmetic', Federal Reserve Bank of Minneapolis, *Quarterly Review,* vol. 5, no. 3, pp. 1–17; reprinted, 1993, in *Rational Expectations and Inflation,* 2nd edn (New York: HarperCollins).

Sims, Christopher A. (1994) 'A Simple Model for the Study of the Determination of the Price Level and the Interaction of Monetary and Fiscal Policy', *Economic Theory,* vol. 4, pp. 381–99.

Sims, Christopher A. (1995) 'Econometric Implications of the Government Budget Constraint', Mimeo, Yale University.

Wicksell, Knut (1936) *Interest and Prices* (London: Macmillan), trans. R. F. Kahn from *Geldzins und Güterpreise: Eine Studie über die den Tauschwert des Geldes bestimmenden Ursachen* (Jena: Gustav Fischer Verlag) (reprinted 1965) (New York: Augustus M. Kelley).

Woodford, Michael (1994) 'Monetary Policy and Price Level Determinacy in a Cash-in-Advance Economy', *Economic Theory,* vol. 4, pp. 345–80.

Woodford, Michael (1995) 'Price-Level Determinacy Without Control of a Monetary Aggregate', *Carnegie-Rochester Conference Series on Public Policy,* pp. 1–46.

Woodford, Michael (1996) 'Control of the Public Debt: A Requirement for Price Stability?', NBER Working Paper No. 5684.

Woodford, Michael (1998a) 'Doing without Money: Controlling Inflation in a Post-Monetary World', *Review of Economic Dynamics,* vol. 1, pp. 173–219.

Woodford, Michael (1998b) 'Public Debt and the Price Level', Mimeo, Princeton University.

Comment

Seppo Honkapohja
University of Helsinki, Finland

1 The fiscal theory of price level determination

Macroeconomics has recently seen a revival of the views that stress the importance of government fiscal behaviour in the determination of the price level. Wealth effects and the form of the (consolidated) government budget constraint play a central role in this fiscal approach; see the key papers by Sims (1994) and Woodford (1994, 1995) for the theoretical underpinnings.[1]

Ramon Marimon's chapter considers the plausibility of the fiscal approach in an intriguing way, and illustrates some of the main principles of the approach by studying their implications in the context of the financial theory of firms and of asset pricing. The chapter is a theoretical contribution and only makes occasional remarks about the interplay between fiscal and monetary policy considerations that are the core of the fiscal approach.

Given this unusual viewpoint, it is worthwhile to devote some space to a summary of the main ideas of the fiscal approach in the context of a standard fiscal and monetary model. Consider the following standard monetary model, exposited in Woodford (1995). There is an infinitely-lived representative consumer making intertemporal consumption and portfolio choices between money and bonds. Real balances are in the utility function. The consumer faces the usual non-negativity and budget constraints, including a borrowing limit that, in each period, his/her wealth must be at least as high as the present value of net obligations; that is, taxes minus future income.

The government faces a financing constraint according to which expenditure on purchases of goods minus tax revenue is equal to the end-of-period money stock *plus* end-of-period bond stock *minus* gross interest payments on money *minus* gross interest payment on bonds. A fiscal and monetary policy regime is specified by fixing four out the six sequences of: expenditure; taxes; rate of return on money; rate of return on bonds; money stock; and bond stock.

In a rational expectations equilibrium, the usual market clearing conditions hold. For this model it is customary to substitute the goods market clearing condition into the money market clearing condition and the intertemporal consumer optimality condition, which then yields the two basic equilibrium equations. In general it is an implication of the consumer's constraints and market clearing that the following present value constraint on government holds: real value of government net liabilities (including interest saving on monetary liabilities) equals the present value of future government surpluses *plus* possible initial (real) wealth.[2]

The fiscal approach to price level determination takes a different track, and goes as follows. Drop the money market clearing condition. In place use, in each period, the present value constraint on government net liabilities as an equation determining the price level for that period (given expectations about current and future values of fiscal and monetary variables in the present-value constraint for the government). This equation determines, for each period, the price level. The money market clearing condition is an implication of the other conditions, but it is not used to solve for the price level.

2 Application of the fiscal ideas to a financial theory of the firm

Let us now explain how the chapter applies this kind of approach to a financial theory of the firm. The basic setup is in many ways similar to the monetary model outlined above. There is a representative infinitely-lived household, whose utility function in each period is separable in consumption and his/her share of the stock of the representative firm. The consumer can also hold debt issued by the firm and faces the usual accounting constraint and a transversality constraint. These constraints can also be written as a present-value budget constraint.

The firm has an investment policy leading to a stream of profits. In addition, the firm must decide on its dividend policy, stock policy and debt policy. These are tied together by the financing or budget constraint which states that the value of stocks *plus* debt *plus* profits must not be less than investment expenditure *plus* value of stock *plus* dividends *plus* gross return payments on debt, each taken in the beginning of the period.

Defining value of the firm as stock price *plus* dividend *multiplied by* amount of stock *plus* gross return on debt, it is possible to obtain the result that current value of the firm (that is, its current liabilities) must be equal to the present value of its net revenues. It should be emphasized that this conclusion is a consequence of the transversality condition stating that the present value of the firm's liabilities is zero.

A rational expectations equilibrium is then defined by the requirements (i) resource feasibility; (ii) that the consumer optimizes and is willing to hold all the stock issued by the firm; and (iii) that the firm's investment, debt–equity and dividend policies are consistent with the price system and satisfies the firm's budget constraint. The key equations defining the equilibrium are Equations (10) and (11) or (15) and (16) in the special case used by Marimon.

The difference between the usual asset pricing theory and the 'fiscal financial theory' can be seen as follows. In standard asset pricing theory Equation (11) or (15) is used to derive the evolution of stock prices, given the stock and dividend policies of the firm. To obtain the usual result that stock price is the present value of future dividends one must assume that dividends are equal to the 'net profits' of the firm in each period. In contrast, the fiscal financial theory is based on the firm's budget constraint, Equation (13) or (16), and it is taken as the key for price determination. Given initial liabilities, it determines the stock price. In conjunction with an accounting constraint for the firm's funds (Equation (8)) this can lead to a different sequence of stock prices. It is important to notice that dividends are not required to be equal to net profits, though – as emphasized by Marimon – in fiscal financial theory all rents are accounted for properly.

The fiscal financial theory has surprising implications. First, the current stock price can even be independent of the firm's stock and dividend policy. In any case, the way asset prices are determined is very different from the usual theory.[3]

Second, the theory is based on the assumption that present value of the firm's total liabilities is zero at the limit, but there is no separate 'no default' constraint on debt. If such a constraint is introduced, the model behaves as the orthodox asset-pricing theory suggests.

Third, the fiscal view leads to a model in which the value of the firm is not independent of the debt-equity mix, that is, the Modigliani–Miller theorem does not hold. This is because the fiscal view imposes the present value constraint only on the firm's total liabilities and not on the debt alone as a no-default constraint.

These last results show that, in the context of the firm, the fiscal view results are based on the notion that it is total liabilities that are constrained by the transversality condition and not debt alone. This makes clear an apparent weakness of the approach when it is applied to the firm: the no-default constraint on debt would seem to be important in practice. Marimon's discussion shows very clearly that one must be very careful about the precise form of the no-default constraints that are part of the model. This would apply to governments as well as to firms.

3 Discussion of the approach

Governments are to some extent different from firms. In particular, they have ways of influencing prices and real interest rates (they also have the right to levy taxes and can issue currency and nominal liabilities). The possibilities for influencing the price level are arguably a key difference between a firm and the government. The fiscal approach relies on price changes and wealth effects for the attainment of equilibrium. This provides a potential test for the approach.

Suppose, as a thought exercise, that the government starts to borrow very heavily. What would be the likely market reaction to this? Is the price level going to rise, as suggested by the fiscal approach, or are interest rates going to rise, which would be the orthodox view? I tend to think that in most cases the reaction happens as interest rates, rather than the price level, rise. However, in some extreme circumstances the reaction might be more in inflation, an example being the hyperinflationary episodes in which a fiscal reform is a major part of the stabilization package.

Towards the end of the chapter Marimon remarks that, while the fiscal approach provides a rationale for fiscal constraints as a check on price stability and avoiding price level indeterminacy, an alternative approach is to postulate that in fact the economic agents learn and try to co-ordinate their expectations about the future. Indeed, in this case, fiscal constraints have a different justification in ensuring price stability in the economy; see Evans *et al.* (2001).

It must be stressed that in the learning approach agents have limited foresight and try to find an equilibrium through trial and error (the trials being done by means of standard statistical inference). The fiscal constraints are then direct limitations on deficits and bond or money issues. These guarantee that inflation does not run high, though high initial expectations do create some inertia in reducing inflation. This role is very different from that envisaged by the fiscal approach, where the mechanism is very indirect. It works through agents' perfect foresight about government present-value budget and the ensuing wealth effects on current behaviour. One feels uneasy about putting so much weight on perfect foresight or rational expectations. It is a non-trivial task for an expert – an econometrician, say – to identify whether a present-value constraint is likely to be satisfied or not. The fiscal approach places a lot of faith in the agent's ability in this respect. The learning viewpoint seems far more appealing on this count.

Notes

1 Recent commentaries of the fiscal approach include Buiter (1998) and McCallum (1998).

2 Note that this discussion is somewhat ambiguous since, in contrast to the consumer, the government is not a priori required to satisfy an intertemporal wealth constraint at each period and at each possible system of prices and all sequences of its variables. As emphasized by Buiter (1998), this feature can be important for fiscalist implications. Broadly speaking, imposing analogous budget constraints for both the consumer and the government will yield the standard theory.

3 Using a monetary model, McCallum (1998) argues that price paths of the fiscal theory involve bubbles.

References

Buiter, W. H. (1998) *The Young Person's Guide to Neutrality, Price Level Indeterminacy, Interest Rate Pegs and Fiscal Theories of the Price Level*, CEPR Working Paper No. 1799.

Evans, G. W., S. Honkapohja and R. Marimon (2001) 'Convergence in Monetary Inflation Models with Heterogeneous Learning Rules', *Macroeconomic Dynamics*, vol. 5, pp. 1– 31.

McCallum, B. T. (1998) *Indeterminacy, Bubbles, and the Fiscal Theory of Price Level Determination*, NBER Working Paper No. 6456.

Sims, C. A. (1994) 'A Simple Model for the Study of the Determination of the Price Level and the Interaction of Monetary and Fiscal Policy', *Economic Theory*, vol. 4, pp. 381–99.

Woodford, M. (1994) 'Monetary Policy and Price Level Determinacy in a Cash-in-Advance Economy', *Economic Theory*, vol. 4, pp. 345–80.

Woodford, M. (1995), 'Price-Level Determinacy Without Control of a Monetary Aggregate', *Carnegie–Rochester Conference Series on Public Policy*, pp. 1–46.

4
Inflation and Welfare*

Robert E. Lucas, Jr
University of Chicago, USA

1 Introduction

In a monetary economy, it is in everyone's private interest to try to get someone else to hold non-interest-bearing cash and reserves. But someone has to hold it all, so these efforts must simply cancel out. All of us spend several hours per year in this effort, and employ thousands of talented and highly-trained people to help us. These person-hours are simply thrown away, wasted on a task that should not have to be performed at all.

Since the opportunity cost of holding non-interest-bearing money is the nominal rate of interest, we would expect that the time people spend trying to economize on cash holdings should be an increasing function of the interest rate. This observation is consistent with much evidence, and suggests that, as long as interest rates are positive, people could be made better off if money growth, and hence the average inflation rate and the interest rate, were reduced. The problems of working out the details of this theoretical idea, and of applying it to estimate the potential gains in welfare from the adoption of the monetary policies that reduce inflation

* This chapter is based on a paper prepared for the 1997 summer meetings of the Econometric Society in Pasadena, Hong Kong, and Toulouse and is reproduced with permission from *Econometrica*, vol. 68, no. 2 (2000), pp. 247–74. Earlier versions, entitled 'On the Welfare Cost of Inflation', were given at the 1993 Hitotsubashi International Symposium on Financial Markets in the Changing World, and at conferences in Bergen and the Federal Reserve Bank of San Franscisco. I am grateful to many colleagues and discussants, but particularly to Martin Bailey, Lars Hansen, Bennett McCallum, Casey Mulligan and Nancy Stokey, for helpful discussion and criticism. Michael Beveridge, Vimut Vanitch-arearnthum and Tomoyuki Nakajima provided able research assistance. The National Science Foundation provided research support.

and interest rates, are classic questions of monetary economics, addressed in a long line of research stemming from the contributions of Bailey (1956) and Friedman (1969). The goal of this chapter is to provide a substantive summary of where this line of research stands today.

The way the analysis of inflation and its consequences has developed over the years is also interesting from a methodological point of view, as an illustration of the extent to which the quantitative, mathematical vision shared by the founders of the Econometric Society has succeeded in transforming the practice of economics. An applied economist today uses explicit theoretical modelling to organize data from a variety of sources, and brings this information to bear on quantitative questions of policy in a way that is almost entirely a development since the 1950s. As compared to older, more literary methods, the explicit theoretical style of post-war economics can lead to sharper questions and better answers, and at the same time expose the limits of current knowledge in ways that can stimulate improvements in both theory and data. I would like this chapter to exemplify these virtues as well.

In the next section, I display and discuss evidence on money, prices, production and interest rates for the twentieth century in the USA. Using this evidence, I replicate essentially Meltzer's (1963a) estimated money demand function, and then use these estimates to replicate Bailey's (1956) welfare cost calculations. The rest of the chapter deals with the theoretical interpretation of these calculations.

Section 3 provides one possible general equilibrium rationale for the welfare estimates reported in Section 2, based on a simplified version of Sidrauski's (1967a, 1967b) model. Section 4 then uses the Sidrauski framework to consider the consequences of dropping the assumption, used in Section 3, that the monetary policy that implements any given interest rate can be carried out with lump-sum fiscal transfers. It re-examines the estimation under the alternate assumption that only flat-rate income taxes can be used, and that a government sector of a given size must be financed either with inflation taxation or income taxation. This modification introduces theoretical complications but does not, I argue, lead to major quantitative differences from the conclusions of Section 2.

Section 5 provides a second general equilibrium rationale for the welfare estimates of Section 2, using as context a model of a transactions technology proposed by McCallum and Goodfriend (1987). This model provides another theoretical justification of the consumers' surplus formulae used in Section 2, one that turns out to be closely related to Baumol's (1952) inventory-theoretic analysis. Section 6 contains concluding remarks.

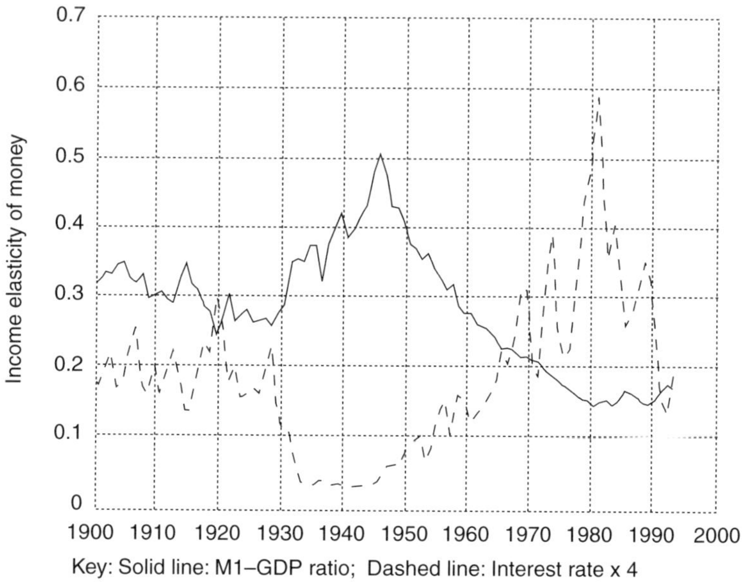

Figure 4.1 US money, income and interest rates, 1900–94

2 Money demand and consumers' surplus

Figure 4.1 shows plots of annual time series of a short-term nominal interest rate, r_t, and of the ratio of M1 to nominal GDP, $m_t = M_t/(P_t y_t)$, for the USA, for the period 1900–94.[1] Over this 95-year period, real GDP grew at an average annual rate of 3 per cent, M1 grew at 5.6 per cent, and the GDP deflator grew at 3.2 per cent. The money-income ratio is thus essentially trendless over the entire century, although there has been a strong downward trend since the Second World War. Technical change in the provision of transactions services would, other things being equal, produce a downward trend in the money-income ratio m_t. An income elasticity of money demand exceeding one would produce an upward trend. Neither trend appears in the data, though of course both might have been present in an offsetting way.

In this section, I interpret these two time series as points on a demand function for real balances of the form $M_t/P_t = L(r_t, y_t)$, where this function L takes the form $L(r,y) = m(r)y$.[2] Figure 4.2 displays a plot of observations (the circles in the figure) on the money-income ratio m_t and the interest rate r_t for the years 1900–94. The figure also plots the curves $m = Ar^{-\eta}$ for

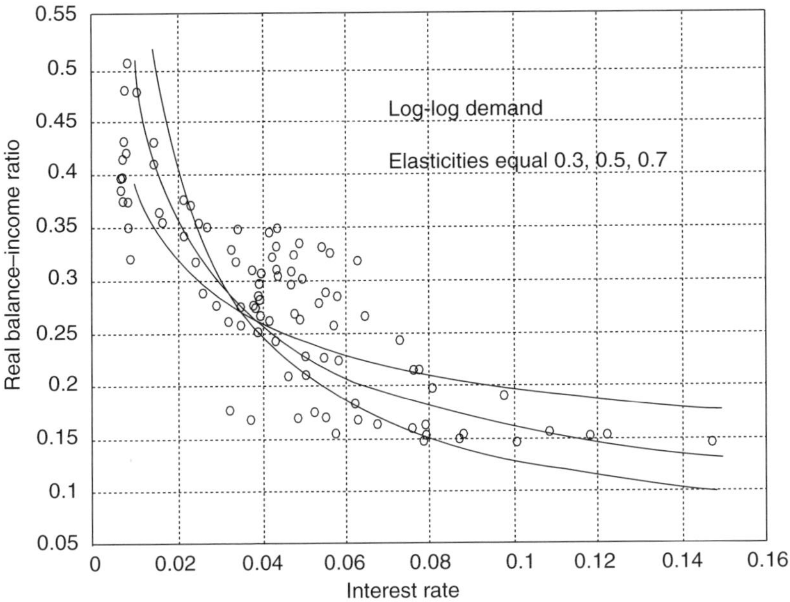

Figure 4.2 US money demand, 1900–94

the η-values 0.3, 0.5 and 0.7, where A is selected so the curve passes through the geometric means of the data pairs. Within this parametric family, it is evident that $\eta = 0.5$ gives the best fit. Figure 4.3 presents the same data, this time along side the curves $m = Be^{-\xi r}$ for the ξ-values 5, 7 and 9. Again, all three curves pass through the geometric means. Within this parametric family, $\xi = 7$ appears to give the best fit. It also clear, I think, that the semi-log function plotted here provides a description of the data that is much inferior to the log-log curve in Figure 4.2.[3]

In order to provide some perspective on these estimates, Figure 4.4 plots actual US real balances (not deflated by income) against the real balances predicted by the log-log demand curve: $Ar_t^{-.5}y_t$. One sees that the fitted values successfully track the secular increase in the money-income ratio prior to the Second World War, including the acceleration of this increase in the 1930s and 1940s. They also track the decrease in m_t as interest rates rose in the post-war period (though they miss the 1990s, when interest rates declined and velocity did not). One can also see, however, that the fitted series exhibits some large, shorter-term fluctuations that do not appear in the actual series. The interest elasticity needed to fit the long-

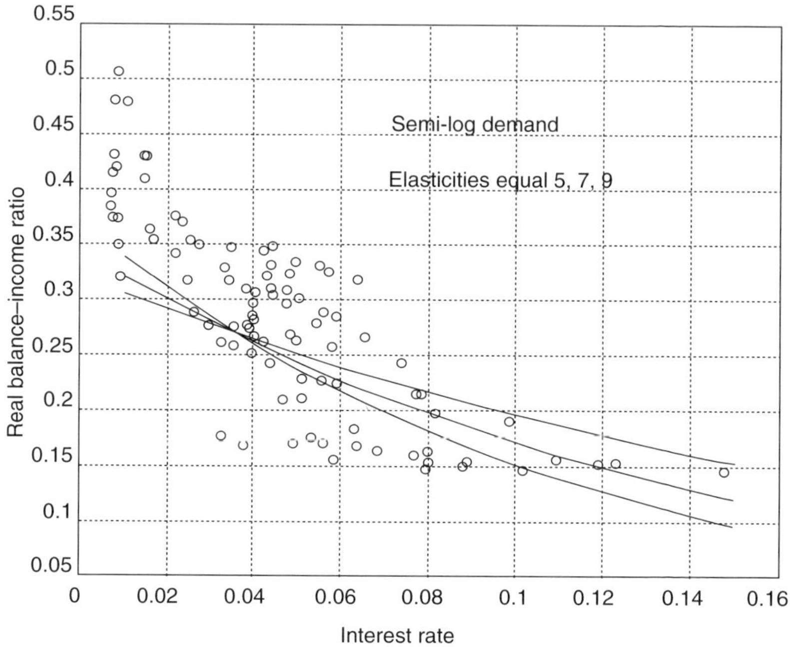

Figure 4.3 US money demand, 1900–94

term trends (and very sharply estimated by these trends) is much too high to permit a good fit on a year-to-year basis. Of course, it is precisely this difficulty that has motivated much of the money demand research since the 1970s, and has led to distributed lag formulations of money demand that attempt to reconcile the evidence at different frequencies. In my opinion, this reconciliation has not yet been achieved, but in any case, it is clear that the functions plotted in Figures 4.2 and 4.3 contribute nothing toward the resolution of this problem.

To translate the evidence on money demand into a welfare cost estimate, we first apply the method of Bailey (1956), defining the welfare cost of inflation as the area under the inverse demand function – the *consumers' surplus* – that could be gained by reducing the interest rate from r to zero. That is, let $m(r)$ be the estimated function, let $\psi(m)$ be the inverse function, and define the welfare cost function $w(r)$ by:

$$w(r) = \int_{m(r)}^{m(0)} \psi(x)dx = \int_0^r m(x)dx - rm(r) \tag{4.1}$$

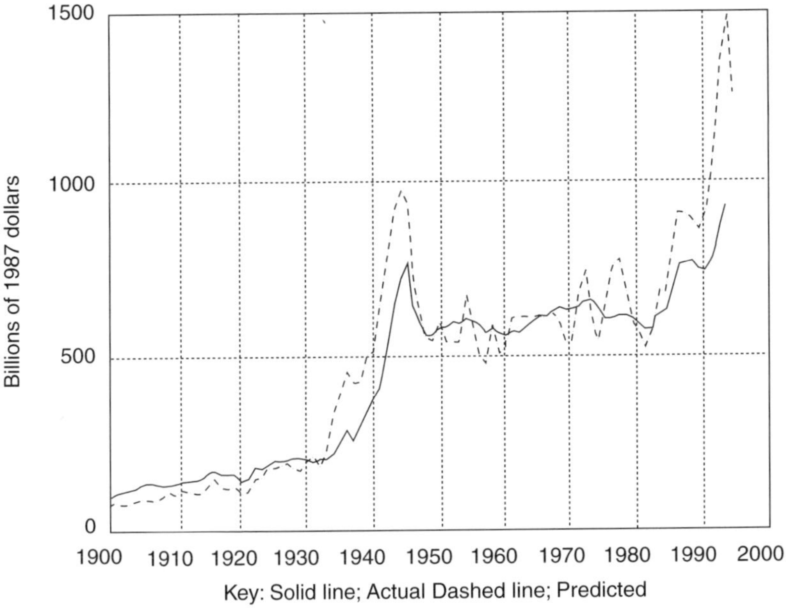

Figure 4.4 Actual and predicted real balances, 1900–94

Since the function m has the dimensions of a ratio to income, so does the function w. Its value $w(r)$ has the interpretation, to be made more precise in later sections, as the fraction of income people would require as compensation in order to make them indifferent between living in a steady state with an interest rate constant at r and an otherwise identical steady state with an interest rate of (or near) zero.

For the log-log demand function $m(r) = Ar^{-\eta}$, Equation (4.1) implies:

$$w(r) = A\frac{\eta}{1-\eta}r^{1-\eta}$$

For $\eta = 0.5$, this is just a square root function. It is plotted in Figure 4.5. For the semi-log function $m(r) = Be^{-\xi r}$, Equation (4.1) implies:

$$w(r) = \frac{B}{\xi}[1 - (1 + \xi r)e^{-\xi r}]$$

This curve is also plotted, for $\xi = 7$, in Figure 4.5. This is the parameterization used by Bailey.

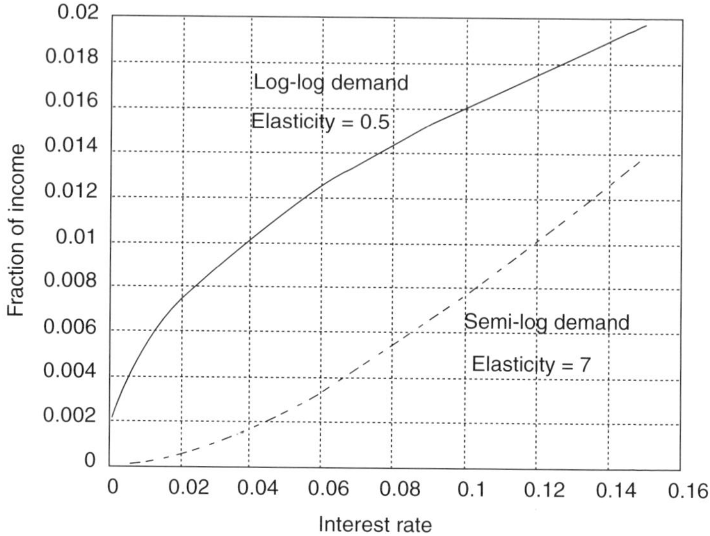

Figure 4.5 Welfare cost functions

Note that the two demand curves imply very different estimates for the welfare cost of moderate inflations. At a 6 per cent interest rate, for example, the log-log curve implies a welfare cost of about 1 per cent of income, while the semi-log curve implies a cost of less than 0.3 per cent. But much of this difference is caused by the difference in behaviour at very low interest rates predicted by these two curves. Figure 4.6 plots the curves $w(r) - w(0.03)$ for both fitted demand curves, where $r = 0.03$ is chosen as the interest rate that would be associated with an inflation rate of zero. Since the two curves on Figure 4.5 are nearly parallel between interest rates of 3 per cent and 10 per cent, the two curves on Figure 4.6 imply very similar estimates of the cost of exceeding an inflation rate of zero by moderate amounts. The main difference, then, is that log-log demand implies a substantial gain in moving from zero inflation to the deflation rate needed to reduce nominal interest rates to zero, while under semi-log demand this gain is trivial.

3 The Sidrauski framework

In order to decide whether we want to view either of the curves plotted in Figure 4.5 as describing the consequences of policy changes in the actual

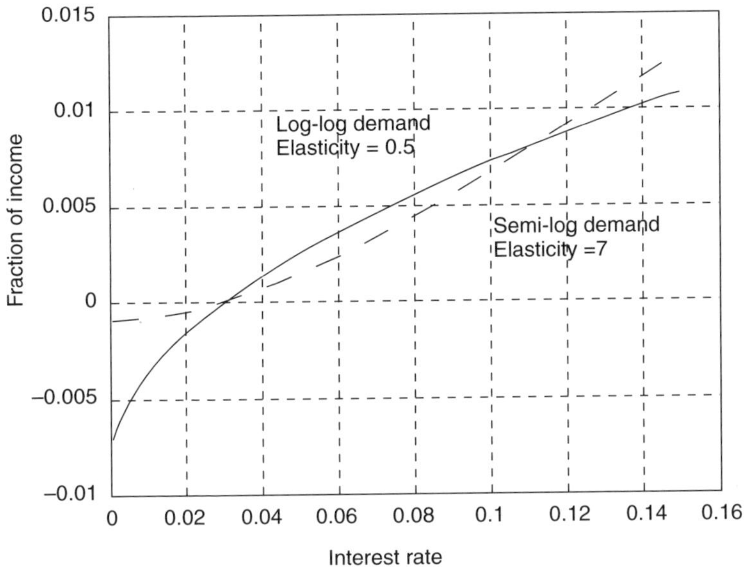

Figure 4.6 Welfare cost relative to 3 per cent interest

US economy, we need to be clear on the nature of the thought experiment of which the outcome is traced out by these curves. For this purpose, we need a model of the entire economy that can let us to see what changes in monetary policy might generate the curve $m(r)$ and the associated welfare costs $w(r)$. Simply labelling the points plotted in Figure 4.2 a 'demand function' does not tell us anything about what we are estimating or how accurate the estimates are: giving colourful names to statistical relationships is not a substitute for economic theory.

The following simplified version of the general equilibrium model of Sidrauski (1967a, 1967b) provides one framework that can provide an explicit rationale for the consumers' surplus formula (Equation (4.1)).[4] Consider a deterministic, representative agent model, in which households gain utility from the consumption c of a single, non-storable good, and from their holdings $z = M/P$ of real balances. Household preferences are:

$$\sum_{t=0}^{\infty}(1+\rho)^{-t}U(c_t z_t) \qquad (4.2)$$

where the current period utility function U is given by:

$$U(c, z) = \frac{1}{1-\sigma}[c\varphi(\frac{z}{c})]^{1-\sigma} \quad (4.3)$$

provided $\sigma \neq 1$. These homothetic preferences are consistent with the absence of trend in the ratio of real balances to income in US data, and the constant relative risk aversion form is consistent with balanced growth.

Each household is endowed with one unit of time, which is inelastically supplied to the market and which produces $y_t = y_0\ (1 + \gamma)^t$ units of the consumption good in period t.[5] Hence one equilibrium condition is:

$$c_t = y_t = y_0(1+\gamma)^t$$

Households begin period t with M_t units of money, out of which they pay a lump sum tax H_t (or, if $H_t < 0$, receive a lump sum transfer). The price level is P_t, so the cash flow constraint for households is:

$$M_{t+1} = M_t - H_t + P_t y_t - P_t c_t$$

in nominal terms. In real terms, it is:

$$(1+\pi_{t+1})z_{t+1} = z_t - h_t + y_t - c_t \quad (4.4)$$

where $h_t = H_t/P_t$ and $1 + \pi_t = P_t/P_{t-1}$.

We consider the decision problem of a household in an economy on a balanced growth equilibrium path, on which the money growth rate is constant at μ, maintained by a constant ratio $v = h/y$ of transfers to income. In this case, the ratio of money to income will be constant, and the inflation factor $1 + \pi_t$ will be constant at the value $(1 + \mu)/(1 + \gamma)$. Let $\tilde{v}(z, y)$ be the value of the maximized objective function (Equation (4.1)) for a household in such an equilibrium that has real balances z when the economy-wide income level has reached y. This function $\tilde{v}$ satisfies the Bellman equation:

$$\tilde{v}(z, y) = \max_c\{\frac{1}{1-\sigma}[c\varphi(\frac{z}{c})]^{1-\sigma} + \frac{1}{1+\sigma}\tilde{v}(z', y(1+\gamma))\} \quad (4.5)$$

where next period's real balances z^l are:

$$z' = \frac{z - h + y - c}{1+\pi}$$

Under the homogeneity assumptions I have imposed, the problem (Equation (4.5)) can be simplified to a single state variable problem as follows. Define the function $v(m)$ by:

$$\tilde{v}(z, y) = v(m)y^{1-\sigma}$$

where $m = z/y$ is the money–income ratio. If we view $w = c/y$ as the household's choice variable, we can see that the function $v(m)$ will satisfy:[6]

$$v(m) = \max_{\omega}\{\frac{1}{1-\sigma}[\omega\varphi(\frac{m}{\omega})]^{1-\sigma} + \frac{(1+\gamma)^{1-\sigma}}{1+\rho}v(m')\} \tag{4.6}$$

where:

$$m' = \frac{z'}{y(1+\gamma)} = \frac{z-h+y-c}{y(1+\gamma)(1+\pi)} = \frac{m-\nu+1-\omega}{1+\mu}$$

The first-order and envelope conditions for the problem (Equation (4.6)), evaluated at $w = 1$ (which will hold along any equilibrium path) are:

$$[\varphi(m)]^{-\sigma}[\varphi(m) - m\varphi'(m)] = \frac{1}{1+r}v'\left(\frac{m-\nu}{1+\mu}\right)$$

and

$$v'(m) = [\varphi(m)]^{-\sigma}\varphi'(m) + \frac{1}{1+r}v'\left(\frac{m-\nu}{1+\mu}\right)$$

where the nominal interest rate r is defined by:

$$\frac{1}{1+r} = \frac{(1+\gamma)^{1-\sigma}}{(1+\rho)(1+\mu)} \tag{4.7}$$

(Note that this nominal interest r approximately equals $\rho + \sigma\gamma + \mu - \gamma$, the familiar sum of the real rate and the inflation premium.) Along the balanced path, m is constant, and eliminating $v'(m)$ between these two equations and simplifying yields:

$$\frac{\varphi'(m)}{\varphi(m) - m\varphi'(m)} = r \tag{4.8}$$

Let $m(r)$ denote the m value that satisfies Equation (4.8), expressed as a function of the interest rate. Throughout the chapter, it is this kind of steady state equilibrium relation $m(r)$ that I call a 'money demand function', and that I identify with the curves shown in Figures 4.2 and 4.3.

The flow utility enjoyed by the household on the balanced path is $U(y, m(r)y)$, where y is growing at the constant rate γ. Provided $m'(r) < 0$, this utility is maximized over non-negative nominal interest rates at $r = 0$: the Friedman (1969) rule of a deflation equal to the real rate of interest.[7] In this section, I define the welfare cost $w(r)$ of a nominal rate r to be the percentage income compensation needed to leave the household indifferent between r and 0. That is, $w(r)$ is defined as the solution to:

$$U[(1 + w(r)y, m(r)y] = U[y, m(0)y]$$

With the assumed functional form (Equation (4.3)), this definition is equivalent to:

$$(1 + w(r))\varphi\left(\frac{m(r)}{1 + w(r)}\right) = \varphi[m(0)] \tag{4.9}$$

An estimated function $m(r)$ can be used to calculate the function $w(r)$ as follows. Let $m(r)$ be given and let $\psi(m)$ be the inverse function. Then Equation (4.8) implies that the function φ satisfies the differential equation:

$$\varphi'(m) = \frac{\psi(m)}{1 + m\psi(m)}\varphi(m) \tag{4.10}$$

Differentiating Equation (4.9) through with respect to r, we obtain:

$$0 = w'(r)\varphi\left(\frac{m(r)}{1 + w(r)}\right) + \varphi'\left(\frac{m(r)}{1 + \omega(r)}\right)\left[m'(r) - \frac{m(r)\omega'(r)}{1 + \omega(r)}\right] \tag{4.11}$$

Now apply Equation (4.10) with $m = m(r)/(1 + w(r))$ to Equation (4.11) and cancel, to obtain the differential equation:

$$\omega'(r) = -\psi\left(\frac{m(r)}{1 + w(r)}\right)m'(r) \tag{4.12}$$

in the welfare cost function w, which has the natural initial condition $w(0) = 0$.

Given any money demand function m (and inverse ψ), Equation (4.12) is readily solved numerically for an exact welfare cost function $w(r)$. But comparing Equations (4.12) and (4.1), one can guess that for small values of r – and hence of $w(r)$ – the solution to Equation (4.12) must be very close to the value implied by the consumers' surplus formula. In fact, on a plot such as Figure 4.5, the exact and the approximate solutions cannot be distinguished. (See also Figure 4.8 in Section 5.)

We can also solve the differential Equation (4.10) for the function φ, reconstructing the utility function. For the particular demand function $m(r) = A/\sqrt{r}$, for example, Equation (4.10) has the solution:

$$\varphi(m) = [1 + \frac{A^2}{m}]^{-1}$$

with the boundary condition $\varphi(0) = 0$. Since the value of A in the USA is empirically about 0.05 (see Figure 4.2), the Sidrauski utility function takes the form:

$$U(c, z) = \frac{1}{1-\sigma}\left([\frac{1}{c} + \frac{0.0025}{z}]^{\sigma-1} - 1\right)$$

The implied elasticity of substitution between goods and real balances is 0.5. The estimated money demand function gives no information on the intertemporal substitution parameter σ.[8]

To interpret the welfare cost functions plotted in Figure 4.5, then, we think of these curves as tracing out different steady states of deterministic economies subjected to different, constant rates of money growth. The differences in interest rates across these economies are attributed *solely* to differences in inflation premia. This interpretation seems to me to rationalize a focus on low-frequency evidence on money demand in twentieth-century US time series, and suggests the possibility that accurate estimates of welfare costs, in the sense of across-steady-state comparisons, may be obtained without a good understanding of the behaviour of velocity at high frequencies.

Using a general equilibrium framework to interpret the welfare estimates of the last section, even one as simple as my version of Sidrauski's, is helpful – essential, really – in exploring the effects of changes in assumptions on these estimates. Many economists, for example, believe that a deterministic framework such as Bailey's or mine misses the important costs of inflation that are thought to arise from price or inflation rate *variability*. It would be a straightforward exercise, today, to add stochastic shocks of realistic magnitude and behaviour to both real productivity and money supply behaviour in this model, and to re-examine the welfare calculations in this new context. Based on the Cooley and Hansen (1989) study of a similar model of the US economy, I am very confident that the effects of such a modification on the welfare costs estimated in Section 2 would be negligible.[9] In the next section, I illustrate in another way this process of modifying the model in order to examine the importance of its simplifying assumptions.

4 Fiscal considerations

In the analysis to this point, the nominal interest rate r has been treated as a policy variable, and the welfare cost of inflation has been defined by a comparison of resource allocations when $r > 0$ to a benchmark case of $r = 0$. In fact, of course, any particular interest-rate policy must be implemented by a specific money-supply policy, and this monetary policy must in turn be implemented by a policy of fiscal transfers, open market operations, or both. This fact raises no difficulties as long as the necessary transfers can be effected through lump-sum payments or assessments, but if this is not possible, the optimality of the Friedman rule may cease to obtain. Aspects of this question have been examined by Phelps (1973), Bewley (1983), Lucas and Stokey (1983a), Kimbrough (1986a, 1986b), Woodford (1990), Cooley and Hansen (1991), Eckstein and Leiderman (1992), Miller (1995), and also by by Chari, Christiano and Kehoe (1993), Guidotti and Vegh (1993), and Mulligan and Sala-i-Martin (1997). This section addresses some of these fiscal questions in the contexts of the Sidrauski model of the last section.

Let $m(r)$ be steady-state real balances. Define the parameter δ by $1 + \delta = (1 + \rho)/(1 + \gamma)^{1-\sigma}$, so that $\delta \cong \rho + \sigma\gamma - \gamma$ is the amount by which the real interest rate exceeds the growth rate of output. Recall that $r = \delta + \mu$ and $v = -\mu m(r)$. Then the consumer budget constraint and the resource constraint together imply that to implement a nominal interest rate r, the fraction:

$$\nu = -\mu m(r) = (\delta - r)m(r) \tag{4.13}$$

of income y_t must be transfered from the private sector to the government in a steady state, in the form of real balances withdrawn from circulation. (If $\delta < r$, the negative of this magnitude is seigniorage revenue, relative to income.)

For the function $m(r) = A/\sqrt{r}$ that fits US data, $m(r) \to \infty$ as $r \to 0$, so if the flow (Equation (4.13)) must be withdrawn using a fractional tax on income, the policy $r = 0$ is not feasible. The need to resort to income taxation thus places a positive lower bound on r. But with $\delta = 0.02$ and $A = 0.05$, an income tax rate of 0.03 would implement an interest rate of 0.001 (that is, one-tenth of 1 per cent). The Friedman rule requires qualification in this case, but the qualification is of no quantitative interest.

The cases considered by most of the authors cited above, however, have the additional complications that labour is supplied elastically, so an income tax distorts resource allocation, and there is a positive amount of government consumption, necessitating a resort to distorting taxation of some kind. In these circumstances, it is not impossible that a positive inflation tax might have a useful role to play in the overall tax structure. In this section, these two features will be added to the model of Section 3, and the welfare cost calculations described there will be redone. The results of these calculations are given in Figure 4.7.

We modify the current period preferences (Equation (4.2)) to include the consumption of leisure, x:

$$U(c, m, x) = \frac{1}{1-\sigma}[c\varphi(\frac{z}{c})\phi(x)]^{1-\sigma}$$

Modify the resource constraint to include government consumption, g_t:

$$c_t + g_t = (1 - x_t)y_t = (1 - x_t)y_0(1 + \gamma)^t$$

Modify consumers' budget constraints to reflect income taxation at a flat rate τ:

$$(1 + \mu)m_{t+1} = m_t + (1 - r)(1 - x_t) - \omega_t$$

where $m_t = z_t/y_t$ is the ratio of money to full income, and $w_t = c_t/y_t$.

If government consumption is a constant ratio g to full income y_t, this model has an equilibrium path with constant ratios of consumption and real balances to income and with leisure constant as well. Using the same normalization employed in Section 3, an individual household's Bellman equation on such a path is:

$$v(m) = \max_{w,x}\{\frac{1}{1-\sigma}[\omega\varphi(\frac{m}{\omega})\phi(x)]^{1-\sigma} + \frac{(1+\gamma)^{1-\sigma}}{1+\rho}v(m')\}$$

where:

$$(1 + \mu)m' = m + (1 - \tau)(1 - x) - \omega$$

The first order and envelope conditions for this problem are:

$$[\omega\varphi(\frac{m}{\omega})\phi(x)]^{-\sigma}\varphi(\frac{m}{\omega}) - \frac{m}{w}\varphi'(\frac{m}{w})]\phi(x) = \frac{1}{1+\tau}v'(m')$$

$$[\omega\varphi(\frac{m}{\omega})\phi(x)]^{-\sigma}\omega\varphi(\frac{m}{\omega})\phi'(x) = \frac{1}{1+\tau}v'(m')(1-\tau)$$

and

$$v'(m) = [\omega\varphi(\frac{m}{\omega})\phi(x)]^{-\sigma}\varphi'(\frac{m}{\omega})\phi(x) + \frac{1}{1+\tau}v'(m')$$

where again the nominal interest rate r is defined by Equation (4.7). Along the balanced path, m is constant, and eliminating $v'(m)$ from these equations and simplifying yields:

$$\tau[\varphi(\frac{m}{\omega}) - \frac{m}{\omega}\varphi'(\frac{m}{\omega})] = \varphi'(\frac{m}{\omega}) \tag{4.14}$$

$$\omega\varphi(\frac{m}{\omega})\phi'(x) = [\varphi(\frac{m}{\omega}) - \frac{m}{\omega}\varphi'(\frac{m}{\omega})]\phi(x)(1-\tau) \tag{4.15}$$

Additional steady state equilibrium conditions are:

$$\omega + g + x = 1 \tag{4.16}$$

$$\mu m = (1 - \tau)(1 - x) - \omega \tag{4.17}$$

Condition (4.14) just repeats Equation (4.7). Condition (4.15) equates the marginal rate of substitution between goods and leisure to the after tax real wage, $1 - \tau$. Conditions (4.16) and (4.17) are the resource and consumer budget constraints; together, they imply the government budget constraint. For any given nominal interest rate r and government consumption rate g, Equations (4.14)–(4.17) are four equations that can be solved for the steady-state allocation (w, x, m) and the income tax rate τ. Any monetary policy dictates a tax policy, depending on the extent to which seigniorage revenues help to finance g, or the extent to which the need to withdraw cash from the public adds to the burden on the tax system.

Figure 4.7 tabulates a welfare cost function $w(r)$, defined as:

$$U[(1 + w(\tau))c(\tau), m(\tau), x(\tau)] = U[c(\delta), , x(\delta)] \tag{4.18}$$

I use $r = \delta$ as a benchmark rather than $r = 0$ because, depending on the assumed functions φ and π, the system (Equations (4.14)–(4.17)) may not have a solution at $r = 0$.

The figure is based on the following parameterization. For the function φ, I used $\varphi(m) = (1 + 1/(km))^{-1}$, which follows from the money demand function $m(r) = A\sqrt{r}/r$; A was set equal to 0.05, to fit the US data. For the function ϕ, I used $\phi(x) = x^{\beta}$. With these assumptions, the definition in Equation (4.18) of the function $w(r)$ implies:

$$(1 + \omega(\tau))\frac{m(\tau)}{1 + k(m(\tau)/\omega(\tau))}x(\tau)^{\beta} = \frac{m(\delta)}{1 + k(m(\delta)/\omega(\delta))}x(\delta)^{\beta}$$

I let the elasticity β range over the values 0.0001, 0.3, 0.6, and 0.9. Reading from bottom to top, these are the four curves plotted in Figure 4.7. I set $1 - g = 0.35$, so that if $x = 0$, $w = 1$. Finally, I set $\delta = 0.02$.

One can see from Figure 4.7 that above about 0.5 per cent, estimated welfare costs are the same as in the inelastic labour supply, lump-sum tax case studied in earlier sections. The effects of distorting taxation appear only at extremely low interest rates. Thus, for a leisure elasticity of $\beta = 0.3$, the optimal interest rate is about 0.03 per cent, while at $\beta = 0.9$, it is about 0.04 per cent. For any $\beta > 0$, the optimal r is strictly positive, but the deviations from $r = 0$ are minute. The differences in welfare are small too. The minimized welfare costs are in all cases less than –0.0045, while the

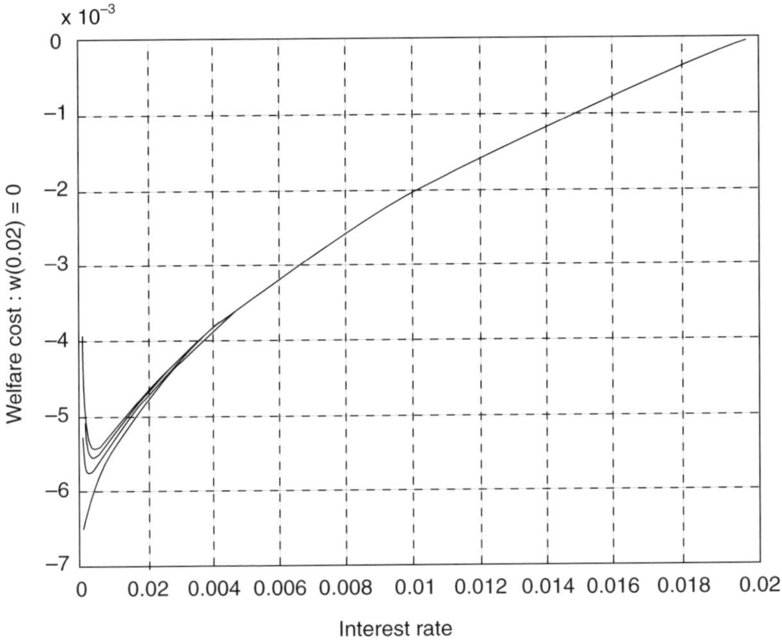

Figure 4.7 Welfare cost with income taxation

intercept of the benchmark curve, $-w(\delta)$, is –0.006, a difference of 0.0015 times income.

These second-best tax problems have so many logical possibilities that I thought it would be useful to work one case through, quantitatively, to see what kind of magnitudes are at stake. But the case I selected for study is, in some respects, arbitrary, and the literature cited above is helpful in isolating crucial assumptions. The model underlying Figure 4.7 is a special case of the model analyzed in Section 2 of Chari, Christiano and Kehoe (1993), where it is shown that the Friedman $r = 0$ policy is optimal in the sense of Ramsey, provided that the private sector begins with a net nominal position (money plus nominal debt) of zero. If, on the other hand, the net nominal position of the private sector is positive, a monetary–fiscal policy that is efficient in Ramsey's sense entails an initial hyperinflation to exploit the capital levy possibilities. In my analysis, there is no government debt and the public holds a positive initial nominal position (its cash), but I have constrained the money growth rate and the tax rate to be constant, precluding a capital levy. Under these assumptions, Woodford (1990) shows that $r = 0$ is not optimal, a fact that Figure 4.7 reflects.

In short, the optimality of the Friedman rule can be studied in a very wide variety of second-best frameworks, with a wide range of different qualitative conclusions. In the specific context I have used, the Friedman rule needs qualification, but the magnitude of the needed amendment is trivially small. The fact is that real balances are a very minor 'good' in the US economy, so the fiscal consequences of even sizeable changes in the rate at which this good is taxed – the inflation rate – are just not likely to be large.[10]

5 The McCallum–Goodfriend framework

The Sidrauski theory takes us behind the estimated money demand function to possible underlying preferences and technology, and by so doing certainly clarifies the welfare interpretation of Figure 4.5. It is also a convenient framework for exploring the consequences of different assumptions that may affect welfare cost estimates, such as the fiscal considerations examined in the last section. It is less helpful in thinking about cash management behaviour at very low interest rates. The same criticism can be raised about Friedman's (1969) argument: What does it mean, exactly, to satiate an economy with cash? To make progress on this question, one needs to think more concretely about what people *do* with their money holdings.

The cash-in-advance formulation used in Lucas and Stokey (1983b) provides a specific image of a cash-using society that could be useful for this purpose. In this section, though, I shall use a version of McCallum and Goodfriend's (1987) proposed variation on the Sidrauski model. In their model, the use of cash is motivated by an assumed transactions technology, rather than by an assumption that real balances yield utility directly. One can also see useful connections between this assumed technology and earlier inventory-theoretic studies of money demand.

In the McCallum-Goodfriend model, household preferences depend on goods consumption only:

$$\sum_{t=0}^{\infty}(1+\rho)^{-t}\frac{1}{1-\sigma}c_t^{1-\sigma}, \quad \sigma \neq 1 \tag{4.19}$$

Each household is endowed with one unit of time, which can be used either to produce goods or to carry out transactions. Call s the fraction devoted to transacting. The goods production technology is assumed to be:

$$c_t = (1 - s_t)y_t = (1 - s_t)y_0(1 + \gamma)^t \tag{4.20}$$

The cash flow constraint in real terms is:

$$(1 + \pi_{t+1})z_{t+1} = z_t - h_t + (1 - s_t)y_t - c_t$$

where $z_t = M_t/P_t$. In terms of the money–income ratio m_t, this constraint reads:

$$(1 + \mu_{t+1})m_{t+1} = m_t - v_t + 1 - s_t - \omega_t$$

where $v_t = h_t/y_t$ and $w_t = c_t/y_t$.

The new element in the model is a transactions constraint, relating household holdings of real balances and the amount of household time devoted to transacting to the spending flow the household carries out. I assume that, in real terms, this constraint takes the form:

$$c_t = z_t f(s_t) \tag{4.21}$$

which will be consistent with a unit income elasticity of money demand.[11]

As in the last section, I consider the decision problem of a household in an economy on a balanced growth equilibrium in which the money growth rate is constant at μ, maintained by a constant ratio $v = h/y$ of transfers to income, the ratio of money to income is a constant m, and the inflation factor $1 + \pi_t$ is constant at the value $(1 + \mu)/(1 + \gamma)$. Think of the household's choice variables as the time allocation s and the consumption–income ratio w. Let $y^{1-\sigma}\, v(m)$ be the value of the maximized objective function in Equation (4.19) for a household in this balanced path equilibrium that has a ratio of money balances to income of $m = M_t/(P_t y)$ when the economy-wide income level has reached y. Then the function v satisfies the Bellman equation:

$$v(m) = \max_{\omega, s}\{\frac{1}{1-\sigma}\omega^{1-\sigma} + \frac{(1+\gamma)^{1-\sigma}}{1+\rho}v(m')\}$$

subject to:

$$\omega = mf(s)$$

where:

$$m' = \frac{m - v + 1 - s - \omega}{1 + \mu} \tag{4.22}$$

We use the transactions constraint to eliminate w as a decision variable:

$$v(m) = \max_s\{\frac{1}{1-\sigma}[mf(s)]^{1-\sigma} + \frac{(1+\gamma)^{1-\sigma}}{1+\rho}v\left(\frac{m-\nu+1-s-mf(s)}{1+\mu}\right)\} \tag{4.23}$$

The value function that satisfies Equation (4.23) need not be concave, so one cannot use standard arguments to show that a time allocation that satisfies the first-order condition for Equation (4.23) is in fact optimal. Even so, I shall begin, as in Sections 3 and 4, by using the first-order and envelope conditions to characterize a balanced-path equilibrium. Then I shall carry out a numerical analysis of Equation (4.23) to determine the conditions under which consumer utility is maximal along this balanced path.

The first-order and envelope conditions for Equation (4.23) are:

$$[mf(s)]^{-\sigma}mf'(s) = \frac{1}{1+r}v'(m')[1+mf'(s)]$$

and

$$v'(m) = [mf(s)]^{-\sigma}f(s) + \frac{1}{1+r}v'(m')[1-f(s)]$$

where, as in Section 3, the nominal interest rate r is given by Equation (4.7). Along the balanced path, $m = m'$, and eliminating $v'(m)$ and simplifying yields:

$$f(s) = rmf'(s) \tag{4.24}$$

A second equilibrium condition follows from the transactions constraint and the fact that $w = c/y = 1 - s$ on a balanced path:

$$1 - s = mf(s) \tag{4.25}$$

Given f, we can solve Equations (4.24) and (4.25) for s and m as functions of r.

In this model, the time spent economizing on cash use, $s(r)$, has the dimensions of a percentage reduction in production and consumption, and hence is itself a direct measure of the welfare cost of inflation, interpreted as wasted time. To estimate this function $s(r)$, we work backwards from the function $m(r)$ as estimated in Section 2, to the transactions technology function f. As in Section 3, we do this by finding a first-order differential equation in the welfare cost $s(r)$.

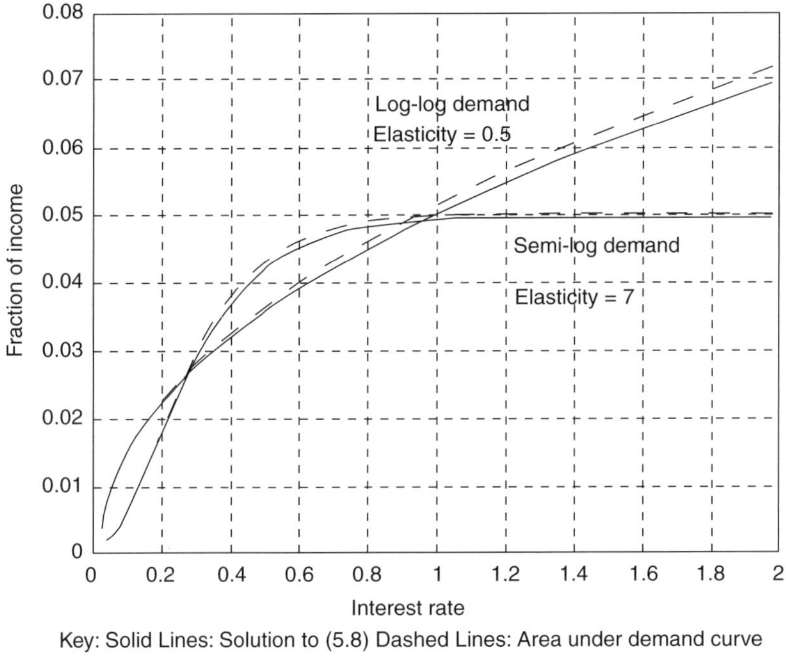

Figure 4.8 Approximate and exact welfare cost functions

Given f, let $m(r)$ and $s(r)$ satisfy Equations (4.24) and (4.25). Then differentiating Equation (4.25) through with respect to r and using Equations (4.24) and (4.25) to eliminate $f(s)$ and $f'(s)$ yields:

$$s'(r) = \frac{rm'(r)(1 - s(r))}{1 - s(r) + rm(r)} \tag{4.26}$$

Comparing Equations (4.26) and (4.1), one can see that for small r – and hence small $s(r)$ – solutions to Equation (4.26) and the area under the inverse money demand function will be very close. Figure 4.8 plots the solution $s(r)$ with initial condition $s(0) = 0$ for the log-log and semi-log demand cases, for interest rates ranging from 0 to 2 (200 per cent). Also plotted are the areas under the two demand curves, as in Figure 4.5. For the semi-log case, the exact and approximate welfare cost estimates cannot be distinguished. For the log-log case, the two curves are also virtually identical at interest rates below 20 per cent. Thus the McCallum–Goodfriend model yields simply a new interpretation of estimates already obtained.

For the log-log case with interest elasticity of 0.5, the implied transactions time function is simply a straight line through the origin, $f(s) = ks$, for some constant k. This case is of particular interest, since a multiplicative transactions technology kms corresponds to the celebrated inventory-theoretic model introduced by Baumol (1952), and developed by Tobin (1956), Miller and Orr (1966), Dvoretzky (1965) and Patinkin (1965), Frenkel and Jovanovic (1980), and Chang (1992).[12] If one can sustain a given pattern of transactions with average balances m and s units of time in trips to the bank, then the same pattern can be sustained by halving average cash and doubling the number of trips. In this special case, the two steady state equations (5.6) and (5.7) become:

$$s = rm$$

and

$$1 - s\,kms$$

and eliminating the money–income ratio m between the two yields a quadratic in the steady state value of s:

$$\frac{k}{r}s^2 = 1 - s \tag{4.27}$$

For large values of the ratio k/r, the unique positive solution to Equation (4.27) is very well approximated by the square-root rule:[13]

$$s(r) = \sqrt{\frac{r}{k}}$$

and the money–income ratio by:

$$m(r) = \sqrt{\frac{1}{rk}} \tag{4.28}$$

The parameter k can be calibrated from the intercept $A = 0.05$ of the money demand function: $k = (.05)^{-2} = 400$.

Could it be simply coincidence that the interest elasticity predicted by Baumol's theory – one-half – is the value the best fits US time series evidence? This is a possibility, certainly, but attributing striking results to coincidence is not the way science tends to move forward![14]

Figures 4.9 and 4.10 report results of numerical calculations designed to check whether consumer utility is in fact maximized along the balanced path I have constructed from the first-order conditions for the dynamic programme in Equation (4.23). In all calculations, the technology $f(s) = ks$ is assumed, with $k = 400$. I assumed the real growth rate $\gamma = 0.02$ and a

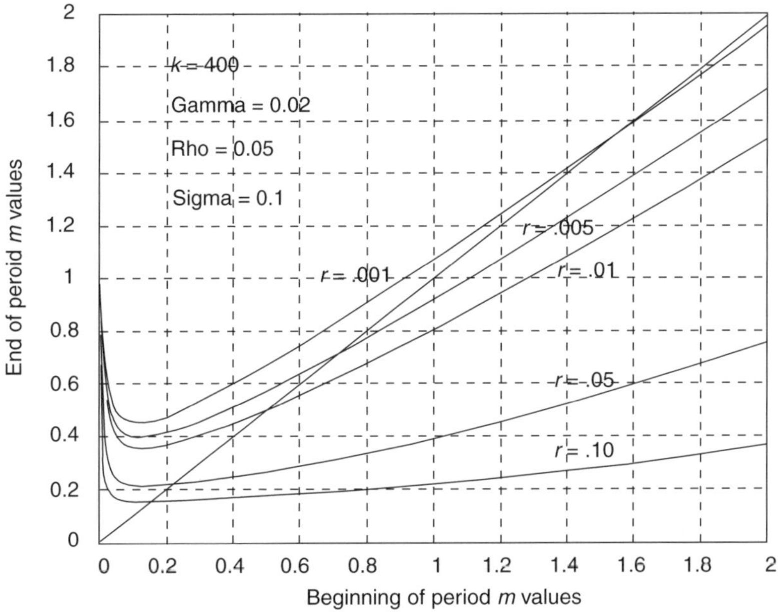

Figure 4.9 Policy functions for different interest rates

subjective discount rate of $\rho = 0.05$. The coefficient of risk aversion σ and the nominal interest rate r were varied over several values, as indicated. For each (σ, r) pair, I used Equation (4.7) to calculate the rate of money growth μ that is implied by given values of γ, ρ, σ, and r. Then I used the condition $\mu m = -v$, with m at the balanced path value given in Equation (4.28), to calculate the implied fiscal policy. These parameter values completely specify the consumer's problem (Equation (4.23)).

To calculate the optimal value and policy functions for Equation (4.23), the values of m and m' were restricted to a grid of 1000 values ranging from 0 to 2 in Figure 4.9, and 0 to 1 in Figure 4.10. Maximization was carried out by comparing values at all points of the grid: no first-order conditions were used. Each figure plots a different family of policy functions (the optimal m' as a function of m) for Equation (4.23).

In Figure 4.9, σ is set at the low value of 0.1, and the nominal interest rate is varied from 0.001 (one-tenth of 1 per cent) up to 0.10. In all cases, the cash holdings of a single consumer with arbitrary initial balances converges to the steady state value given by Equation (4.28). As the

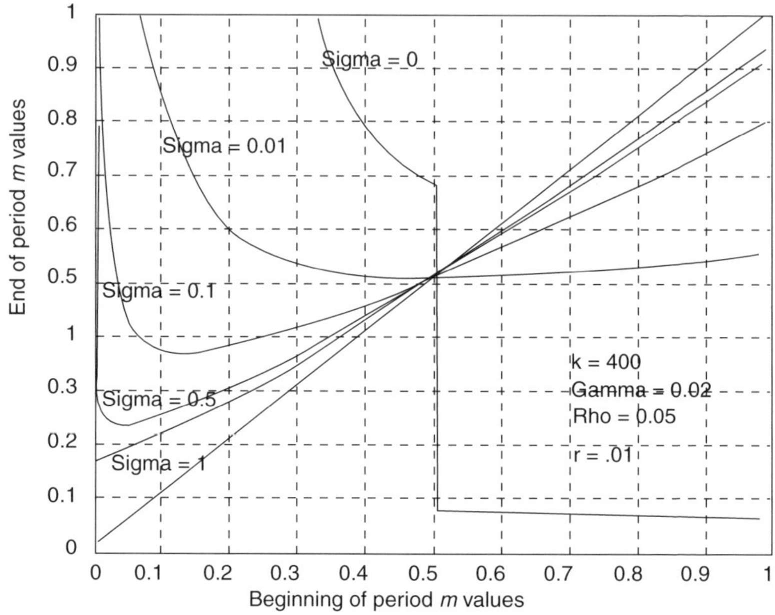

Figure 4.10 Policy functions for different sigma values

interest rate rises above 0.10, the policy function continues to flatten above balanced path values, reflecting the fact that, at high interest rates, consumers very quickly reduce cash holdings to long-run levels. Similar results are obtained at higher values of σ.

In Figure 4.10, the interest rate is held fixed at 0.01 and the parameter σ is varied from the linear case $\sigma = 0$ through the log utility case $\sigma = 1$. For $\sigma > 0$, all these policy functions have a fixed point at $m = 0.5 = 1/\sqrt{rk} = 1/\sqrt{(400)(.01)}$, consistent with the analysis based on first-order conditions that leads to Equation (4.28). For linear utility, however, the policy function has a discontinuity at $m = 0.5$: the optimal policy in this case is to set $s = 0$ for a time, consuming nothing, earning maximum income, and accumulating cash, and then to enjoy a consumption orgy in which all cash is spent at once. The consumer then returns to the cash-accumulation phase, and the cycle is repeated. Similar behaviour emerges at positive but very small (smaller than 0.01) values of σ.

In summary, then, it *is* possible that in this non-convex problem the first-order conditions can fail to hold under optimal behaviour. In such cases, the McCallum–Goodfriend theory cannot be used to rationalize the money demand function in Equation (4.28). But these difficulties arise only under near-linear utility, with values of σ far below any available estimates. For realistic values of the risk-aversion parameter, and in particular even for very low interest rates, Equation (4.28) is an implication of the theory.

6 Conclusions and further directions

There are several research developments I have not yet mentioned that hold promise for sharpening our knowledge on the cost of inflation. I shall discuss these briefly, and then offer some conclusions.

I have emphasized that money-holding behaviour at very low interest rates is central for estimating welfare costs. In this chapter I have pursued the idea that models parameterized to fit time series behaviour under interest rates as low as 2 per cent could be used to predict behaviour at interest rates in the zero to 2 per cent range. Recent work by Mulligan and Sala-i-Martin (1996) provides reason to believe that this extrapolation will not be reliable, and proposes a quite different empirical approach to the problem. They begin from the hypothesis that there is a fixed cost (renewable annually, say) of holding positive amounts of interest-bearing securities, and that households who hold only cash do not incur this cost. In this case, if a monetary policy driving interest rates to zero were implemented, more and more households would decide not to incur this fixed cost, which is to say that fewer and fewer households would be using resources to economize on cash holdings. The presence of such a cost might be undetectable in aggregate time series, yet important enough to completely negate any welfare gain from reducing interest rates from, say, 1.5 per cent to zero.

Mulligan and Sala-i-Martin then observe that, in deciding whether to incur the fixed cost, a household will compare it to something like the *product* rA of the interest rate r and asset holdings A. If so, then the portfolio behaviour of people with low asset holdings should resemble behaviour at low interest rates, and we should be able to see the effects of the fixed cost by looking at people with low financial wealth in a cross section. According to the Survey of Consumer Finances, as described in Avery *et al.* (1984), about 59 per cent of American households in 1989 had no financial assets besides cash and their cheque account. Mulligan and Sala-i-Martin interpret this fact as evidence that the fixed costs described in the previous paragraph are sizeable. I think this interpretation is right, and conclude that the construction of models that can utilize cross-section and time series evidence together has real promise for learning about behaviour under very low interest rates. If so, then there is good reason to doubt that accurate estimates of cash holding at very low interest rates can be obtained from aggregate US time series evidence alone.

Another set of questions about the time series estimates concerns the fact that M1 – the measure of money I have used – is a sum of currency holdings that do not pay interest and demand deposits that (in some circumstances) do. Moreover, other interest-bearing assets beside these may serve as means of payment. One response to these observations is to formulate a model of the banking system in which currency, reserves and deposits play distinct roles. Such a model seems to be essential if one wants to consider policies such as reserve requirements, interest on deposits, and other measures that affect different components of the money stock differently. See Yoshino (1993) for a promising step in this direction.[15]

A second response to the arbitrariness of M1, more fully developed so far than the first, is to replace M1 with an aggregate in which different monetary assets are given different weights. The basic idea, as proposed in Barnett (1978, 1980), and Poterba and Rotemberg (1987), is that if a treasury bill yielding 6 per cent is assumed to yield no monetary services, then a bank deposit yielding 3 per cent can be thought of as yielding half the monetary services of a zero-interest currency holding of equal dollar value. Implementing this idea avoids the awkward necessity of classifying financial assets as either entirely money or not monetary at all, and lets the data do most of the work in deciding how monetary aggregates should be revised over time as interest rates change and new instruments are introduced. The Divisia monetary aggregates constructed by Barnett and others can behave quite differently from 'simple sum' aggregates such as M1 or M2.[16] For most of the US time series data used in this chapter, though, demand deposits were required by law not to pay interest. I doubt that this issue is of much importance for Meltzer's (1963b) estimates, nor do I think it is of much importance for my extension of Meltzer's estimation to later years. But one can see from Figure 4.4 that my estimated money demand functions do very badly in the 1990s. I share the widely-held opinion that M1 is too narrow an aggregate for this period, and I think that the Divisia approach offers much the best prospects for resolving the difficulty.

As in any active research area, then, there are many interesting avenues left to pursue. But I began this chapter with the substantive question of the estimation of the welfare gains available to a society that reduces the long-run growth rates of money and prices, and I owe the reader a summary of what is known, now, on this question.

In all of the models I have reviewed, the estimated gains of reducing inflation and interest rates are positive, starting from any interest rate above, say, one-tenth of 1 per cent. Even when fiscal considerations make a strictly positive interest rate optimal, the necessary qualification to the Friedman (1969) rule is quantitatively trivial. According to Figure 4.5 (or 4.6) reducing interest rates from 14 per cent to 3 per cent would yield a benefit equivalent to an increase in real income of about 0.008 – eight-tenths of 1 per cent. This estimate is about the same whether one uses the fitted log-log demand curve for money or the semi-log version. It is based on observations that contain a great deal of information on behaviour over this entire range of interest rates. I have argued that this estimate is not at all sensitive to assumptions about the fiscal policy used to effect the interest rate reduction, and that adding realistic productivity or money supply shocks to the model of Section 3, or to that of Section 5, will not alter the estimated welfare cost greatly. I regard all these conclusions as solidly, though of course not conclusively, established.

A 3 per cent interest rate is about the rate that would arise in the US economy under a policy of zero inflation. The optimal monetary policy, within the class of theories discussed in this chapter, entails a *deflation* consistent with interest rates at or near *zero*. Based on the theory and evidence I have reviewed, the estimated welfare gain of a reduction in interest rates to near-zero levels can vary considerably, depending on the specific model one uses. According to the estimates based on a log-log demand curve, as reported in Figure 4.5, the welfare gain from a monetary policy that reduces interest rates from 3 per cent to zero, measured as a fraction of real GDP, is about 0.009, which is to say, slightly larger than the gain from reducing rates from 14 per cent to 3 per cent! Using the semi-log estimates, however, the estimated gain from reducing interest rates from 3 per cent to zero is less than 0.001. In so far as the fixed costs postulated by Mulligan and Sala-i-Martin are important, even this figure may be an overstatement.

Successful applied science is done at many levels, sometimes close to its foundations, sometimes far away from them, or without them altogether. As Simon (1969) observes, 'This is lucky, else the safety of bridges and airplanes might depend on the correctness of the "Eightfold Way" of looking at elementary particles.' The analysis of sustained inflation illustrates this observation, I think: though monetary theory notoriously lacks a generally accepted 'microeconomic foundation', the quantity theory of money has attained considerable empirical success as a positive theory of inflation. Beyond this, I have argued in this survey that we also have a normative theory that is quantitatively reliable over a wide range of interest rates. There are indications, however, that theory at the level of the models I have reviewed in this chapter is not adequate to let us see how people would manage their cash holdings at very low interest rates. Perhaps, for this purpose, theories that take us further on the search for foundations, such as the matching models introduced by Kiyotaki and Wright (1989), are needed.

Notes

1 The interest rate is the short-term commercial paper rate. For 1900–75, it is from Friedman and Schwartz (1982), table 4.8, col. 6. For 1976–94, it is from the *Economic Report of the President* (1996), table B-69. The money supply is M1 in billions of dollars, December of each year, not seasonally adjusted. For 1900–14, it is from *Historical Statistics of the United States* (1960) Series X-267. From 1915–47, it is from Friedman and Schwartz (1982), pp. 708–18, col. 7. For 1948–85, it is from the *International Financial Statistics Tape*. From 1986–94, it is from the Federal Reserve Bank of St. Louis *FRED Database*. Real GDP is in billions of 1987 dollars. From 1900–28, it is from Kendrick (1961), table A-III. From 1929–58, it is from the *National Income and Product Accounts of the U.S., 1929–1958*, table 1.2. From 1929–94, it is from *Citibase*, Series GDPQ. The GDP deflator equals 1.0 in 1987. For 1900–28, it is from *Historical Statistics of the United States* (1960), Series F-5. For 1929–58, it is from the *National Income and Product Accounts of the U.S., 1929–1958*, table 7.13. For 1959–94, it is from *Citibase*, Series GDPD.

2 Estimates of the income or wealth elasticity of money (M1 or M2) demand obtained from long US time series tend to be around unity: Meltzer (1963a), Laidler (1977), Lucas (1988), Stock and Watson (1993). Ball (1998), using methods similar to Stock and Watson's but applied to data through 1996, obtains an income elasticity near 0.5. Meltzer (1963b) reports estimates near one for sales elasticities in a cross-section sample of firms. Estimates from post-war quarterly data are generally below one: Goldfeld (1987). Recent estimates by Mulligan and Sala-i-Martin (1992) from panel data on US states are higher, around 1.3.

3 Cagan (1956) used the semi-log form in his classic study of European hyperinflations. It is interesting that the paradox that Cagan noted, of inflation rates during hyperinflations that exceeded the revenue-maximizing levels, is specific to semi-log money demand. With log-log demand, seigniorage is always an increasing function of the money growth rate.

4 Here I follow Brock's (1974) perfect-foresight version of the Sidrauski model.

5 Throughout this chapter I take the real growth rate γ to be independent of monetary policy. The role of inflation when real growth is endogenously determined is examined in De Gregorio (1993), Gomme (1993), Jones and Manuelli (1995), Chari, Jones and Manuelli (1995), and Dotsey and Ireland (1996).

6 If a function v satisfies Equation (4.6), then it is easy to see that the function $\tilde{v}(m, y) = y^{1-\sigma} v(m/y)$ satisfies Equation (4.5). Ruling out other solutions to Equation (4.5) is more difficult. In general, I will not provide a rigorous treatment of the Bellman equations that arise in this chapter.

7 Depending on the way the holding of real balances is motivated, the equilibrium in the limiting economy where $r = 0$ may be ill-defined, or there may be equilibria with $r = 0$ that are not close to equilibria with r positive but arbitrarily small. I shall confine attention here to economies with $r > 0$. By referring to 0 as the optimal rate in this context I mean that reducing r is welfare-improving for any $r > 0$.

8 The irrelevance of the intertemporal substitution parameter for money demand reflects the fact that, in this model, money is dominated as a store of value by nominal bonds.

9 Burdick (1997) contains an interesting analysis of transition dynamics in a model closely related to Cooley and Hansen's.

10 In the US tax structure, inflation also has an indirect effect on the effective tax rates on income from capital (because of its effects on allowable deductions for depreciation, for example). These effects, if not offset by indexing or legislative changes, can be sizeable. See Feldstein (1996) and Bullard and Russell (1997).

11 Brock (1974) proposes a similar formulation, and shows that it is equivalent to a utility-based formulation in which utility depends on leisure as well as goods and real balances.

12 Karni (1973), Kimbrough (1986a, 1986b), Den Haan (1990), Cole and Stockman (1992) and Gillman (1993) have also used monetary models featuring a time-using technology for transactions. Karni is explicit about the links with the inventory-theoretic literature I am here using to motivate a specific form for this technology. The construction of an explicit general equilibrium model in which agents solve Baumol-like cash management problems has not been carried out in any of these papers, nor is it here. See Fusselman and Grossman (1989) or Grossman (1987) for interesting results along this line. A useful recent contribution is Rodríguez (1996).

13 Jovanovic (1982) contains another derivation of thez square-root formula from an aggregative general equilibrium model.

14 Depending on the way one interprets the Baumol theory, one may take it as also predicting that the *income* elasticity of money demand is one-half. If this is right, the theory fails badly on US time series evidence. The issue is whether we interpret the growth in the economy's aggregate production as growth in the size of the cash flows to be managed, or in the number of flows, or somewhere in between. The constant returns, unit income elasticity that I have built into the aggregate theory requires the assumption that it is the *number* of cash flows to be managed that doubles whenever real GDP doubles, and not their average size.

15 Other recent work that treats components of M1 separately includes Dotsey (1988) and Marty (1993).

16 See, for example, Belongia (1996).

References

Avery, Robert B., Gregory E. Elliehausen, Arthur B. Kennickell and Glenn Canner (1984) 'Survey of Consumer Finances, 1983', *Federal Reserve Bulletin*, vol. 70, pp. 679–92.

Bailey, Martin J. (1956) 'The Welfare Cost of Inflationary Finance', *Journal of Political Economy*, vol. 64, pp. 93–110.

Ball, Laurence (1998) 'Another Look at Long-Run Money Demand', Working paper, Johns Hopkins University, Baltimore, Md.

Barnett, William A. (1978) 'The User Cost of Money', *Economics Letters*, vol. 1, pp. 145–9.

Barnett, William A. (1980) 'Economic Monetary Aggregates: An Application of Index Number and Aggregation Theory', *Journal of Econometrics*, vol. 14, pp. 11–48.

Baumol, William J. (1952) 'The Transactions Demand for Cash: An Inventory Theoretic Approach', *Quarterly Journal of Economics*, vol. 66, pp. 545–56.

Belongia, Michael T. (1996) 'Measurement Matters: Recent Results from Monetary Economics Reexamined', *Journal of Political Economy*, vol. 104, pp. 1065–83.

Bewley, Truman (1983) 'A Difficulty with the Optimum Quantity of Money' *Econometrica*, vol. 51, pp. 1485–1504.

Brock, William A. (1974) 'Money and Growth: The Case of Long Run Perfect Foresight', *International Economic Review*, vol. 15, pp. 750–77.

Bullard, James and Steven Russell (1997) 'How Costly is Sustained Low Inflation for the U.S. Economy?', Working paper, Federal Reserve Bank of St. Louis, Miss.

Burdick, Clark A. (1997) 'A Transitional Analysis of the Welfare Cost of Inflation', Working paper, Federal Reserve Bank of Atlanta, Ca.

Cagan, Phillip (1956) 'The Monetary Dynamics of Hyperinflation', in Milton Friedman (ed.). *Studies in the Quantity Theory of Money* (University of Chicago Press).

Caplin, Andrew and John Leahy (1991) 'State-Dependent Pricing and the Dynamics of Money and Output', *Quarterly Journal of Economics*, vol. 106, pp. 683–708.

Chang, Fwu-Ranq (1992) 'Homogeneity and the Transactions Demand for Money' Working paper, Indiana University.

Chari, V. V., Lawrence J. Christiano and Patrick J. Kehoe (1993) 'Optimality of the Friedman Rule in Economies with Distorting Taxes'. Federal Reserve Bank of Minneapolis Working Paper.

Chari, V. V., Larry E. Jones, and Rodolfo E. Manuelli (1995) 'The Growth Effects of Monetary Policy', *Federal Reserve Bank of Minneapolis Quarterly Review*, vol. 19, pp. 18–32.

Cole, Harold L. and Alan C. Stockman (1992) 'Specialization, Transactions Technologies, and Money Growth', *International Economic Review*, vol. 33, pp. 283–98.

Cooley, Thomas F. and Gary D. Hansen (1989) 'The Inflation Tax in a Real Business Cycle Model', *American Economic Review*, vol. 79, pp. 733–48.

Cooley, Thomas F. and Gary D. Hansen (1991) 'The Welfare Costs of Moderate Inflations', *Journal of Money, Credit, and Banking*, vol. 23, pp. 483–503.

Correia, Isabel and Pedro Teles (1997) 'The Optimal Inflation Tax, Working paper, Federal Reserve Bank of Minneapolis, Minn.

De Gregorio, José (1993) 'Inflation, Taxation, and Long-run Growth', *Journal of Monetary Economics*, vol. 31, pp. 271–98.

Den Haan, Wouter J. (1990) 'The Optimal Inflation Path in a Sidrauski-Type Model with Uncertainty', *Journal of Monetary Economics*, vol. 25, pp. 389–409.

Dotsey, Michael (1988) 'The Demand for Currency in the United States', *Journal of Money, Credit, and Banking*, vol. 20, pp. 22–40.

Dotsey, Michael and Peter Ireland (1996) 'The Welfare Cost of Inflation in General Equilibium', *Journal of Monetary Economics*, vol. 37, pp. 29–47.

Dvoretzky, Aryeh (1965) 'The Probability Distribution Generated by the Random Payments Process' Special Appendix to ch. v in Patinkin (1965).

Eckstein, Zvi and Leonardo Leiderman (1992) 'Seigniorage and the Welfare Cost of Inflation', *Journal of Monetary Economics*, vol. 29, pp. 389–410.
Economic Report of the President (1996) (Washington, DC: US Government Printing, Office).
Feldstein, Martin (1996) 'The Costs and Benefits of Going from Low Inflation to Price Stability', Working paper, National Bureau of Economic Research.
Frenkel, Jacob and Boyan Jovanovic (1980) 'On Transactions and Precautionary Demand for Money', *Quarterly Journal of Economics*, vol. 95, pp. 25–43.
Friedman, Milton (1969) *The Optimum Quantity of Money and Other Essays* (Chicago: Aldine).
Friedman, Milton and Anna J. Schwartz (1982) *Monetary Trends in the United States and the United Kingdom, 1867–1975* (University of Chicago Press, for the National Bureau of Economic Research).
Fusselman, Jerry and Sanford J. Grossman (1989) 'Monetary Dynamics with Fixed Transactions Costs', Working paper, Princeton University, NJ.
Gillman, Max (1993) 'The Welfare Cost of Inflation in a Cash-in-Advance Economy with Costly Credit', *Journal of Monetary Economics*, vol. 31, pp. 97–115.
Goldfeld, Stephen M. (1987) 'Demand for Money: Empirical Studies' in John Eatwell, Murray Milgate and Peter Newman (eds) *The New Palgrave: A Dictionary of Economics* (London: Macmillan New York: Stockton Press), pp. 770–5.
Gomme, Paul (1993) 'Money and Growth Revisited' *Journal of Monetary Economics*, vol. 32, pp. 51–77.
Grossman, Sanford J. (1987) 'Monetary Dynamics with Proportional Transactions Costs and Fixed Payment Periods', in William A. Barnett and Kenneth J. Singleton (eds), *New Approaches to Monetary Dynamics* (Cambridge University Press).
Guidotti, Pablo E. and Carlos A. Vegh (1993) 'The Optimal Inflation Tax When Money Reduces Transactions Costs: A Reconsideration', *Journal of Monetary Economics*, vol. 31, pp. 189–206.
Historical Statistics of the United States (1960) (Washington, DC: US Government Printing Office).
Jones, Larry E. and Rodolfo E. Manuelli (1995) 'Growth and the Effects of Inflation', *Journal of Economic Dynamics and Control*, vol. 19, pp. 1405–28.
Jovanovic, Boyan (1982) 'Inflation and Welfare in the Steady State', *Journal of Political Economy*, vol. 90, pp. 561–77.
Karni, Edi (1973) 'Transactions Costs and the Demand for Media of Exchange', *Western Economic Journal*, vol. 11(1), pp. 71–80.
Karni, Edi (1977) 'The Transactions Demand for Cash: Incorporation of the Value of Time into the Inventory Approach', *Journal of Political Economy*, vol. 81, pp. 1216–25.
Kendrick, John W. (1961) *Productivity Trends in the United States* (Princeton, NJ: Princeton University Press, for the National Bureau of Economic Research).
Kimbrough, Kent P. (1986a) 'Inflation, Employment, and Welfare in the Presence of Transactions Costs', *Journal of Money, Credit, and Banking*, vol. 18, pp. 127–40.
Kimbrough, Kent P. (1986b) 'The Optimum Quantity of Money Rule in the Theory of Public Finance', *Journal of Monetary Economics*, vol. 18, pp. 277–84.
Kiyotaki, Nobuhiro and Randall Wright (1989) 'Money as a Medium of Exchange', *Journal of Political Economy*, vol. 97, pp. 927–54.
Laidler, David E. W. (1977) 'The Rate of Interest and the Demand for Money', *Journal of Political Economy*, vol. 74, pp. 545–55.

Lucas, Robert E. Jr (1988) 'Money Demand in the United States: A Quantitative Review', *Carnegie–Rochester Conference Series on Public Policy*, vol. 29, pp. 137–68.

Lucas, Robert E. Jr, and Nancy L. Stokey (1983a) 'Optimal Fiscal and Monetary' Policy in an Economy without Capital', *Journal of Monetary Economics*, vol. 12, pp. 55–93.

Lucas, Robert E. Jr, and Nancy L. Stokey (1983b) 'Money and Interest in a Cash-in-Advance Economy', *Econometrica*, vol. 55, pp. 491–513.

Marty, Alvin L. (1993) 'The Inflation Tax, and the Marginal Welfare Cost in a World of Currency and Deposits', Working paper, City University of New York.

McCallum, Bennett T. and Marvin S. Goodfriend (1987) 'Demand for Money: Theoretical Studies', in John Eatwell, Murray Milgate and Peter Newman (eds), *The New Palgrave: A Dictionary of Economics* (London: Macmillan New York: Stockton Press), pp. 775–81.

Meltzer, Allan H. (1963a) 'The Demand for Money: The Evidence from Time Series', *Journal of Political Economy*, vol. 71, pp. 219–46.

Meltzer, Allan H. (1963b) 'The Demand for Money: A Cross-Section Study of Business Firms', *Quarterly Journal of Economics*, vol. 77, pp. 405–22.

Miller, Merton H. and Daniel Orr (1966) 'A Model of the Demand for Money by Firms', *Quarterly Journal of Economics*, vol. 80, pp. 413–35.

Miller, Preston J. (1995) 'The Jointly Optimal Inflation Tax, Income Tax Structure, and Transfer', Working paper, Federal Reserve Bank of Minneapolis, Minn.

Mulligan, Casey B. and Xavier Sala-i-Martin (1992) 'U.S. Money Demand: Surprising Cross-Sectional Estimates', *Brookings Papers on Economic Activity*, vol. 2, 1992, pp. 285–343.

Mulligan, Casey B. and Xavier Sala-i-Martin (1996) 'Adoption of Financial Technologies: Technologies and Implications for Money Demand and Monetary Policy', Working paper, National Bureau of Economic Research.

Mulligan, Casey B. and Xavier Sala-i-Martin (1997) 'The Optimum Quantity of Money: Theory and Evidence', Working paper, National Bureau of Economic Research.

National Income and Product Accounts of the United States (annual) (Washington DC: US Government Printing Office).

Patinkin, Don (1965) *Money, Interest, and Prices*, 2nd edn (New York: Harper and Row).

Phelps, Edmund S. (1973) 'Inflation in the Theory of Public Finance', *Swedish Journal of Economics*, vol. 75, pp. 67–82.

Poterba, James M. and Julio J. Rotemberg (1987) 'Money in the Utility Function: An Empirical Implementation', in William A. Barnett and Kenneth J. Singleton (eds), *New Approaches to Monetary Dynamics* (Cambridge University Press).

Rodríguez Mendezibál, Hugo (1996) 'The Variability of Money Velocity in a Modified Cash-in-Advance Model', Working paper, University of Chicago.

Sidrauski, Miguel (1967a) 'Rational Choice and Patterns of Growth in a Monetary Economy', *American Economic Review*, vol. 57, pp. 534–44.

Sidrauski, Miguel (1967b) 'Inflation and Economic Growth', *Journal of Political Economy*, vol. 75, pp. 796–810.

Simon, Herbert A. (1969) *The Sciences of the Artificial* (Cambridge Mass.: MIT Press).

Stock, James H. and Mark W. Watson (1993) 'A Simple Estimator of Cointegrating Vectors in Higher Order Integrated Systems', *Econometrica*, vol. 61, pp. 783–820.

Tobin, James (1956) 'The Interest Elasticity of the Transactions Demand for Cash', *Review of Economics and Statistics*, vol. 38, pp. 241–7.

Woodford, Michael (1990) 'The Optimum Quantity of Money', in Benjamin M. Friedman and Frank H. Hahn (eds), *Handbook of Monetary Economics*, vol. II (Amsterdam: North Holland).

Yoshino, Joe A. (1993) *Money and Banking Regulation: The Welfare Costs of Inflation*, Doctoral dissertation, University of Chicago.

Comment

David Laidler
University of Western Ontario, Canada

Robert Lucas's chapter takes important policy questions – what is the optimal inflation rate, and what are the costs of deviating from it? – and uses state-of-the-art monetary theory to address them, and to organize relevant empirical evidence. Following Friedman (1969), the optimal rate of inflation is shown to be that which reduces the nominal rate of interest to zero, but if it were achieved we would be in unknown territory. Economic theory, as deployed by Lucas, allows us to extrapolate beyond the boundaries of empirical experience, and warns us when we approach the limits of our established knowledge. Specifically, he shows that when the opportunity cost of holding money is very low, the size of the further gain to be had from pushing it towards zero depends crucially on the form of the demand for money function, and he reminds us that our knowledge here is shaky.

Lucas's approach ensures that, at every stage in the argument, we know exactly where we are, and how we got there. Furthermore, anyone who has lived through a policy experiment which has carried an economy into new territory will appreciate the benefits of trying such things out first on a well-specified model economy constructed on the basis of the best available theoretical and empirical knowledge. On reading Lucas's paper, one cannot help but feel that his is the way economics should always be done. Even so, while such work is surely necessary for competent policy analysis, it may not always be sufficient. To use old-fashioned vocabulary, the application of economic *science* to policy questions remains an *art*, for reasons inherent in the nature of the science itself.

Lucas stresses that the technical skills of its practitioners impose limits upon what economic analysis can achieve at any particular moment, and that it makes progress over time. This implies: first, that today's state-of-the-art formal model is at best the latest, but not the last, word on any topic; and second, that currently available technique will inevitably limit the range of factors that model takes into account, perhaps to the neglect of some that are important. Let me illustrate the dangers here with a brief, and therefore highly simplified, reference to the not so distant history of macroeconomics.

The early 1930s saw much discussion of the role of endogenous forward-looking expectations in economic life, but that discussion ran well ahead of theorists' capacity to analyse the phenomenon formally. In an important sense, the static IS–LM model of the later 1930s was a step forward. It allowed the best of then generally available analytic techniques to be brought to bear systematically on important macroeconomic issues, but one factor permitting this was that model's treatment of expectations as exogenous. In due course, some economists forgot that this simplification underlay what they were doing, and the 'Keynesian' economics of the 1960s and 1970s was the result. Before we had Robert Lucas's work (for example, 1972), we did not know how to incorporate endogenous forward-looking expectations into formal analysis, but in the 1960s and 1970s would economic policy not have been better had some attention been paid to what had earlier been informally known about these issues?

Perhaps we are now in a similar situation *vis-à-vis* the costs of inflation. Lucas emphasizes that variations in the opportunity cost of holding money affect the volume of resources devoted to portfolio management in an economy in which markets for goods, services and assets exist and clear with equal ease, regardless of the inflation rate. He is quite right to insist that these are the questions that economic analysis in its present state of development is able to address; but Lucas himself finds it helpful to go beyond putting the services of money into the utility function, to ask just what is the nature of those services. He stresses money's means of exchange role. Money, however, is also a unit of account, and we have extensive empirical evidence that inflation interferes with its capacity to perform this function.

To be sure, the most dramatic and costly effects here – the disruption and, at the limit, the disappearance of longer-term capital markets, and of the arbitrage that is needed to maintain a coherent structure of relative prices – occur in conditions of what Daniel Heymann and Axel Leijonhufvud (1995) have termed 'high inflation', and Lucas's chapter is not directly concerned with such a state of the world. Even so, a substantial literature, surveyed by Peter Howitt (1990, 1997) suggests that such problems also occur in a less dramatic, but still costly, fashion at low inflation rates. Menu costs do exist, and, more important, it seems to be impossible to adapt the accounting procedures upon which the data needed for intelligent business decisions depend, and upon which tax codes are based, to variations in the purchasing power of money. These facts give rise to resource misallocations which probably reduce both the level, and perhaps also the rate of growth, of real income.

To put matters in the language of the neoclassical theory on which Lucas's analysis rests, a *fully anticipated* inflation rate is not merely one that is accurately *expected* by all agents; it is also one to which all contracts and market institutions have been *fully adapted*. In the current state of knowledge, we cannot be sure that a *fully anticipated* inflation rate in this sense is anything more than a theoretical construct, and ought to bear in mind that ongoing inflation imposes more costs than Lucas's model enables us to discuss. Howitt (1990) has noted that, while neoclassical analysis of the costs of inflation suggests that mild deflation is optimal, arguments about inflation's capacity to disrupt money's unit of account role point to zero as the right number. And now, in the wake of a recent study by Akerlof *et al.* (1996) of money wage stickiness in the region of zero – surely the result of a particular kind of menu cost – some would argue that mildly positive inflation is desirable. There is, then, a trade-off among costs to be taken into account in fixing an inflation target.

Seen in this light, Lucas's empirical conclusion that the benefits in terms of portfolio management economies of driving the opportunity cost of holding down money from a starting value of 6 per cent per annum are initially large, but shrink, and indeed become problematic, the closer that opportunity cost gets to zero, lend weight to pragmatic arguments against driving inflation into negative territory. I suspect that Lucas would not want to be associated with such an interpretation of his work, and would prefer to confine the discussion to the results yielded by his well-organized formal analysis. But perhaps in due course economic theory will advance to the point that inflation's effects on money's capacity to act as a unit of account can be analyzed as rigorously as its means of exchange and store of value functions, and he will then change his mind. In the meantime, however, policymakers have decisions to make, and in my view those decisions are likely to be better if they are based on all the evidence that economists have amassed, rather than only on the subset that can be incorporated in a formal model.

References

Akerlof, G. A., W. T. Dickens and G. I. Perry (1996) 'The Macroeconomics of Low Inflation', *Brookings Papers on Economic Activity*, no. 1, pp. 1–59.

Friedman, M. (1969) 'The Optimum Quantity of Money', in M. Friedman, *The Optimum Quantity of Money and other Essays* (London: Macmillan).

Heymann, D. and A. Leijonhufvud (1995) *High Inflation* (Oxford University Press).

Howitt, P. W. (1990) 'Zero Inflation and a Long-Run Target for Monetary Policy', in R. G. Lipsey (ed.), *Zero Inflation: The Goal of Price Stability* (Toronto: C. D. Howe Institute).

Howitt, P. W. (1997) 'Low Inflation and the Canadian Economy', in D. Laidler (ed.), *Where We Go from Here: Inflation Targets in Canada's Monetary Policy Regime* (Toronto: C. D. Howe Institute).

Lucas, R. E. Jr (1972) 'Expectations and the Neutrality of Money', *Journal of Economic Theory*, vol. 4, no. 2, pp. 115–38.

Comment

Hans-Werner Sinn
University of Munich, Germany

1 The basic problem

Robert Lucas modestly calls his paper a 'summary' of the literature on the welfare cost of inflation, but in fact it is more than that. It is a synthesis of various theoretical approaches combined with an attempt to estimate the magnitude of the welfare loss.

Lucas basically follows Bailey's (1956) definition of the welfare cost of inflation. He defines 'the welfare cost of inflation as the area under the inverse demand function – the consumer surplus – that could be gained by reducing the [nominal] interest rate ... to zero'. Figure 4.11 illustrates this concept. The demand for real money balances is a decreasing function of the nominal rate of interest because people choose their real money balances in order to equate their marginal benefit in terms of liquidity services with their marginal opportunity cost. The marginal opportunity cost of real balances is given by the nominal rather than the real rate of interest, because inflation is a burden on both money balances and interest-bearing bonds and will therefore not affect the portfolio decision. Given the real rate of interest, the nominal rate can be reduced by lowering the rate of inflation, possibly even to negative values. If the rate of deflation equals the real rate of interest, the nominal rate of interest is zero, and money demand is at the Friedman (1969) optimum. The marginal benefit from money holding then equals its marginal social cost, which is about zero, since it is merely determined by the negligible cost of printing the money. Integrating the marginal benefits from money holding over the entire range where they are positive, starting with the balances held under the existing inflation–interest combination, gives the total benefit from a transition to a deflation rate that equals the real rate of interest or, equivalently, gives the welfare cost of inflation.

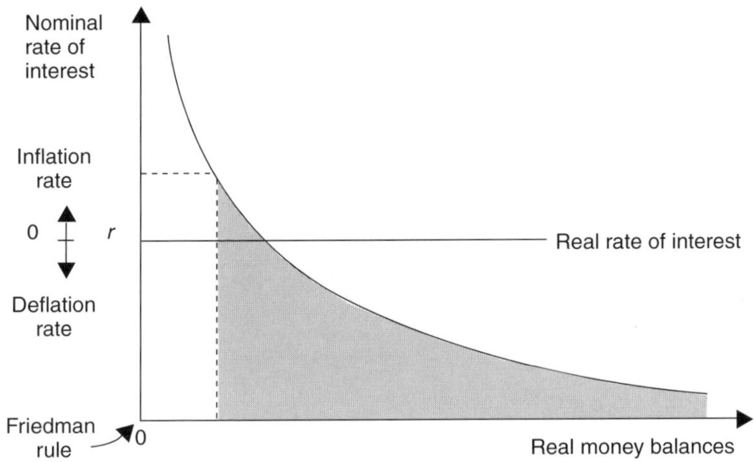

Figure 4.11 The welfare cost of inflation

Definitions are always arbitrary, so they should not be criticized. It is, however, important to note that the welfare cost of inflation according to the Bailey–Lucas definition is not the welfare cost of raising the price level beyond some initial level, but rather of not letting it shrink at an annual rate that equals the economy's real rate of interest. In Figure 4.11, this means that the welfare cost is measured by the total shaded area under the curve, and not just by the part of this area above the real rate of interest marker.

Robert Lucas does not confine himself to the partial-analytic model of Bailey, but also studies more sophisticated intertemporal general equilibrium approaches. In particular, he interprets the money-demand curve in terms of Sidrauski's (1967a, 1967b) model, where money is an argument in the utility function, and the McCallum–Goodfriend (1987) model, where money balances serve the purpose of reducing Allais–Baumol–Tobin type transactions costs. Interpreting a rich set of money-demand data that stretch from 1900 to 1994 on the basis of these models, he estimates the welfare cost of inflation at an interest rate of 6 per cent to be about 1.2 per cent of GDP.

Lucas does not believe in this estimate however, since, as he points out, it relies uncomfortably on the shape of the money-demand function in the range of very low interest rates where no empirical evidence is available. If the functional forms of the money-demand schedule resulting from the theoretical models are bad approximations of the true demand schedule in the range of small interest rates, the true welfare loss from inflation may differ significantly from the 1.2 per cent figure.

2 The role of transactions costs

The money-demand schedules resulting from the Sidrauski model or the McCallum-Goodfriend model have the property of approaching the abscissa asymptotically as the stock of money balances goes to infinity. This is certainly not a plausible property.

Lucas points to the fact that Mulligan and Sala-i-Martin (1996) found that a surprising 60 per cent of American households in 1989 held no financial assets besides cash and cheque accounts. He attributes this observation to the presence of a significant transactions cost that renders a policy of diversifying portfolios inefficient, and concludes that this cost makes the money-demand function inelastic beyond a certain stock of money balances.

His argument is based on the Allais–Baumol–Tobin model. In that model, costly trips to the bank are necessary to convert interest-bearing assets into liquid money balances, and the lower the rate of interest, the longer the time-span between trips to the bank, the larger the amount of money withdrawn per trip, and the larger the average amount of money held. Lucas argues that the time-span cannot be increased indefinitely by reducing the rate of interest to zero, because a certain minimum number of trips to the bank will always be necessary for other purposes, and that the time spent on this minimum number of trips is the transactions cost that explains the low degree of asset diversification among American households.

While I find the assumption of a certain minimum number of trips to the bank to be realistic, I do not see how it could explain the lack of portfolio diversification. If people go to the bank in any case, they should have little difficulty in optimizing their asset portfolios and holding a variety of different assets. Transactions costs that limit portfolio diversification appear to be commission charges, consulting fees, uncertainty premia and similar items that reduce the net benefit from holding interest-bearing assets. Such costs do not make the money-demand curve more inelastic; on the contrary, they make it more elastic. These are the kinds of costs that Keynesian theory postulates with the liquidity trap in the money-demand function.

In fact, the non-observability of low interest rates suggests the existence of such a liquidity trap. If the money-demand function were inelastic for small rates of interest, as Lucas claims, occasionally we should observe extremely low interest rates when the economy is in a deep recession. However, if the curve is perfectly elastic at a certain interest level, we can never observe interest rates below this level.

Figure 4.12 makes clear what the alternative views on the shape of the money-demand function for low interest rates imply. From the empirical data on money demand as reported in Lucas's Figure 4.9, it is obvious that the nominal interest rate has a floor at about 0.75 per cent. Using a variant of the McCallum–Goodfriend model with different household types and the assumption of a minimal number of trips to the bank, Lucas estimates a vertical branch[1] of the money-demand function at a money–GPD ratio of 0.44, so that the area to the right of this branch no longer contributes to the welfare loss from inflation. Including this area, the estimated welfare loss would be 1.2 per cent of GDP. Excluding it, the loss is only 0.6 per cent of GDP.[2] The Keynesian interpretation of the empirical interest floor at a rate of 0.75 per cent is that at this level there is a liquidity trap that adds a horizontal branch to the money demand function: since the cost of holding bonds is 0.75 per cent of their value, no one would ever hold bonds if their rate of return were equal to, or less than, 0.75 per cent.

To further clarify the difference between the Keynesian view and Lucas's view, consider the Allais–Baumol–Tobin function $T(M, Y)$ with $T_M \leq 0$ and $T_Y > 0$, where T is the cost of the trips to the bank, M the stock of real money balances and Y the transactions volume (income). According to Lucas, people choose their money balances in order to equate the marginal saving in the cost of visiting the banks with the nominal rate of interest (r),

$$T_M(M, Y) = r \qquad \text{(Lucas) (1)}$$

The marginal cost of bank visits is a declining function of real balances with a positive second derivative, $T_{MM} > 0$. As M approaches some critical level M^*, T_{MM} even approaches infinity. In other words, the marginal benefit from money holding, $-T_M$, falls sharply to zero when M approaches M^*.

According to the Keynesian interpretation, on the other hand, $T(M, Y)$ is well behaved, but, instead of Equation (1), the marginal condition for an optimal choice of real money balances is:

$$T_M(M, Y) = r - k \qquad \text{(Keynes) (2)}$$

where k is the transactions cost of holding the bonds. When there are transactions costs of holding bonds, people will choose their money balances to equate their marginal benefit to the nominal rate of interest net of these transactions costs.

This has significant implications for the size of the welfare cost, although it does not confirm the increase in this cost that the horizontal branch of the money-demand curve might at first sight suggest. In Figure 4.12, only the vertical distance between the money demand curve and the value of 0.75 per cent is the marginal benefit from money-holding, and the Friedman optimum where this marginal benefit is zero is reached at a money–GDP ratio of about 0.44. The integral over the marginal benefit up to the Friedman optimum, which in general should be the measure of the welfare cost of inflation, is the area Lucas estimates minus the hatched rectangle shown in Figure 4.12. With a nominal interest rate of 6 per cent, Lucas's data imply that money demand is 0.21 per cent of GDP. Thus the welfare loss of inflation that Lucas calculates needs to be reduced by an amount equal to (0.44 – 0.21)·0.75 per cent, which is about 0.17 per cent. Subtracting this from Lucas's figure (0.6 per cent) gives a welfare loss from inflation equal to 0.43 per cent of GDP.

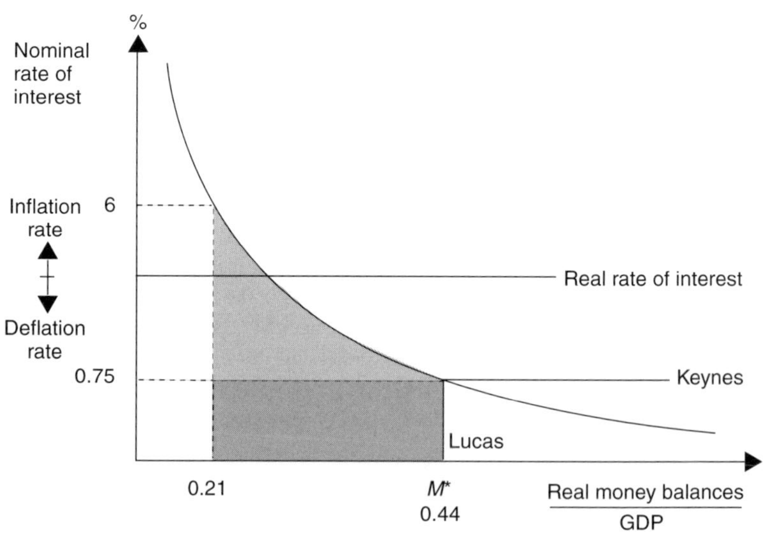

Figure 4.12 Two alternative views on the money demand at low interest rates

3 Taxation of interest income

One reason why the nominal rate of interest does not measure the marginal benefit from money-holding is that the transactions cost of holding bonds has to be taken into account in an optimal portfolio decision. Another reason is the tax burden that bond holders have to bear.

In most countries, including the USA, interest income is subject to income tax. Abstracting from the transactions cost of bond holding, one should therefore expect the marginal benefit from money holding to be equal to the net-of-tax nominal rate of interest rather than the nominal interest rate as such. If τ is the income tax rate, the marginal condition for an optimal choice of real money balances becomes:

$$T_M(M, Y) = (1 - \tau)r \tag{3}$$

It follows that only the fraction $(1 - \tau)$ of the area under the money demand curve can be equated with the welfare cost of inflation. With $\tau = 0.5$, this in itself would mean that the welfare cost is only 50 per cent of what Robert Lucas has measured.

A combination of the tax and transactions cost effects would substantially reduce the welfare cost of inflation. For example, with a 50 per cent tax rate and a tax-deductibility of the cost of bond holding, the welfare loss from inflation in the sense of deviating from the modified Friedman optimum by allowing for a nominal interest rate of 6 per cent, would then be only 0.215 per cent. This is a small number by any standard.

4 Other reasons for a welfare loss

While the Bailey–Lucas type of welfare cost from inflation seems negligible, there are other types of welfare cost from inflation that could potentially be important. In this section I briefly sketch a few of them.

4.1 Money in the production function

Suppose the Allais–Baumol–Tobin type of money demand is exerted by firms rather than households, so that real money balances become a factor of production.

A simple formulation of the production function could be:

$$Y = f(K, L) - T[M, f(K, L)] \tag{4}$$

where $f(K, L)$ is the usual production function with capital and labour as arguments, and T is the cost of trips to the bank in terms of absorbing labour and capital which otherwise could have been used for production. A profit-maximizing firm will, as before, choose its money balances to equate the marginal benefit from money holding, in terms of reducing the cost of the trips to the bank, to the nominal rate of interest:

$$-T_M(M, f) = r \tag{5}$$

In addition, it will employ capital up to the point where its marginal product net of the cost of making the bank trips is equal to the real rate of interest, $r - \pi$, where π is the inflation rate:

$$f_K(1 - T_f) = r - \pi \tag{6}$$

In this formulation, the trips to the bank drive a wedge between the marginal product of capital and the real rate of interest. This is similar to a tax wedge and implies that inflation generates distortions similar to tax distortions. Assuming that $T_{fM} < 0$ and $T_{MM} > 0$, it can easily be shown from Equations (5) and (6) that an increase in the inflation rate reduces the stock of real money balances for any given values of K and L:

$$\frac{dM}{d\pi} = \frac{1}{T_{fM} - T_{MM}} < 0 \tag{7}$$

Because of Equation (5), this implies that the real rate of interest declines with an increase in inflation:

$$\frac{d(r - \pi)}{d\pi} = f_K \frac{T_{fM}}{T_{MM} - T_{fM}} < 0 \tag{8}$$

In an open economy, this will tend to drive out capital to other countries,[3] and in an economy with capital accumulation it will reduce the rate of growth.

These distortions may be more severe than the ones analyzed by Lucas, but they cannot be measured by moving along the money-demand curve and calculating the change in the area underneath that curve, because they are induced by a decline in the real rate of interest rather than an increase in the nominal one.

Of course, this denies the Fisher effect, but that effect has a weak empirical basis in any case. In an extensive study covering 120 years of US history, Lawrence Summers (1983) has provided overwhelming evidence that inflation does not translate into a higher nominal interest rate on a one-to-one basis.

4.2 The nominality principle

Another reason for inflationary welfare costs is the nominality principle: the fact that credit contracts, wage contracts, tax laws and other rules that define financial payments are typically set up in nominal rather than real terms. After all, money, and not commodities, is the unit of account in a modern economy.

Unforeseen, and even *foreseen*, inflation will under these circumstances be able to generate real distortions because the real meaning of a nominal contract will change with the price level. For example, a fixed nominal wage may be above the marginal product of labour at the beginning of the contract period and below it at the end, generating welfare-reducing distortions in either case.

In principle, the distortions can be avoided by frequent adjustment of the rules of payment, but this involves menu costs that could be substantial. Similarly, an indexation could induce prohibitive information costs.

In fact, the periods during which financial payment rules are fixed despite inflation can be substantial. In some countries, fixed interest credit contracts extend over twenty years or more, and in most countries tax laws are revised after decades rather than years.

Among potential distortions, those resulting from historical cost accounting seem particularly important. The tax law fixes depreciation rules for real assets invested by firms on the basis of their historical purchasing value rather than their current reproduction cost. When there is inflation, this means that the real depreciation over the lifetime of an asset will always be below 100 per cent of the asset's real value. Even when the tax law allows for accelerated depreciation, this typically will discriminate the investment process and induce both a slowdown of economic growth and an expulsion of capital to other countries.[4]

The government's extra revenue from historical cost accounting is about ten times the revenue from the inflation tax on money-holding.[5] It would not be surprising if the real economic distortions created by historical cost accounting were also much bigger than the Bailey–Lucas type of inflationary welfare loss.

4.3 Uncertainty

More inflation means not only a more rapid change in the price level, but also a larger variance of the future price level, if only because zero is a neutral focusing point for monetary policy that exhibits some commitment value. A central bank which announces an inflation goal of 0 per cent will deviate by fewer percentage points from its goal than one that announces a goal of 12 per cent. It is difficult to explain why this is so; there may be deeper psychological reasons. Nevertheless, to me it seems to be an obvious fact of life.

If more inflation also means more inflationary risk, inflation is bad because it destroys the long-term capital market. Buyers and lenders will then mutually demand risk premia in their contracts which limit the scope for welfare-improving contracts as such. This may be a serious impediment to investment and growth, because it will limit the possibility of financing long-term investment projects.

The risk problem may be one of the reasons why, in the United States, for example, hardly any long-term housing loans with fixed interest rates are taken up, while in Germany, which traditionally has been a low-inflation country, contracts with repayment periods of up to thirty years are not unusual. The absence of long-term fixed-interest housing loans may have had adverse implications for the durability of the American housing stock – something which would be worth investigating further.

Apart from that, the price level uncertainty may have severe distributional consequences that might even threaten the stability of society itself. Germany's experience in the 1920s should be a warning. German inflation expropriated the middle class and deprived the German society of one of the pillars on which its political system was built. The political implications in 1933, and the resulting welfare loss for the whole world, have dwarfed all the other welfare losses that might possibly result from inflation.

5 Welfare gains from inflation

My final point is to question the basic presumption that inflation as such is bad. Lucas's normative starting point is the Friedman rule, where the price level declines at a rate given by the real rate of interest. Any lower deflation, and a fortiori a true inflation is bad.

The nominality principle and the risk argument I discussed in the previous two sections deny that view by implying that the optimal rate of inflation, or deflation, is zero. There is another argument that even suggests that a moderate rate of inflation is desirable. I do not mean the Phelps (1973) argument that some inflation may be useful to generate some inflation tax revenue for the government, which could then be used to lower distortive taxes. Lucas has rightly dismissed this argument as empirically insignificant. I mean instead the argument recently renewed by Truman Bewley (1998) in his Marshall lecture to the European Economic Association.

The argument refers to the downward stickiness of wages and prices, again an issue where economic theory has as yet not been able to offer a full explanation. Truman interviewed 300 firms to find out about their wage setting, hiring and dismissal rules. His conclusion from these interviews was that nominal wage cuts are typically not made within an existing employment relationship because they would be considered an insult and a sign of mistrust. If a wage cut is necessary, the only way to achieve it is to dismiss the existing employees and hire new ones at lower wages. This confirms the old observation of Keynes (1936) that workers resist a direct wage cut because they are afraid that this would worsen their relative income position, but they would not object strongly to an indirect wage cut brought by a general inflation because this would leave their relative income positions intact.

If the Bewley view is true, and if a market economy needs structural change accompanied by wage cuts in declining sectors, then some inflation would be useful. It would effectively make the wages flexible and facilitate structural change. I mention this argument for the sake of completeness, not in order to finish with a plea for an inflationary policy. The arguments I have put forward all have some merits, but it is difficult to make a judgement about their net effect. That applies also to Robert Lucas's arguments. They are correct, but not complete. Nothing is complete in this world.

Notes

1 I have changed the axes of Lucas's Figure 4.9 so that I can draw the money-demand function in its usual form.
2 Part of the decline in the welfare loss is also attributable to a downward shift of the money-demand curve in the neighbourhood of the kink, which results from the differences in household wealth. The effect is nevertheless not essential for my discussion.
3 See Sinn (1991).
4 Sinn (1987, 1991).
5 Sinn (1983).

References

Bailey, Martin J. (1956) 'The Welfare Cost of Inflationary Finance', *Journal of Political Economy*, vol. 64, pp. 93–110.

Bewley, Truman F. (1998) 'Why Not Cut Pay?', *European Economic Review*, vol. 42, pp. 459–90.

Friedman, Milton (1969) *The Optimum Quantity of Money and Other Essays* (Chicago: Aldine).

Keynes, John M. (1936) *The General Theory of Employment, Interest and Money* (London: Macmillan).

McCallum, Bennett T. and Marvin Goodfriend (1987) 'Demand for Money. Theoretical Studies', in J. Eatwell, M. Milgate and P. Newman (eds), *The New Palgrave. A Dictionary of Economics* (London: Macmillan), pp. 775–81.

Mulligan, Casey B. and Xavier Sala-i-Martin (1996) 'Adoption of Financial Technologies: Technologies and Implications for Money Demand and Monetary Policy', Working paper, National Bureau of Economic Research.

Phelps, Edmund S. (1973) 'Inflation in the Theory of Public Finance', *Swedish Journal of Economics*, vol. 75, pp. 67–82.

Sidrauski, Miguel (1967a) 'Rational Choice and Patterns of Growth in a Monetary Economy', *American Economic Review*, vol. 57, pp. 534–44.

Sidrauski, Miguel (1967b) 'Inflation and Economic Growth', *Journal of Political Economy*, vol. 75, pp. 796–810.

Sinn, Hans-Werner (1983) 'Die Inflationsgewinne des Staates', in E. Wille (ed.), *Beiträge zur gesamtwirtschaftlichen Allokation. Allokationsprobleme im intermediären Bereich zwischen öffentlichem und privatem Wirtschaftssektor* (Frankfurt and Berne: Lang), pp. 111–66.

Sinn, Hans-Werner (1987) 'Inflation, Scheingewinnbesteuerung und Kapitalallokation', in D. Schneider (ed.), *Kapitalmarkt und Finanzierung* (Papers and proceedings of Verein für Socialpolitik) (Berlin: Duncker and Humblot), pp. 187–210.

Sinn, Hans–Werner (1991) 'The Non-neutrality of Inflation for Internationl Capital Movements', *European Economic Review*, vol. 34, pp. 1–22.

Summers, Lawrence (1983) 'The Nonadjustment of Nominal Interest Rates. A Study of the Fisher Effect', in J. Tobin (ed.), *Macroeconomics, Prices, and Quantities. Essays in Memory of Arthur M. Okun* (Oxford: Basil Blackwell), pp. 201–44.

Part II

Monetary and Financial Instability

5
Business Cycles in a Financially Deregulated America

Albert M. Wojnilower
The Clipper Group and Craig Drill Capital, New York, USA

A very long time ago, in 1980, Brookings published my paper entitled 'The Central Role of Credit Crunches in Recent Financial History' (Wojnilower (1980)). Presumably the emphasis of this and subsequent articles on the transcendent role of financial institutions and credit in business fluctuations is what led the chairman to invite the present contribution, although I am an economist practising in the financial rather than the scholarly or government community.

The 1980 article concluded that 'cyclically significant retardation or reduction in credit and aggregate demand occur only when there is an interruption in the supply of credit – a "credit crunch"'. Such interruptions may be prompted, intentionally or accidentally, by the destruction of lenders' incentives through regulatory rigidities ... or the emergence of serious default problems in major institutions or markets. Following such episodes ... the authorities ... and the private markets ... have deliberately reshaped the financial structure so as to prevent the recurrence of that particular form of credit supply interruption'. It went on to argue that removal of the regulatory constraints would lead to more frequent and inherently much more dangerous default crises. In fact this *has* happened, as will be recounted here, necessitating a series of breathtaking lender-of-last-resort rescues by central banks and governments. The potential for such crises continues to multiply, while the means for dealing with them are diminshing.

Although the Brookings paper included the business cycles of the essentially non-inflationary period 1953–65, while it was being written and published US inflation was racing towards double digits. American political and economic hegemony was eroding, and the chronically depreciating dollar spread the inflationary bias world-wide. Commodity prices in general and oil prices in particular were multiplying. Labour unions in the USA and elsewhere applied relentless upward pressure on money wage rates.

Crucial to furthering the inflationary outcome, financial deregulation was inhibiting the tightening of Federal Reserve monetary policy. Removal of official interest rate ceilings kept credit flowing despite successive upsurges in nominal interest rates to unheard-of levels – levels so high that most experts took for granted that they must be severely restrictive, when in actuality they were not. Meanwhile the new competition among deregulated financial institutions led to bankruptcies with potential for systemic disruption, deterring the authorities from pressing home tight policies.

How changed are today's circumstances! The Cold War is over. The hegemony of the dollar is unchallenged; left to its own devices, it tends to appreciate. American business and technology are viewed as leading a world economy globalized to an extent that would have been incomprehensible in 1980. In the industrial countries, inflation is subdued. Oil and other commodities are abundant: their relative and absolute prices have fallen. In the USA, labour union power has collapsed, part of a pervasive rightward shift in political tastes.

With such a sea-change in political and economic climate, it is not surprising that the US business cycle has been gentler and kinder. From 1953 to 1982, as registered by the National Bureau of Economic Research, there were seven business downturns (plus at least one 'close call'), each associated with a credit crunch caused by governmental regulations or actions. Since then, notwithstanding ample turbulence and failures in financial markets, only a single mild recession of eight months has been recognized, and the timing of its onset was unrelated to any serious credit disruption. With the dollar free of pressure or challenge, and inflation markedly decelerated, it is an easy path of least resistance for the Federal Reserve to forestall recessions by responding openhandedly to threatened or actual financial crises. And so it has.

Thus, for the USA, the narrow business-cycle aspect of my Brookings paper has been inapplicable. To this distant American observer, however, the model appears to have remained useful in explaining cyclical setbacks in many other nations that suffered severe banking shocks after 1980. The list, not necessarily accurate or complete, might include: Australia, New Zealand and Japan; Scandinavia and the United Kingdom; as well as Canada, Brazil, Argentina and Mexico. Obviously I am unqualified to pronounce detailed judgement on these instances.

But even for the USA, the approach remains a useful way of examining the macroeconomic consequences of financial change. Although recessions have largely been avoided, the financial system continues to play a prominent role in shaping business fluctuations. Depending on its particular organization and response, real shocks will result in different economic outcomes. Reciprocally, shocks that originate in the financial sector can and do affect the path of the real economy. The process of mutual adaptation between finance and the economy never comes to rest. Nor, consequently, do asset prices or business conditions.

This chapter undertakes a highly selective review of the period since the mid-1980s from this standpoint, focusing on the changes in financial institutions, instruments and practice most influential on the ebb and flow of credit expansion and general business.

1 Demolishing the financial zoo

From the 1930s on into the 1980s, the American financial system resembled a well-run and orderly zoo. The various species – banks, securities dealers, insurance companies and so on – were neatly caged within functional and geographical specialties, prevented and protected from competition with one another. Although competition remained active within each cage, specialized and benign keepers made sure it did not assume lethal proportions. And as in a real zoo, it was just as safe for the public to view a lion as a rabbit: deposit insurance and other safeguards were firmly in place.

This arrangement, which reflected the country's traditional agrarian localism and hostility toward bankers and monopoly, intensified by the disaster of the 1930s, worked well for the thirty years or more during which it was free from serious internal or foreign challenge. Inflation and interest rates remained low, and the rate of saving higher than it has been subsequently. But the tranquil zoo was doomed by technological innovations that rendered the geographical and functional separations grossly inefficient and impossible to preserve. The zoo was technologically and ideologically obsolete in a world increasingly dedicated to freedom and hostile to authority (Wojnilower (1992b)).

Deregulation smashed the constraints on deposit and lending rates, geographical scope, portfolio behaviour and other practices that had segregated and sheltered the various financial intermediaries. Each previously secure and tame animal suddenly became both prey and predator. The population within the cages, already excessive by competitive standards, was hardly suited to life in the wild. And now each species had to compete with every other. Some fell extinct, others adapted, and new ones emerged. Although institutions named banks, insurance companies, securities dealers and so on, survive to this day, their appearance and behaviour would be largely unrecognizable to a 1960s observer.

For firms suddenly facing vanishing profit margins, finding new revenue sources became a desperate matter of survival. The predictable consequence was a rush of lending in unfamiliar fields, unfamiliar instruments, and to unfamiliar clientele. The risks were unavoidably enormous, but preferable to the certain death most deregulated financial businesses faced were they to stand still.

2 The explosion of credit

Just when the inflationary experience of the 1970s and early 1980s was generating virtually insatiable credit demand, financial deregulation made it easy for would-be borrowers to obtain command over 'other people's money' cheaply and with few strings attached. Inordinate credit demand was matched by extraordinary eagerness to lend.

During the first half of 1980, the USA experienced a sharp but brief recession triggered by 20 per cent loan interest rates and the imposition of direct credit controls on an already shaky economy. As soon as the recession became visible, however, interest rates were lowered and the controls lifted soon after. The resurgence in credit growth and economic activity – and inflation – was immediate and substantial (see Figure 5.1).

Notably failing to participate in the recovery, however, were the thrift institutions and homebuilding industry which depended on these

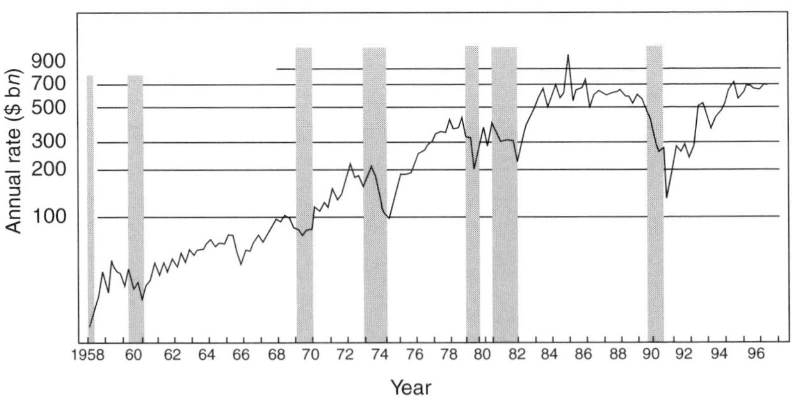

Source: The Conference Board, *Business Cycle Indicators*.

Figure 5.1 Funds raised by private non-financial borrowers in credit markets

intermediaries for mortgages. Savings banks, and savings and loan associations were hampered in attracting deposits because the rates they were allowed to pay remained partly regulated. Meanwhile, their income from fixed-rate mortgages, mostly acquired in the low-interest-rate past, was barely adequate to meet interest-rate expense. The 'crunch' in the mortgage industry became crippling as short-term interest rates rebounded to nearly 20 per cent by mid-1981, touching off yet another, more severe and longer-lasting recession (Wojnilower (1985)).

Renewed easing of monetary policy in 1982 launched a strong and durable business expansion that lasted almost eight years until the oil price eruption caused by the Iraqi seizure of Kuwait in 1990. The 1982 business revival featured a virtual explosion in credit. At the trough of the recession and onset of the recovery, consumer price inflation collapsed down to 2 per cent, while virtually all except money-market interest rates remained in double digits. But even in this economy just emerging from recession, double-digit real rates did not deter credit expansion perceptibly. It happened to be the time when the regulatory authorities, frightened by the consequences of their own measures, explicitly intended to exterminate specialized home-mortgage lending institutions, undertook to liberalize the prudential rules and to ignore, if not encourage, violations. From a severely depressed 1.06 million housing starts in 1982, homebuilding vaulted to 1.70 million starts a year later. Consumer credit also surged, fuelled in part by new legislation that forbade (previously pervasive) discrimination against female borrowers, a liberalization propitiously timed to suit lenders frantically seeking new clients. Similar credit eruptions took place later in the 1980s, in the financing of mergers and acquisitions, so-called 'leveraged buy-outs', junk (low-quality) bond issuance, real-estate investment trusts (REITs), and even 'emerging markets', notwithstanding the proximity to the Mexican crisis of 1982 and other country credit disasters that effectively decapitalized several of the largest banks.

With so much lending to novel borrowers in novel instruments, pushed by inexperienced lenders spurred by high liquidity and desperate need for income, major defaults were to be expected – and they materialized. The authorities, rightfully concerned about systemic collapse, were kept busy putting out fires. Each time they succeeded, market participants became more complacent with respect to risk-taking. With widespread economic slack prompting relatively easy monetary policies in much of the industrial world, and the dollar appreciating strongly until late 1985, the US authorities had little difficulty in cauterizing the problems (the most serious of which was the failure of the Continental Illinois Bank, the seventeenth largest in the country). By the same token, however, market participants had little difficulty in accumulating fresh tinder to ignite.

3 The Plaza inflation

In the fall of 1985, at the notorious 'Plaza' meetings in New York, the major powers agreed on policies to bring down the dollar in the context of world-wide monetary easing. Thus was the stage set for a classic credit-inflation business cycle, including a boom in stock prices.

But as we know from hindsight, the game did not play out quite so simply. In the early stages, the inflationary implications were overwhelmed by a collapse in oil prices. Also, the US and Japanese monetary authorities were initially reluctant and laggard participants (Volcker and Gyohten (1992, chs 8 and 9)). But after mid-1986, US inflation began to creep up. The falling dollar (eventually down 40 per cent from its peak) became a matter of serious international concern and dispute, and the Federal Reserve raised short-term interest rates several times. Nevertheless, stock prices continued to advance until August 1987, when US Treasury bond yields began one of the most intense rises in history, shooting up nearly 3 percentage points to almost 10.5 per cent in October.

It appeared that some sort of credit panic, to be followed by recession, was in the offing, just as had happened at previous business cycle peaks. What gave way first, however, was neither the credit structure nor the economy, but the stock market. From the August peak to the low plumbed early afternoon of Tuesday, 20 October, New York stock prices plummeted 37 per cent, of which 23 percentage points took place on notorious Black Monday, 19 October 1987 (Brady (1988)). Virtually instantly, the crash spread world-wide.

The plunge threatened to bring down both the credit and the payments systems. The natural reaction for banks and others who normally finance securities dealers and clearing houses would have been to reduce credit lines, an action that would have precipitated still more forced sales of stock and, probably, some spectacular bankruptcies. The danger was, if anything, most pronounced late on Tuesday morning, when it appeared as though the previous day's catastrophic losses might be repeated. It was conceivable that cheques due from some brokers and clearing houses might not be forthcoming or honoured, and that the banks failing to pay such cheques might themselves come under suspicion.

Had this disaster been allowed to happen, subsequent economic history might have been very different. The episode would have fitted neatly into the 'credit-crunch-to-business-downturn' schema. But there was no crunch and there was no downturn.

Federal Reserve Chairman Greenspan publicly guaranteed the liquidity of the market. The White House persuaded major companies to buy back their own stock. Around 2 pm on Tuesday the tide was turned by major buying in the stock option and futures markets from sources that have not been identified. What rules may have been bent or broken to prevent disaster, and who made these resolute decisions (perhaps against the advice of legal counsel) is not known.

Soon market functioning was back to normal. But central banks understandably feared the drop in asset values might lead to a recession and a stock market relapse. The Federal Reserve relaxed its posture of restraint and lowered interest rates. The economy continued onward and upward. In such odd fashion, the stock market crash in fact forestalled the cyclical downturn the authorities had earlier been prepared to accept.

4 Derivatives – a warning

Because there was so little economic impact, some important lessons from the experience are in danger of being overlooked. The key propellant of the headlong plunge was selling by some fifteen 'portfolio insurers', institutional investors who were following a programme of automatically selling futures in response to declines in the market value of their portfolios. Three such institutions and one mutual fund reportedly accounted for a major proportion of total market sales (Brady (1988)). Every successive drop in value triggered an exponentially increasing quantity of such sales.

Actual (as opposed to textbook) markets consist of human dealers willing to risk capital on bids and offers, and of lenders willing to finance them. Facing a literal selling avalanche, these mortals figuratively, and often literally, refused to answer the telephone. Trading breakdowns and halts occurred in all stock-related markets. Some of these interruptions are believed to have accentuated the decline, while others may have helped to cushion it. Be that as it may, markets are a human institution and as such have limited ability to withstand unbounded waves of one-way orders.

The experience exemplifies the systemic risk inherent in the practice of multiplying 'derivative' securities – futures, options, and mixes thereof – which embolden market participants to take larger and more leveraged positions (partly by using derivatives to circumvent rules designed to limit risky exposures). By now the 'notional' value of derivatives contracts is in the trillions (millions of millions) of dollars. To be sure, today's leading derivative-market participants have developed more sophisticated computer models to guide their operations, which extend far beyond the stock markets. Although these models are for the most part proprietary and not subject to outside examination, they are constructed by leading experts and probably are as good as the state of the art permits. Whether that is good enough may be questioned, but is not the critical issue. The lesson of 1987 is that such programmes are apt to be quite similar to one another. In times of stress they give identical instructions to all users, to sell the same or similar instruments on a grand scale. But when market makers are overwhelmed, the instantaneous liquidity assumed by the models vanishes, and with it the allegedly hedged character of the portfolios.

In so far as financial futures, options and derivatives have a function beyond offering enticing betting opportunities, it is to enable the public to buy insurance, however illusory, against macroeconomic risks such as tight money or recessions. To the extent that market participants thereby feel relieved of the need to worry about such eventualities, the authorities' difficulties in economic stabilization are escalated. That a derivatives crisis will occur sooner or later, I regard as virtually certain. Whether the economic consequences turn out to be small or large will depend, as in 1987, not on the monetary regime but rather on (among other random factors) the willingness, competence and freedom of the relevant officials to provide immediate and effective lender-of-last-resort relief.

5 The recession of 1990

With monetary policy eased world-wide after the crash, and stock markets regaining their footing, the US economy barely paused in its climb. In Spring 1988 the Federal Reserve had to resume pushing rates up, as growth and inflation re-accelerated. The consumer price index reached a year-on-year increase of 5.5 per cent in the summer. (This may seem low relative to the double-digit increases of 1980–2, but recall that in 1971 the Nixon Administration had felt impelled to impose wage and price controls at a time when inflation was 4 per cent and abating.)

The rise in short rates brought to a head the savings-and-loan-association crisis, as it became evident that vast numbers of depositors stood to lose their money. But so serene was the public's confidence in deposit insurance, that no runs developed. This gave time to marshal a political consensus for a huge governmental bail-out that protected depositors successfully.[1] Many commercial banks also came under pressure, the smaller ones because they too were essentially thrift institutions orientated toward real estate, and the larger ones mainly because of involvement in real estate and other financing undertaken on unrealistic assumptions, including permanently low short-term interest rates. Through merger and failure, eventually thousands of depository institutions were liquidated. Yet despite some sensational bankruptcies, nothing resembling a credit crunch transpired.

Nor, until August 1990, was there a recession. Until then, business fluctuated narrowly, while aggregate labour and industrial capacity utilization held at high pitch. For most of 1988 and 1989, the dollar tended higher, particularly against the yen. World stock markets soared, with New York surpassing its 1987 high in August 1989 on the way up to a crest reached a year later.

The US economy is judged by the National Bureau of Economic Research to have started to contract in August 1990, immediately before the Iraqi invasion of Kuwait and the rise in world oil prices. Was the minimal August decline just noise, or was it the onset of a genuine cyclical recession that would have unfolded even had there been no oil shock? I share the opinion expressed by Chairman Greenspan that, without the oil crisis, no recession would have begun then. Whether, when and in what circumstances a recession might have developed had there been no oil shock (or for that matter, 1987 stock market crash) will for ever remain a mystery.

6 The 'headwinds'

The analysis is muddied by the contemporary emergence of a new regulatory phenomenon. It was expedient for politicians and the public to blame the supervisors for the financial turbulence and its costs. Although these charges were partly warranted, it was at least equally true that the supervisors' warnings often went unheeded, and that their preventive efforts were sometimes thwarted by political pressure. To forestall a repetition of yesterday's disasters and to deflect future criticism, the authorities reacted by developing more formal regulatory criteria. The most notable instance was the 1988 Basle accord among the major financial powers. This set an 8-per-cent-of-risk-assets capital requirement for commercial banks. The accord pleased the major Western commercial banks because it was seen as restraining competition from Japanese banks, and it also suited the Japanese authorities trying to rein in their financial bubble.

American bank examiners applied a harsher standard. The Basle accord defined government securities holdings as being free from default risk, and therefore requiring no capital. The US authorities imposed an additional 'leverage ratio' standard that stipulated capital against all assets, and in a rising proportion as a bank's soundness was deemed to be threatened (Syron and Randall (1991)). Subsequent legislation added an interest-rate risk factor (penalizing holdings of longer-dated maturities) to the capital requirement.

How much, if at all, this 'revenge of the supervisors' might have slowed credit expansion and the economy in the run-up to the 1990–1 recession is unclear. But there is ample statistical and anecdotal evidence that it impeded the economy materially during the recession and the unusually sluggish early years of the subsequent recovery. Bank stock prices gave little warning that particular banks were in trouble. But once the lightning began to strike, almost all banks found it difficult to raise additional capital, whether from the public or through increased earnings. With higher capital ratios being aggressively enforced, the only available response was to reduce risk assets, notably loans. The best loans were terminated first – because they were the ones that borrowers could repay. New business and mortgage lending, especially to smaller customers, was severely curtailed. The sale of securitized packages of consumer and other loans, which improved capital ratios by removing these assets from balance sheet totals, accelerated greatly. Since they were trying to reduce rather than to expand assets, banks also bid much less aggressively for deposits and other funds, opening the door wider for mutual funds (of which more below) (Wojnilower (1992a)).

The insistence on higher capital ratios when capital was inaccessible forced banks to shrink their balance sheets, with adverse consequences for the flow of credit. The impact paralleled that of a central bank open-market sale of securities that absorbs bank reserves and compels banks to reduce assets and liabilities. Although the economic effects were particularly severe (and well documented) in the north-eastern part of the USA known as New England, where banks had been deeply involved in financing a defunct real estate boom, they were national in scope (Brown and Case (1992)). It was to these problems that Chairman Greenspan was referring when, on several occasions, he described the economy as battling 'a fifty mile an hour headwind'. The bank capital squeeze was an important reason why the Federal Reserve kept short-term rates unusually low for a long time, enabling banks to refurbish capital from earnings generated by the large differential between money market and other interest rates.

The state of affairs became known as the 'credit crunch'. Any resemblance to the crunches of earlier years, however, was in name only. Coming during a time of easy money, the early 1990s *capital* crunch was fundamentally different from the earlier *liquidity* crunches triggered by monetary tightening. In the early 1990s the Federal Reserve would have preferred faster expansion of credit. The previous crunches were credit contractions desired by the authorities, but which got out of hand.

In the course of administering all these rules, the official supervisors became involved in detailed private managerial decisions to a degree that, in the days of the financial zoo, would have been regarded as intolerable government meddling. Not surprisingly, the private-sector managers became determined to rebuild capital to levels that would rule out vulnerability to such official interference in the future. This prolonged the crunch, but in the event they largely succeeded. Thus a classic pattern was repeated: supervisors were determined to avoid recurrence of a loss of control – and those supervised to avoid loss of self-determination.

At the time of writing, many banks view themselves as overcapitalized and again have become aggressive lenders at exceptionally low returns for added risk.

7 The rise of mutual and hedge funds

The prolonged weakness of the depository institutions – thrifts and commercial banks – opened the door to new competitors. Of these, so-called money market funds are probably the most important, not only because of their success in attracting household balances, but also for their significant role in drawing consumers into other mutual funds, especially equity investment funds.

In the USA, retail money-market fund balances, which comprised over $600 billion in September 1997, typically are subject to cheque-writing for transactions of over $500. As such, they are included in, and account for, some 15 per cent of M2. Money market funds are useful also to many wholesale investors: so-called 'institutional' money market funds held another $335 billion. Money market funds were created in the early stages of deposit-rate deregulation, when banks were allowed to pay market rates only on deposits of at least $100,000, for the purpose of pooling smaller amounts into sums exceeding that threshold. The decision of the authorities not to prohibit such pooling, as they could have done, reflected their desire for the eventual abolition of all deposit-rate regulation, which has now substantially been accomplished. In this, as in other instances (Eurodollars come easily to mind), a device designed to circumvent regulation turned out to have strong staying power long after the regulatory obstacle had lapsed. But unlike at the beginning, only a small fraction of money market funds is invested currently in domestic bank deposits. The bulk is in commercial paper and other short-term credit instruments, replacing funds that used to be provided by commercial banks.

Although the market value of money-market fund investments necessarily fluctuates, individual subscribers always buy and redeem shares, on demand, at exactly $1. In the few instances in which market values of the underlying assets have dropped materially below $1, the fund sponsors have contributed additional capital to make up the difference. Unlike the other components of M2 or M3, the funds are backed neither by an official lender of last resort nor by deposit insurance. Nor are there legally required reserves, only some prudential investment rules.

By introducing millions of people to mutual funds, money-market funds spearheaded an enormous expansion of mutual fund investment. Bond-type mutual funds are now about as large as money-market funds, and equity mutual funds somewhat larger than money and bond funds put together, for a combined aggregate of over $4200 billion – exceeding 10 per cent of the country's total financial assets. At the beginning of the 1980s mutual fund assets were a mere $50 billion. Over 40 per cent of US households now own equities through mutual funds or directly (indirect holders through defined contribution pension plans or variable annuities issued by insurance companies not included). Fewer than 3 per cent of the population, a US Treasury official estimated at the time, may have owned stock in 1927 (Sobel (1968, p. 355)).

Within most of the large mutual fund groups, shareholders may make overnight transfers by telephone at minimal or no cost between stock and other funds, including money-market funds, subject to check. Much of the stock acquisition by mutual funds has necessarily come from the household sector, and is an intra-sector transfer in the flow-of-funds accounting sense. But, from the public's point of view, there is a large gain in liquidity. It is much simpler and cheaper to rearrange or liquidate mutual fund than stock portfolios. How volatile might be the public's management of fund shares during a time of persistent inflation, recession or stock price decline has not been tested, because we have not experienced such times since mutual funds became so important. In the aftermath of the 1987 crash, withdrawals were small and did not continue for long. But after the Japanese stock market crash two years later, Japanese mutual funds suffered prolonged major outflows.

The risk of selling panics is probably more pronounced among the funds' youthful professional managers, whose median age is said to be under thirty. Their compensation depends on outperforming one another and they have prompted many large securities price fluctuations by their herd-like response to 'news'. But whether the panic originates with mutual fund shareholders or managers, this is yet another sector in which the Federal Reserve's lender-of-last-resort responsibilities are liable to be tested.

An interesting question is whether the novel political configuration in which a powerful segment of voters owns shares may eventually constrain monetary policy. The criticism hurled at Chairman Greenspan from all political sides (and his lack of defenders) for mild cautions as to the elevated stock price level, and for an 0.25 per cent federal funds rate increase in March 1997 at a time of full employment, is ominous.[2]

Another financial intermediary that, like mutual funds, is not new but has grown to global importance is the hedge fund. A hedge fund is, in effect, a private, unadvertised mutual fund limited to wealthy investors willing to incur high risk for high return. Unlike US mutual funds, hedge funds may engage in unlimited short-term trading, take short positions, and borrow.[3] Because hedge funds are essentially unregulated and many are legally domiciled in Caribbean and other tax havens, there are few reliable data. Their aggregate capital is said to be about $200 billion (Bernheim (1997)), divided roughly equally between US and offshore funds. Of course, this capital can be and has been leveraged several-fold on occasion. It is, however, their mobility and freedom to trade in any instrument, rather than their size, that makes hedge funds a market factor of such consequence. By moving all their funds suddenly in the same direction, perhaps accompanied by publicity impelling other money managers and speculators to join the stampede, hedge funds may overwhelm the market. (Of course the funds do not always operate in mob-like fashion; anecdotes relate how, near quarterly statement dates, managers have engaged in uneconomic transactions for the purpose of damaging the market valuation of competitors' holdings.)

In most hedge funds, investors must put up sizeable minimum investments, but in an interesting analogy to the birth of money-market mutual funds, there are instances of investors in non-US funds fractionating their holdings and reselling them in smaller participations. US-domiciled hedge funds hitherto were limited to a maximum of 100 investors to avoid having to register and be regulated as a mutual fund, but this limit has just been raised to 500 for individuals with financial assets of at least $5 million and fiduciaries with $25 million. Significantly, institutional investment in hedge funds is increasing rapidly, and the formation of new funds is being facilitated by sophisticated servicing provided by some securities dealers assuming the transactional burdens.

There is thus the potential for this intermediary to become significant for its mass as well as its velocity.

8 The slope of the yield curve

Hedge funds provide perhaps the purest illustration of how the spread between short- and long-term interest rates acts as a pivotal incentive for the financial sector to expand or contract the quantity of credit. A market participant able to borrow at or only slightly over the money market rate is virtually always able to reinvest at a higher rate, but the wider the 'spread', the more likely it is to exceed transactions, information and other costs of business. This is the case not only for hedge funds but for all market 'insiders'. The money market for wholesale participants is, of course, world-wide. The lowest cost of funds is that which happens to prevail anywhere, although for borrowings in one currency destined for investment in another, the foreign exchange risk (or its cost of hedging) must be taken into account.

From late 1992 to early 1994, a prodigious incentive for such 'transformation' of short-term funds into longer credits was provided by the low 3 per cent federal funds rate maintained by the Federal Reserve to bolster a sluggish economy and, as described earlier, the banking system. When to the surprise (one wonders why?) of money-market participants this rate was raised in early 1994 under circumstances auguring further increase, the market shock was profound. Distress selling of government bonds was widespread, sharply lifting long-term rates around the world with little respect for the substantially differing fundamentals from country to country (Massaro (1999)). In the USA, the drop in bond prices precipitated a number of financial failures, principally through a panic in the market for mortgage-related securities. Treasury bond prices suffered severely because markets for mortgage-backed and some other interest-bearing securities dried up under the selling pressures. Not being able to raise required cash by selling the securities they would have liked to sell, many managers had to liquidate what could be sold, namely US government obligations. This is exactly what we should expect whenever a broad sell signal is given by the derivatives models.

After the shock of the 1994 rate increase had worn off, the situation became in some respects even more attractive for hedge funds. US longer-term rates had gone up but, despite the higher money rates, the cost of wholesale financing fell. This was because of the problems of Japan, which produced an extraordinary and destructive rise in the yen/dollar exchange rate. In September 1995 the Bank of Japan responded by lowering its discount rate to a mere half of 1 per cent – and while this was labelled an 'emergency measure', the rate long remained. Both the persistence of low money rates in Japan and a fall in the yen seemed assured – the yen did in fact plunge from a summer 1995 peak of 80 per dollar to a trough of 127 in March 1997. Thus, borrowing yen and investing outside Japan was hugely profitable. Punctuated by the occasional interruption, the proceeds of this 'carry trade', as it became known in market parlance, poured into the securities and credit markets of the world . In this way, low Japanese rates generated a world-wide bubble in securities prices and credit growth resembling the earlier 'bubble economy' in Japan itself.

More generally, whenever the spread between the relevant short and long rates widens, the quantity of short-term funds demanded by the financial sector, consisting of the individuals, firms and institutions seeking income from interest-rate spreads, enlarges. A wider spread induces such 'arbitrageurs' to borrow more at short-term for the purpose of lending more at longer term. Their additional demand for longer-term claims tends to lower long-term rates. A narrowing of the spread, conversely, discourages the lengthening of asset maturities and raises long-term rates. These financial sector reactions explain why short and long rates usually move in the same direction. The opening and folding of the interest rate accordion, the changes in rate levels, and the associated flux in credit extensions and contractions move nominal and real GDP.

As is well documented, the spread between US long-term and short-term interest has arguably been the best (though far from precise) single leading indicator of business downturns (Estrella and Mishkin (1995)). A narrowing or, more reliably, inverting of the normally positive spread foretells an impending recession. The financial sector is under restraint. Conversely, a widening spread signals greater credit supply and economic revival (see Figure 5.2).

When interest rate ceilings still prevailed, a rise in short rates beyond certain thresholds impaired, or literally cut off, the ability of depository institutions to hold and attract deposits. Because (1) many assets held by the institutions were non-marketable, (2) the Treasury was legislatively restrained from issuing new longer-dated obligations, (3) Treasury obligations were 'locked in' by having to be valued at least at par on bank balance sheets, and (4) there were no futures and options markets, and so on, long-term bond yields tended to rise much less than short-term rates. The long-term markets simply ceased to function normally. Actual inversion of the yield curve corresponded to near-paralysis of financial intermediaries, since any activity in such conditions produced losses. Recessions followed. But because these began before financial institutions

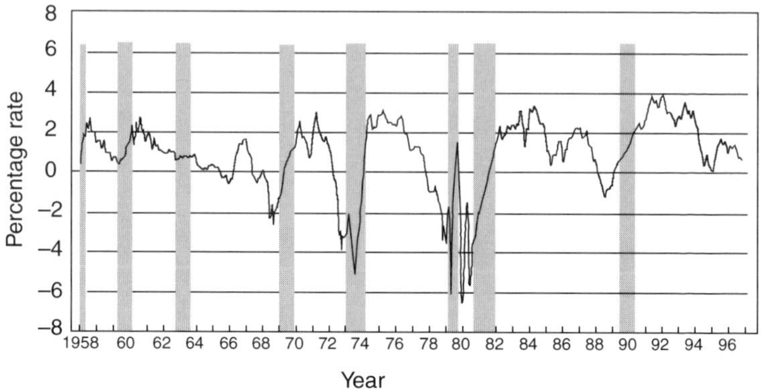

Source: The Conference Board, *Business Cycle Indicators*.
Figure 5.2 Interest rate spread, 10-year Treasury bonds less federal funds

had the time and opportunity to become badly overextended, and were immediately accompanied by lower short-term interest rates, there were no serious financial failures.

Since 1982, with deregulation and the growing perfection of the markets, no deep inversion has occurred. This is partly because there has been no draconian tightening of money. But also, in the deregulated environment, rises in short rates are translated quickly into higher long rates, although not necessarily on a one-for-one basis. When the cost of inputs rises simultaneously for all firms in the financial industry, why would they not raise their prices? Since the amount of reserves the monetary authority stands ready to supply at the official short rate is unlimited, the constraint on the economy now operates primarily through the interest elasticity of the demand for credit.

An interesting paradox lurks here. When the authorities raise the short-term rate, to restrain an actually or potentially overheating economy, should they prefer long-term rates to rise a good deal, not at all, or even to decline? The larger the rise in long rates, the more the public's spending decisions will be deterred. On the other hand, the wider the spread between long and short rates, the greater the incentive for the financial sector to continue to borrow at the new short rate and to extend credit, on easier non-interest terms if need be. Should long rates happen to rise more than short rates, the economy may even be stimulated, the predictive power of the long–short differential suggests. Conversely, a fall in long rates might in fact be contractionary if it sharply curtails borrowing and lending by the financial sector.

Suppose that demand for credit is elastic to the level of rates, but supply to the long–short differential. Keeping in mind that the supply of funds at the official short rate is theoretically infinite, all sorts of outcomes are possible depending on the (potentially highly variable) shapes of the curves. In actuality, long and short rates move in the same direction most of the time, the long rate moving less (although, of course, with larger effect on the value of long-term assets). An implication is that short-term rate increases may be of little moment until they no longer provoke significantly higher bond yields, presumably because only then have the latter reached a level at which credit demand is highly elastic. If long rates keep rising in step with short, then credit growth may persist substantially unrestrained – until short rates soar high enough to cause default problems.

In today's USA, where mutual fund shares have replaced deposits in household portfolios to a considerable extent (see Figure 5.3), stock as well as bond returns may need to be considered. If short-term rates rise but stock prices rise as fast or faster (the cost of capital falls), is policy restrictive? In the Estrella and Mishkin study cited above, stock prices are the next most successful predictor to the interest-rate spread, and the two used together dominate all other combinations.

In addition, as pointed out above in relation to the Japanese money rate, central banks cannot afford to focus solely on domestic interest-rate and stock-price levels and differentials, but need to consider (and influence, but how?) their important international permutations.

Central bankers tend to be elasticity optimists, but I have not been a central banker since 1963. In good times, it seems to me, borrowers tend to be insensitive to rising interest rates until they rise enough to create cash flow problems. Then default problems are generated, rendering it difficult to discriminate between the price and the credit-quality consequences of the higher rates. At high rates, lenders perceive higher credit risk and become more reluctant. This is consistent with the observation that, at the onset of recessions, the decline in other rates lags behind the peak in short rates which, ever since the creation of the Federal Reserve, has tended to coincide with the business cycle peak (see Figure 5.4). At, and immediately after, the upper business-cycle turning point, everyone knows that the economy and inflation will soon be declining, yet long-term and loan rates fall late and reluctantly. It must be because the financial sector is inhibited from responding to its improved incentives by its own capital and credit concerns. That is what I found for the pre-deregulation period, and nothing in the subsequent experience suggests any change.

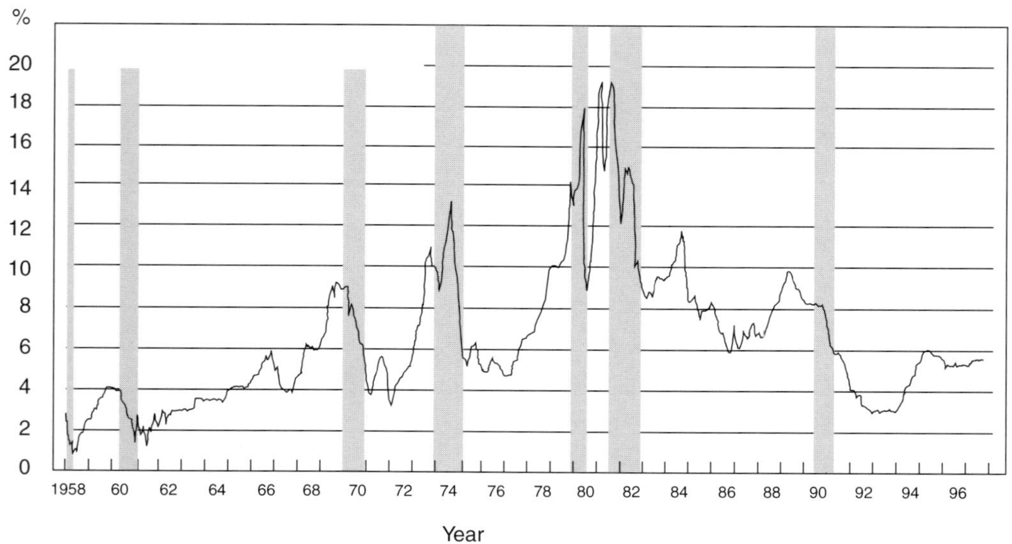

Source: The Conference Board, *Business Cycle Indicators*.
Figure 5.3 Federal funds rate (per cent)

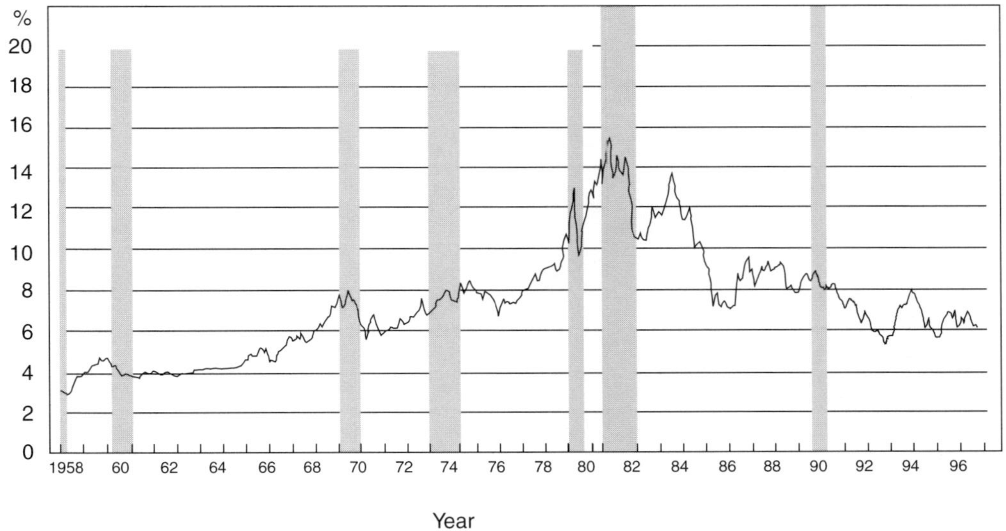

Source: The Conference Board, *Business Cycle Indicators*.
Figure 5.4 Yield on 10-year Treasury bonds (per cent)

How else to explain the curious result that subtracting a series coincident with the business cycle (short rates) from a lagging one (long rates), produces a leading indicator (the spread)?

In sum, the economic impact of an increase in official short rates is difficult to predict because so much depends on what happens to long rates, and the reaction of the financial sector. To the extent that credit demand is inelastic, and large borrowers have hedged themselves against interest-rate increases, large increases in rates will be needed to achieve restraint. Large rises in rates mean large drops in asset prices, which in turn render major defaults and serious recessions – and lender-of-last-resort interventions – more likely.

9 Is the safety net shrinking or expanding?

The problems of assessing the thrust of monetary policy when the policy instrument is the short-term rate have led all central banks to seek a quantitative intermediate money or credit aggregate to target. However, the deregulation and innovation of recent years have rendered such targets largely useless. They are likely to remain so until there is a return to a more orderly (that is, regulated) environment. Ironically, the most ardent advocates of narrow (as opposed to broad) money definition and targeting were also the most ardent enthusiasts for deregulation – which, step by step, has forced central banks to broaden the definition of money. This in turn has led back to more emphasis on targeting credit and, indeed, national income or price aggregates that are almost impossible for monetary policy to fine-tune. In the USA, M2, the principal monetary aggregate still being monitored, albeit perfunctorily, now includes eight components in addition to the currency, demand deposits, and travellers cheques that defined is original M1 (Anderson *et al.* (1997)). None of these eight, it may be noted, is identical to any of the ten components that were added to M1 to arrive at M2 during 1982–5.

Deregulation has made it more difficult for central banks to maintain control over the quantity of the means of payment as it is perceived by the public. In the financially advanced countries, we have become accustomed to take for granted that cheques will be honoured regardless of the institution on which they are drawn, and that the total quantity of money can and will be modulated in order substantially to preserve its purchasing power and maintain economic stability. We also assume that certain assets are immediately convertible into universally accepted means of payment at minimal risk and cost. But it is only reluctantly conceded, if at all, that accomplishing this requires a degree of governmental control over the relevant institutions.

Not everyone can be allowed to accept or create chequing deposits and, in effect, to print money. The system has to be protected, just as people cannot hook up indiscriminately to the electricity grid, or dump waste into or draw on the water reservoirs. The club of institutions which are allowed access, and which long consisted exclusively of commercial and central banks, is obliged to accept certain constraints that are costly. If others not subject to such constraints are allowed to mimic the privileges, they will be more profitable and better able to raise capital (Wojnilower (1991)). The current tendency, perversely, is not only to let outsiders enjoy the benefits of the club without paying dues, but also, in the name of free markets, to take away from or charge the members for their special privileges, such as direct access to central bank credit and payments facilities, governmental deposit insurance, and monopoly over the chequing-account business.

For the USA, the rise of money-market mutual funds is probably the most egregious example of this trend. Money-market funds are not subject to reserve requirements and other expensive constraints imposed on banks. Nevertheless, they are allowed to offer 'deposits' fixed in nominal value and subject to cheque. Although money-market fund balances are not covered by deposit insurance, the public nevertheless assumes that prominent funds are as much within the governmental safety net, as are banks falling into the too-large-to-fail category, since the systemic risk from a fund or a bank failure would be identical. (Perhaps even stock index funds are coming to be perceived as quasi-insured.) When outsiders over whom the central bank has no jurisdiction proliferate and flourish, how are the members of the club (the banks) to preserve their profitability, access to capital and, indeed, their lives, except by resigning? Yet the public continues to hold central banks and governments responsible for the integrity of the payments machinery and the currency, as well as for the maintenance of stable prosperity. That is a tall order for central banks to accomplish solely through adjustments in the overnight interest rate.

The process illustrates an historical pattern. All societies have restricted the privilege of money creation, in the past mainly to harvest seigniorage, and in modern times to protect the integrity of the payments system and to limit price level and business-cycle fluctuation. The private sector tries to circumvent these restrictions by creating means of payment alternative to, or routinely convertible into, the officially-recognized money. Unless the authorities stamp out these alternatives, or at least refrain from supporting them in times of trouble, the innovations take root and become established. They become money, much as bank notes and deposits emerged as money in environments in which coins were the only officially-recognized legal tender. If the authorities wish to maintain control over the quantity of money, they must in some way bring the innovations under their regulation. The world-wide broadening of money supply concepts in recent years displays this process, although the authorities may not fully appreciate the implications because there has been little occasion for severe monetary restraint. If, when money is tightened, it is mainly the growth of the traditional component that is inhibited but not that of the newer alternatives (which, not being 'taxed', offer the higher returns), then eventually the traditional regulated sector will atrophy and only the free-riding newcomers will survive.

One sometimes hears it argued that if the market were left unregulated without a governmental safety net, the need to preserve reputation would inhibit undue risk-taking by agents and intermediaries, and make investors more cautious about where they placed their funds. This is a curious reading of financial history. At best, perhaps some smaller crises would be self-correcting without severe systemic damage, but the large ones would be cataclysmic. Even small crises claim many innocent victims and, not least because they often threaten to become big ones, are politically intolerable.

10 How things are

With the growing size and scope of markets and transactions, the value of a good reputation is diminishing. No longer is it unusual to see bankrupt firms or countries raising large sums within a few years (sometimes months) of having defaulted. From the standpoint of the individuals who make the markets, the need for a good reputation to attract a steady stream of business is much reduced. Much as with athletic or entertainment stars in a global market, the rewards to be gained from a single major success (such as one outstanding season or recording album) often suffice to make the performer rich for life. The temptations to bend ethical standards to score such a deal approach the irresistible.

Reflecting excesses by individual employees, several major institutions have recently incurred colossal losses (Aglietta (1996)). Since the environment has been one of easy money and the victims were strongly capitalized, the firms involved did not default or could be absorbed by competitors who assumed their obligations. In times of tight money and wobbly stock markets, such events are systemically much more dangerous. That is when weak credits are forced to default even without fraud coming into play, and when defensive fraud – fraud for the sake of institutional and personal survival – proliferates.

Economists and regulators stress the need to enforce prompt disclosure of honest information. That is all to the good, but why has the market not compelled firms to make such disclosure? Often investors do not care: few people are thieves, but many (or most) do not seem to mind doing business with thieves thought to be offering a bargain price. Disclosure does not matter as much as the will and authority of the police to inhibit unacceptable behaviour.

So hungry are debt and equity investors these days to place their overflow of funds that credit standards and risk differentials have narrowed to the vanishing point. Huge loans are made on cursory investigation and documentation. The financial sector once again considers itself immune to supervisory restraint. Participants feel secure that political pressures and the great potential for calamity because of market interlinkages will bring prompt lender-of-last-resort support in case of trouble.

In a profound recent analysis, Joseph Bisignano (1997) emphasizes that 'technologies subject to increasing returns, which also includes financial intermediary structures, have the property that the resulting market configuration is unpredictable'. Increasing-returns industries are hard to keep competitive and are at risk of over-expansion. In the financial sector, competitive over-expansion contributes to excessive credit growth and eventually financial-sector defaults that may necessitate lender-of-last-resort intervention.

It is not only the supply side of credit that tends to excess, but the demand side as well. Myopia, optimism and inclination to gamble are hardwired into humanity and have proved highly resistant to legal and social efforts to contain them, and in the financial markets the constraints on these propensities are fewer than elsewhere. As a result, quantities of many times GDP are traded daily. Speculation offers better odds than any other gambling I know of, and is much more respectable to boot. There can be no doubt that, literally like narcotics, speculation attracts and creates many addicts. Together these form a crowd and sometimes a mob, albeit the crowd is 'virtual', connected mainly electronically rather than by physical proximity. Individuals in crowds take 'irrational' actions they would never elect to take on their own. And it is common knowledge that it is suicidally irrational to stand in the way of a mob.

There has been no good opportunity to retest my 1980 hypothesis as to the central role of credit crunches – partly because of the stock crash of 1987 and the oil shock of 1990, and partly because world-wide upswings in aggregate demand have been infrequent. But even though credit crunches have not triggered a recession for a long time, disruptions in credit markets have continued to exert strong influence on business conditions. I remain convinced that liquidity 'crunches' will occur again, most probably as a result of unexpected bankruptcies. With the regulatory restraints that used to serve as early 'circuit breakers' abolished, the burden on lenders-of-last-resort is greater. And with central banks no longer commanding a powerful club of 'inside' institutions through which to respond to trouble, future financial embolisms will be more dangerous than the regulatory crunches of the past.

Notes

1 More recently in Japan under similar circumstances, it has not been possible to reach such a consensus. What model would have predicted that homogeneous Japan would find this more difficult that heterogeneous USA?

2 In the light of current debates as to which objectives central banks should target, it is intriguing to note that the 1929 stock market crash occurred at a time of no inflation, and the subsequent debacle despite substantial central bank interest rate reductions soon after the crash. Every monetary regime spawns its own 'subversive' financial sector incentives.

3 The tax penalty that inhibited short-term trading by mutual funds was removed by legislation included in the summer 1997 Federal budget package.

References

Aglietta, Michel (1996) *Financial Market Failures and Systemic Risk*, CEPII, Paris, Working paper 96–01 (revised version in *Economie internationale*, vol. 76 (1998), pp. 41–67).

Anderson, R. G., B. E. Jones and T. D. Nesmith (1997) 'Building New Monetary Services Indexes: Concepts, Data and Methods', *Review*, Federal Reserve Bank of St. Louis, vol. 70, no. 1, pp. 53–82.

Bernheim, Anatole (1997) Publisher and editor, *Hedge Fund News* and *U.S. Offshore Funds Directory*, personal communication.

Bisignano, Joseph (1997) 'Toward an Understanding of the Changing Structure of Financial Intermediation: An Evolutionary Theory of Institutional Survival', written for a Banco de España seminar 4 June, and an Expert Meeting of the Committee on Financial Markets, OECD, Paris, 7–8 July.

Brady, Nicholas (1988) *Report of the Presidential Task Force on Market Mechanisms, January 1988* (known as the Brady Report) (Washington, DC: US Government Printing Office).

Brown, Lynn E. and Karl E. Case (1992) 'How the Commercial Real Estate Boom Undid the Banks', *Real Estate and the Credit Crunch*, Federal Reserve Bank of Boston, Conference Series No. 36.

Estrella, Arturo and Frederic S. Mishkin (1995) *Predicting US Recessions: Financial Variables as Leading Indicators*, Working Paper No. 5379, National Bureau of Economic Research.

Massaro, Vincent G. (1999) 'Economic Theory, Domestic Policies and Long Rate Behavior: 1994, A Case Study', *International Journal of Commerce and Management*, vol. 9, nos 3–4.

Sobel, Robert (1968) *Panic On Wall Street* (New York: Macmillan).

Syron, Richard and Richard E. Randall (1991) 'The Procyclical Application of Bank Capital Requirements', *Annual Report, 1991*, Federal Reserve Bank of Boston, Mass.

Volcker, Paul and Toyoo Gyohten (1992) *Changing Fortunes* (New York: Times Books).

Wojnilower, Albert M. (1980) 'The Central Role of Credit Crunches in Recent Financial History', *Brookings Papers on Economic Activity*, vol. 2, pp. 277–339.

Wojnilower, Albert M. (1985) 'Private Credit Demand, Supply, and Crunches: How Different Are the 1980's?', *American Economic Review*, vol. 75, no. 2, pp. 351–6.

Wojnilower, Albert M. (1991) 'Some Principles of Financial Deregulation: Lessons from the United States', in Ian Macfarlane (ed.), *The Deregulation of Financial Intermediaries* (Sydney: Reserve Bank of Australia), pp. 203–16.

Wojnilower, Albert M. (1992a) 'Credit Crunches', 'Financial Zoos', 'Interest Rate Ceilings', three articles in *The New Palgrave Dictionary of Money and Finance* (London: Macmillan).

Wojnilower, Albert M. (1992b) 'Discussion' of paper by Joe Peek and Eric S. Rosengren, 'Crunching the Recovery: Bank Capital and the Role of Bank Credit', *Real Estate and the Credit Crunch*, Federal Reserve Bank of Boston, Mass., Conference Series No. 36, pp. 178–85.

Comment

Lars Jonung
Stockholm School of Economics, Sweden

This is an inspiring chapter to read. It is a report by a man who has made his living on Wall Street observing the US financial system for more than thirty years. It is a story about evolution, and more specifically about financial sophistication and deregulation. The study forces the university economist living in the equilibrium world to think about the effects of institutional change.

I focus on two issues in this chapter, both related to the macroeconomic consequences of the process of financial deregulation: first, the effects on the business cycle; and second, the effects on the deregulation on the power of central banks or on the efficiency of monetary policy. These issues are not novel ones; they have been with us for a long time.

The first theme is associated with the old question: has the business cycle changed its character? There are variations on this theme. One school argues that the business cycle has been dampened, even suggesting that the end of the business cycle is near. The position of the author is unclear on this point: on the one hand, he suggests initially that the US business cycle has been 'gentler and kinder' since the mid-1980s; but on the other, at the end of the chapter he voices fears that the future will see growing financial instability because of the rise of non-bank financial intermediation. From this I would expect him to argue that the business cycle will display greater cyclical instability.

Basically, there are two schools concerning the effects of financial deregulation on macroeconomic stability. One school maintains that financial sophistication will allow households and firms to adjust more easily and quickly to economic disturbances, thus smoothing the business cycle and reducing its amplitude, while the other school holds the opposite view: the enormous growth of financial markets has increased instability and volatility on a international scale, and disturbances will spread more rapidly in the world economy through well-integrated financial markets. We shall thus see a future with larger volatility than at present. This is the view of Wojnilower.

Which hypothesis is correct, ignoring the 'status quo' view, where there is no change? How shall we approach this issue? One approach is to look at the history of business cycles during different financial regimes, preferably comparing periods of deregulated financial markets with periods where financial regulations are in place. By now there is a number of empirical studies of the amplitude of the business cycle, covering, for example, the pre-1914 gold standard, a period of 'free' and well-functioning capital markets, and the Bretton Woods period, a period of far-reaching controls of financial markets, both of domestic and foreign flows of credit and capital. These studies do not suggest that the business cycle has been dampened by financial controls as far I have seen.

Let us look at the post-Bretton Woods period. What has been the role of financial markets since the early 1970s? The existence of financial markets facilitated the adjustment of the world economy to the macroeconomic shocks of OPEC I and II. I shall conjecture that financial deregulation has contributed to stability in this sense, facilitating the recycling of debt after the oil crisis, and allowing governments to borrow in periods of financial strain.

In another sense, the process of deregulation (that is, the movement from a non-market system of controls to 'freely functioning' capital markets) has caused a number of severe transition problems in many countries – a process similar to the march from the planned economy to the market economy in the former USSR. Events in Sweden and Finland illustrate such developments nicely. In these two countries deregulation was initially accompanied by a credit expansion, asset inflation and euphoria, and then by a credit crunch, asset deflation, financial instability and economy-wide depression in the early 1990s. I would like to stress that this process of sudden major financial deregulation was not an ordinary business-cycle event. It was a structural shift or, more precisely, a change of the financial regime that was not counter-balanced by appropriate economic policies.

The second major issue raised by Wojnilower deals with the power of monetary policies and thus of the monetary authorities. He suggests that the US central bank had stronger control over the volume of credit, money and interest rates, as well as over financial institutions during the system of financial regulation in the 1950s and 1960s than is the case at the time of writing. Wojnilower says that the financial jungle was controlled by having all the animals locked into separate cages in the zoo.

Since the mid-1970s, the Federal Reserve system has moved to a monetary policy regime based on influencing short-term interest rates. The animals have been let out of their cages and now roam freely. The growth of non-bank financial intermediaries relative to commercial banks has weakened the efficiency of monetary policy. The volume of credit relative to the monetary base is ballooning, implying growing financial fragility of the financial structure. The system is moving towards Knut Wicksell's vision of a pure credit economy.

Is the Fed now (i.e at the end of twentieth century) losing its power to control? At present, it seems that the US Federal Reserve system is successful in containing inflation and fostering a climate of financial stability. Wojnilower's chapter is a testimony in favour of this view. Inflation rates have come down from two-digit levels in the 1970s and are now at an historically low level, while US employment and US economic growth are high. Non-inflationary growth seems to prevail, at least for the present. The Federal Reserve system and the US economy are regarded with envy and admiration outside the USA. So far, the US central bank does not appear to have lost its capacity to control monetary and credit conditions and to influence the US economy.

To sum up, I have discussed two issues raised by Wojnilower's chapter: first, the effects of financial deregulation on economic stability; and second, on the power of the monetary policymakers. I do not share Wojnilower's guarded pessimism. I would prefer to be a guarded optimist. However, we know only one thing for certain: time will tell us more about the macroeconomic effects of financial deregulation. I hope that the lesson-learning will not come through major disasters.

6

Learning about Trends: Spending and Credit Fluctuations in Open Economies*

Daniel Heymann
UN Economic Commission for Latin America, Torcuato di Tella Institute and University of Buenos Aires, Argentina

Martin Kaufman
International Monetary Fund, Washington DC, USA

and

Pablo Sanguinetti
University Torcuato di Tella, Buenos Aires, Argentina

1 Introduction

This chapter is inspired by an old theme. The view that misperceptions about the future outcomes of current plans can generate business fluctuations has a long tradition in the literature. Theories that allow for the existence of intertemporal co-ordination failures can have different specific features (see Leijonhufvud (1968, 1981)). They have in common the argument that agents decide on the basis of a less than perfect knowledge of the 'laws of motion' of the environment, and that the consequent difficulties in forming expectations can have noticeable macroeconomic consequences. In particular, a class of cyclical ups and downs may emerge when agents cannot forecast accurately the characteristics of the economy's growth path.

---

* Special thanks are due to P. Azcue for the advice and help he gave in performing the simulations which are reported in Section 3 of the chapter. The comments received from S. Galiani, F. Guerrero, A. Leijonhufvud and J. P. Nicolini are gratefully acknowledged. The views expressed are not necessarily those of the institutions where the authors serve.

Identifying growth trends is generally problematic. Still, when economies are evolving more or less smoothly, agents can rely on extrapolating past performance in order to predict future opportunities. This does not apply in the case of rapid transitions. Events such as policy or institutional reforms, shifts in external conditions, or technological changes can drastically alter the behaviour of an economy, in ways that agents (and analysts) need not be able to anticipate precisely. Expected returns on investment, wealth perceptions and the anticipated profitability of lending would then vary as individuals revised their beliefs according to the information they receive and the rules of inference they use. The resulting dynamics of expectations translates into movements in aggregate spending and output.

This line of reasoning seems likely to be relevant to interpreting some particular cyclical episodes. In the Latin-American experience of the last decades of the twentieth century, there was a number of instances in which wide-ranging policies of stabilization and economic reform were associated with large fluctuations in domestic demand, relative prices and the balance of trade, as an initial phase of rapid increase in aggregate spending was followed by a sharp contraction. Indeed, those cycles have been analyzed in different ways (some alternative arguments are discussed briefly in Section 5). The conjecture that we explore in our work is that revisions of expectations (on the part of both domestic agents and foreign lenders) about the prospects of the economies play an important part in episodes of that type. In Section 2 we present a brief description of some cases to motivate the analysis that follows; the preliminary evidence suggests that there is room for large movements in forecasts of output flows and, consequently, in wealth perceptions.

In Section 3, which is based on Heymann and Sanguineti (1998),we specify the basic argument through a simple model. We use an analytical framework with points in common with that of the literature on real business cycles for open economies in intertemporal equilibrium. The fluctuations we represent are of a real nature, in the sense that they originate from a shift in real opportunities, and the behaviour of the system is simulated without imposing restrictions on price adjustments. Current markets clear. However, we differ from the equilibrium analysis in treating future income flows (and, therefore, wealth), as variables that agents must predict by using the knowledge they have obtained from some learning procedures that will not automatically reveal to them the actual features of the relevant processes.

In the model, the investment opportunities of an individual agent (and, in an extended version that incorporates non-traded goods, his or her sales prices) depend on aggregate output. Each agent must therefore form expectations about the aggregate performance of the economy in order to plan his/her capital accumulation and consumption. The purpose of the model is to analyze the response of the system to a 'singular' real shock. Specifically, in the simulation exercises we consider the effects of a productivity shift that takes place in the current period; with slight changes, the analysis would apply also to 'news' that would signal that such a shift will occur in the future. We want to represent agents who are alert to the properties of the environment, but who fall short of being all-knowing: the individuals in the model may recognize when there has been a change of fundamentals, but they do not have immediate access to the 'true model' of the economy. Agents are assumed to base their expectations about aggregate production on an auto-regressive function whose form is similar to the one which would (approximately) describe the convergence to the steady state along a perfect foresight path. Starting with some initial guess about the shape of the function, the agents update its parameters using a standard adaptive-learning algorithm (see Sargent (1993), Evans and Honkapohja (1995)).

For some initial configurations of the parameters, the model can generate transitional cycles in spending. The system eventually approaches a steady state, but the convergence may be non-monotonic. For example, if individuals initially overestimate their wealth (because they have exaggerated expectations about the growth in economy-wide output), their consumption will exceed the perfect foresight value. The error need not be corrected at once: the aggregation of individual actions can generate realizations of total output which, for a certain number of periods, are larger than individuals anticipated. This, in turn, would lead to an upward revision of wealth perceptions; that is, to a movement 'in the wrong direction'.

The agents in the model do make mistakes, but not 'systematic' ones. The shock they are responding to is a unique event, and the learning procedure finally takes the system to a steady state where expectations are accurate. Moreover, as shown in Section 3, for a given shock, certain sets of initial beliefs generate sizeable cycles, while others do not. Without a good knowledge of the structure of the model, and without a good knowledge of aggregate expectations, an individual cannot easily infer that the system is following a cyclical path only by observing its behaviour in a few periods. Agents could, indeed, realize that the system they inhabit is undergoing a transition, and that it may go through a period of 'excessive' or 'insufficient' expansion. However, the observable aggregate information does not provide a simple way of revising in one direction or the other the expectations derived from the learning algorithm. One could say that it is precisely the fact that agents may confuse non-equilibrium behaviour with a movement along a well co-ordinated path that sustains for some time the misperceptions which result in the spending cycles.

In the model just sketched, changes in spending are associated with movements in the demand for credit at an exogenously given interest rate. The argument serves to highlight the role of income expectations in the determination of aggregate demand and the trade balance in an open economy. However, it is clearly incomplete, from both an analytical point of view and for the purpose of interpreting concrete episodes: swings in credit conditions are salient features of the fluctuations we are concerned with.

There is a sizeable recent literature that analyzes 'credit cycles'. This literature has stressed the links between the value of the assets held by prospective borrowers and their access to credit; changes in the tightness of financial restrictions generate a mechanism by which the effects of shocks are amplified and persist over time. We are interested in a related issue: how perceptions about the evolution of future income act on the supply of and the demand for credit. In Section 4 we analyze possible extensions of the basic model that endogenize the supply of credit and incorporate financial effects. Although the analysis is carried out within a very schematic framework (a standard two-period, two-state, consumption–loan model allowing for default) and it is not fully integrated with the multi-period learning model of capital accumulation previously presented, we can identify several channels through which expectations influence current expenditures, pointing to different cyclical scenarios. When lenders revise their expectations about the performances of the economy in 'bad states' (when partial default will occur), the consequent shift in the supply of credit appears to 'initiate' the upswing or downswing; the credit demand schedule varies with the forecasts of prospective borrowers of their income in 'good states'. This suggests that, depending on the conditions of each case, interest rates and aggregate demand can be related in different ways.

In Section 4 we comment briefly on how the previous results could be of use in analyzing cyclical episodes. Interpretations based on alternative approaches are discussed in Section 5, with reference to recent fluctuation in Latin America. In that section, we also deal briefly with policy implications; the point we make is that, irrespective of whether policy-makers have 'superior knowledge' about the behaviour of the economies, their decisions are in fact predicated on judgements, not only about the future evolution of fundamentals, but also about the way in which the private sector determines its own expectations.

2 A brief review of some episodes

The Latin-American experience of the recent decades offers a number of examples of very wide economic fluctuations. Several of these took place in the midst of major changes in economic policies. Such policy reforms aimed specifically at price stabilization, but they were also motivated by disappointment in the growth performance of the economies, and tried purposefully to modify the environment for private decisions. There is a vast literature analyzing these episodes; we rely on it in the brief discussion that follows. Clearly, we cannot present a full picture: this would require a detailed study of each case. The purpose of this section is simply to provide a broad view of a set of cyclical episodes, indicating the nature of the changes the economies were undergoing, and suggesting that the observed performance may have been linked to significant revisions in agents' perceptions of the growth prospects of income.

2.1 Chile 1977–82

Between 1970 and 1975, the Chilean economy contracted by an average of more than 2 per cent a year, during a period of political turmoil. Large-scale economic reforms started in 1974, with the privatization of banks and public enterprises, followed soon after by measures that liberalized international trade: non-tariff barriers were eliminated, and the government announced a schedule of tariffs converging to a flat 10 per cent rate in 1979. The removal of restrictions on financial transactions induced a large expansion in the banking sector. In 1975, the government implemented a large fiscal adjustment by cutting expenditure and raising taxes.

After a sharp recession in 1975, real output showed a rapid recovery, with growth at over 7 per cent in 1976–8. In order to attack the still very high inflation (84 per cent in 1977), in June 1978 the government decided to apply a policy of preannounced devaluations at a declining rate, converging towards a peg to the dollar. Also, international financial movements were further liberalized. Other reforms launched at this time were the introduction of a private pension system and various measures of deregulation in goods markets.

Real growth continued to be quite strong: again, over 7 per cent on average in 1978–81. Edwards and Cox Edwards (1987) have stated: 'This new growth pattern together with the reduction of inflation ... generated a sense of prosperity and of improved future economic perspectives for the general public ... This, in turn, resulted in a perception of substantially high wealth'. Moreover, the large supply of funds in world markets stimulated lending to the region, and particularly to Chile. Such conditions were reflected in dramatic increases in asset prices and in private spending: the savings rate fell sharply. The consumption boom was asociated with a large current-account deficit, which averaged 7 per cent of GDP in 1978–80, and reached nearly 19 per cent in 1981. In addition, a large real appreciation was observed.

The expansion in output and aggregate demand started to slow down in 1981. Interest rates rose, and highly indebted firms had difficulties in making repayments. This created problems for banks.

By the beginning of 1982, real output was declining, and the expectations of devaluation brought about a capital outflow. Around that time, financial flows to the region were suddenly cut. A balance of payments crisis forced a devaluation in September 1982; in that year, real GDP fell by 14 per cent, and by 0.7 per cent the following year, before the long (and lasting) recovery that started in the mid-1980s.

2.2 Argentina 1978–82

After more than a decade of moderate but sustained growth in real GDP, the Argentine economy went into recession in 1975, as the policies of high budget deficits and rapid monetary expansions followed at that time by the government led to a balance of payments crisis and to a succession of large devaluations. The drop in real incomes and the acceleration of inflation aggravated the political crisis. After the military takeover in March 1976, the government eliminated price controls and abolished the system of multiple exchange rates. Many restrictions on foreign exchange transactions were eliminated, and tariff rates were reduced (although this mainly meant a reduction in redundant protection). Various changes were introduced in the tax system (for example VAT was applied to a wider set of activities, and income tax was reformulated). In June 1977, a financial reform liberalized interest rates.

Real output increased more than 6 per cent in 1977 (with a sharp increase in investments, both private and public), but fell again the following year, probably as a result of tighter monetary conditions. The inflation rate was still much higher than 100 per cent a year. In December 1978, the government initiated a policy of preannounced devaluations. This was combined with tariff reductions.

In 1979, domestic demand and real output increased quickly, and the inflation rate fell, but remained well above the rate of devaluation. There was a substantial revaluation in the dollar value of incomes.[1] At the same time, public spending continued to rise. The higher expenditures of both the private and public sectors contributed to the generation of a sizeable current-account deficit in 1980, despite the sharp increase in export prices.

By 1980, some domestic firms were making losses. Early in that year, bank failures induced a movement of funds away from deposits and into foreign currencies. The government was able to stop an incipient run on the banks, but the level of foreign reserves declined while real output stagnated. Exchange rate speculation put pressure on interest rates. Capital flight became rapid at the beginning of 1981. The exchange rate policy was eventually abandoned. The large depreciation of the currency in 1981 and 1982 aggravated the financial situation of firms and individuals with dollar debts. The contraction of GDP accumulated over those two years reached around 8 per cent.

2.3 Uruguay 1978–82

From the mid-1970s, the Uruguayan government adopted policies of economic liberalization by gradually eliminating price controls, doing away with the system of multiple exchange rates, removing interest rate ceilings, reducing barriers to entry in banking, abolishing restrictions on capital flows, and progressively lowering taxes on traditional exports. In 1975–8, the annual growth of GDP accelerated to an average of 4 per cent,[2] with a marked increase in the investment ratio. In October 1978, the exchange rate was fixed, and together with this, the government established a new schedule of tariff reductions. At the end of 1978, legal reserve requirements on bank liabilities were unified at 20 per cent, and totally eliminated the following May. The fiscal deficit was already low (less than 1 per cent of GDP); in any case, new measures to raise tax revenues were taken in 1979.

In 1978–80, GDP growth (5.7 per cent on average) improved upon the previous performance. Domestic demand rose sharply (more than 10 per cent in 1979). As happened in other countries, there was a considerable real appreciation and a growing current-account deficit.[3] However, in 1981, output growth was only around 1 per cent, and domestic demand had already contracted (see Talvi (1995)). This contraction became rapid in 1982 (when real GDP fell by 10 per cent). Although lower real expenditure led to a reduction in the current-account deficit, the demand for foreign currencies increased sharply, as the budget deficit soared (to nearly 9 per cent of GDP, compared with 0.1 per cent of GDP the previous year), and the public formed strong expectations of a devaluation in the near future. In fact, the devaluation occurred in November 1982, and was followed by further falls in output and severe difficulties in the financial system (Vaz (1997)).

2.4 Mexico 1987–95

The Mexican stabilization plan which started at the end of 1987 was part of a comprehensive programme of economic reforms that was initiated as a reaction to the 1982 foreign debt crisis. The measures taken in the 1983–87 period were aimed at reducing the budget deficit and liberalizing foreign trade. Real growth was slow and unsteady. Despite the fiscal adjustment, however, inflation remained high, and accelerated in 1986 when a fall in the price of oil led to a more rapid rate of depreciation of the currency.

The 1987 disinflation stategy included the preannouncement of the exchange rate and measures aiming at synchronizing a deceleration of wages and prices (see Ortiz (1991), Santaella and Vela (1996)). In addition, the government took new action to cut the fiscal deficit and quickened the pace of reforms, especially in the areas of privatization and trade liberalization (import tariffs were reduced, to a maximum of 20 per cent, ahead of schedule). Inflation fell and the real recovery, weak at first, then gained speed between 1989 and 1991, with an average GDP growth of 4 per cent. Observers of the Mexican economy pointed out that this performance was influenced by the success of disinflation, the economic reforms, the renegotiation of the foreign debt in 1989 and the prospects of trade integration within NAFTA (see Ortiz (1991)). Higher rates of output growth went together with still more rapid increases in domestic expenditure; this was associated with a real appreciation and larger current-account deficits.

Economic activity decelerated in 1992 and 1993 (with increases in GDP of 2.8 per cent and 0.4 per cent, respectively). Santaella and Vela (1996) mention that concerns about the approval of NAFTA affected expectations negatively in 1992. In any case, the current-account deficit exceeded 7 per cent of GDP in 1993. Relatively high interest rates and slow sales had an impact on the cash flow of firms, with repercussions on the financial system. In 1994 state development banks expanded their credit to commercial banks and private firms and real output rose by around 3 per cent. However, in addition to the weakening of the economy's performance, the rise in US interest rates and internal political events increased the programme's fragility. Diminishing foreign reserves induced the new administration that took office at the end of 1994 to let the currency depreciate. In 1995, GDP fell by 6 per cent. The sharp recession and the real depreciation of the currency caused widespread problems in the repayment of debts to the banks. Still, output recovered in 1996, led by a rapid increase in exports.

2.5 Argentina 1991–5

Following a period of extreme monetary instability in 1989 and the early part of 1990, in 1991 the government passed a law fixing the exchange rate to the US dollar and requiring the issue of base money to be tightly linked to foreign reserve flows. In the course of the early 1990s, the authorities privatized most state enterprises. The government tended to concentrate its revenues on broad-base taxes, particularly value added tax (VAT). Import tariffs were reduced, and harmonized with those of neighbouring countries in the context of the Mercosur agreements, which established free trade conditions within the area. In addition, a private pensions system was introduced, and various activities were deregulated. In 1993, the authorities completed a Brady-plan agreement with foreign creditors. Interest rate spreads measuring 'country risk' premia decreased substantially.

The inflation rate converged to very low figures (less than 4 per cent a year in 1994); in the process, however, domestic prices rose substantially relative to the exchange rate. Real output showed a very strong recovery. In the 1991–4 period, GDP increased at an annual average of nearly 9 per cent, and real consumption rose even faster, with an average rate of 10 per cent a year. The investment rate grew, starting from very low levels. The rapid increase in domestic spending was financed by large capital inflows. In 1990, the trade balance had had a US $8 billion surplus (equivalent to around two-thirds of the value of exports); the deficit in 1994 approached US $6 billion (36 per cent of exports that year).

The rise in US interest rates in 1994 had some effects on domestic financial markets. By the middle of that year there were some indications that the growth in domestic demand was levelling off; in contrast, exports (especially those going to Brazil) accelerated their growth. However, following the Mexican devaluation at the end of 1994, the demand for domestic assets suddenly fell. The central bank lost reserves, and the volume of bank deposits declined; withdrawals accelerated to a near panic by March 1995. The government maintained the convertibility system with a fixed exchange rate and negotiated loans from the IMF and other multilateral organizations. The banking panic stopped. However, there was a sharp credit contraction. The economy went into a recession: GDP fell by 4.5 per cent in 1995 and the unemployment rate (which had been rising even during the expansion) jumped to a peak of more than 18 per cent. Larger exports and reduced imports resulted in a trade surplus. The demand for financial assets recovered after mid-1995, but the cycle of real output reached a trough in the second half of that year. Activity increased in 1996 and 1997, although the unemployment rate remained very high.

The bare-bones description of these episodes shows that each one had specific features, both in terms of the process leading to the crisis, and the behaviour of the economies after this had happened. However, the various cases also show important common aspects. The literature has focused mainly on the consequences of exchange rate pegging and the influence of international credit conditions (see, for example, Kiguel and Liviatan (1992), Calvo and Vegh (1993), Calvo *et al.* (1993), Reinhart and Vegh (1995)). Clearly, these elements cannot be left out in a full analysis of the episodes. Still, elementary calculations show that changes in projected growth rates and in the terms of borrowing can lead to substantial movements in individuals' perceived wealth. In all these episodes, at some point agents had reasons to believe that their incomes would grow at a faster rate than in the past, while foreign lenders were willing to provide financing, probably on the basis of optimistic evaluations of the economies' prospects. In the aftermath of crises, it seems likely that at least some of these expectations were disappointed. In the following sections we present some simple models with the objective of making the argument more precise.

3 A simple model

We consider first an open economy producing a single good, which faces a perfectly elastic supply/demand for foreign credit at an interest rate that equals the rate of time preference of the representative individual. The model is specified in a standard fashion. The economy is populated by infinitely-lived individuals who produce the good, which can be consumed, sold abroad or 'planted' as capital. The preferences of the representative agent are assumed to be time-separable, and the individuals are supposed to decide as if they had perfect foresight:[4]

$$U_{it} = \Sigma_{j=t}^{\infty} \beta^{j-t} U_i({}_t c_{ij}) \qquad (6.1)$$

The specification of preferences is such that the individual will choose a path with constant consumption. Therefore, ${}_t C_{ij}$, the planned consumption in period j chosen by individual i in period t, will be equal to the return on perceived wealth:[5]

$$ {}_t c_{ij} = {}_t [W^i_{it}](1-\beta) = \frac{r}{1+r} {}_t [W^i_{it}],\ j = t, t+1 \ldots \qquad (6.2)$$

It is well known that consumption according to Equation (6.2) implies that the individual plans to maintain a constant level of wealth (see Obstfeld and Rogoff (1994)).

Each individual produces the good using capital and a fixed input (for example, specific labour). We assume that there are externalities in production, so that the output of a given individual varies positively with the aggregate level of output.[6] Production also depends on a shift variable. We shall interpret this variable as being influenced by economic policies, and by other shocks. The production function is then specified as (with y_{it} being the output of individual i in period t; z_{it} the shift parameter; k_{it-1} the beginning of the period capital stock held by individual i in period t; and y_t aggregate output):

$$y_{it} = z_{it} k_{it-1}^{\alpha} y_t^{\eta} \tag{6.3}$$

As is usually done in the literature, we suppose that changes in the capital stock have associated adjustment costs. For simplicity, these are taken to be a symmetric (quadratic) function of the gradient of the capital stock during the period. The productive decisions of the individual are governed by the objective of maximizing the present value of net output. This results in the following problem:

$$\max \sum_{j=t}^{\infty} \beta^{j-t} \left[{}_t y_{ij} - ({}_t k_{ij} -_t k_{ij-1}) - \frac{\phi}{2} \frac{({}_t k_{ij} -_t k_{ij-1})^2}{{}_t k_{ij-1}} \right] =_t [W_{it}^{iy}] \tag{6.4}$$

Here ${}_t y_{ij}$ denotes the level of individual output in period j planned at t by agent i (and similarly for ${}_t k_{ij}$), ${}_t[W_{it}^{iy}]$ indicates the expected present value, perceived by individual i, of his/her production plan (net of investment and adjustment costs) defined at t.

Because of the externality, the path for the capital stock, the value of perceived wealth and consumption will depend on the expectations that the individual forms about aggregate output. Given the accumulation and production plan derived from the programming problem in Equation (6.4), and given those expectations, the individual estimates the present value of the planned flow of output, net of investment and adjustment costs. Perceived wealth equals that value of net output, less the agent's financial liabilities:

$${}_t[W_{it}^{i}] =_t [W_{it}^{iy}] - (1+r) b_{it-1} \tag{6.5}$$

We assume that initially (at $t = 0$), those liabilities are zero; thereafter, the realized level of debt evolves according to the difference between actual spending and output:

$$b_{it} = b_{it-1}(1+r) + c_{it} + (k_{it} - k_{it-1}) + \frac{\phi}{2}(k_{it} - k_{it-1})^2\, k_{it-1} - y_{it} \qquad (6.6)$$

The system defined by Equations (6.2)–(6.6) determines the production, consumption and financing plans of the individual for a given set of expectations. Assuming that z_{it} is a deterministic variable, a perfect foresight solution can be obtained by making anticipated future aggregate output equal to the value that the model delivers for each period. We have assumed that the externality in production is not too strong (that is, $(\alpha + \eta) < 1$), so that the perfect foresight paths for output and the capital stock converge to a steady state.[7]

Figure 6.1 shows the simulated paths of the main variables after an upward (permanent) productivity shift which raises steady-state output by 15 per cent.

These solutions have standard qualitative features. The adjustment costs in investment delay the increase in the capital stock, and cause it to be gradual. However, starting from a previous steady state, wealth perceptions are revised immediately after the arrival of the news about

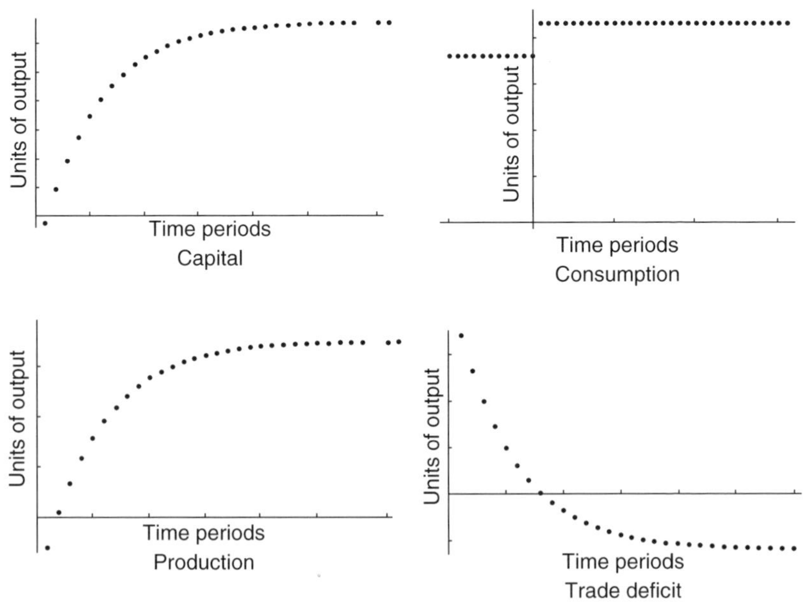

Figure 6.1 Simulated paths of the main variables

the productivity shift. Consumption thus moves at once to the new steady-state level. During the first periods of the transition, investment is also high, while production is still far from the new steady state. The economy then shows trade and current-account deficits, as foreign credit is used to finance the higher level of spending. After its initial jump, aggregate expenditure falls during the transition path (because of the gradual decrease in investment), while output increases. Eventually, the trade balance becomes positive. As the economy approaches the steady state, the trade surplus becomes close to the value of the interest services on the accumulated debt. Wealth remains constant after being re-evaluated when the shock is observed; as should be the case along a perfect foresight path, this validates the expectations that sustained the initial increase in consumption.

In this perfect foresight case, changes in output near the steady state can be approximated by a first-order auto-regressive equation:

$$y_t = \lambda y_{t-1} + (1 - \lambda)\bar{y} = \lambda y_{t-1} + y^* \tag{6.7}$$

According to Equation (6.7), the value of aggregate output in a given period is a convex combination of its observed value in the previous period and of the steady-state output $\bar{y}$. The parameter λ is a measure of the speed of the transition: if it is small, the auto-regressive term is also small, and consequently output converges swiftly to its steady state.

Although the perfect foresight evolution of the hypothetical economy is qualitatively simple, the numerical results depend on the values of various parameters, which need not be known by all the agents. From the point of view of an individual trying to anticipate the future behaviour of output for the purpose of drawing up his/her own plans, finding the path generated by the fundamentals of this simple model of the economy would imply knowing the aggregate shock, the strength of the externality effect, and the adjustment costs of investment for the average firm (in order to predict the rate of investment of other agents). These parameters are likely to be difficult to specify, particularly if the economy is going through a structural change, in which the coefficients can be supposed to be shifting.

The scenario we are interested in analyzing is one where agents realize that there has been a productivity shock (both for their own specific activity and for the economy as a whole), and they are able to determine in broad terms how the system will react, but they must learn about the quantitative performance of the economy through some learning procedure.

For the purposes of this exercise, we use a relatively simple adaptive algorithm to model the way in which individuals update their expectations of aggregate output. This learning scheme seems reasonably well adapted to the case we are studying. As we showed before, the perfect foresight model generates a solution with a gradual relaxation of output towards the steady state. This solution is approximated by Equation (6.7). We assume that agents form their expectations on the basis of this equation, which implies that they can identify the general form of the equilibrium output path: even if they do not consider the way in which fundamentals and expectations interact to generate output, they employ a reduced form approach that is appropriate for the problem they are facing. Agents use the observations of actual aggregate output to revise their estimates of the parameters y^* and λ. In period 0, when they receive information about the occurrence of the productivity shock, individuals make a conjecture about the values of these parameters. These conjectures could in practice be based on the history of the economy itself, on similar episodes of other economies, or upon 'influential opinions'. In this exercise, we take the initial conjectures as given.

A commonly used learning scheme is based on the stochastic approximation algorithm (see Sargent (1993), Evans and Honkapohja (1995)). According to this scheme, the parameters of a linear function relating a variable y with a vector of variables x are to be determined by:

$$\begin{aligned} \beta_t &= \beta_{t-1} + \gamma_t R_t^{-1} x_t (y_t - x_t' \beta_{t-1}) \\ R_t &= R_{t-1} + \gamma_t (x_t x_t' - R_{t-1}) \end{aligned} \tag{6.8}$$

The coefficient γ_t can be a function of time. When γ_t diminishes with t (a decreasing gain algorithm), this means that successive forecast errors have less weight in determining the parameters. In a recursive regression, $\gamma_t = 1/t$. The constant gain algorithms result by setting the parameter γ_t at a given, fixed value. Such algorithms will find a use when it is believed that the process generating the variable y is subject to frequent changes (see Evans and Honkapohja (1993)). In our case, the agent must learn about the values of y^* and λ of Equation (6.7), so that the vector β_t includes both parameters. The learning procedure implies that the agent uses the forecast errors s/he makes over time to recompute the estimates of the coefficients on which s/he bases the expectations of future aggregate output of the good. In particular, if the individual has underpredicted total production during this period, s/he will revise upwards his/her estimate of long-run aggregate output. The intuition seems clear: the agent interprets the event of a higher-than-expected output as an

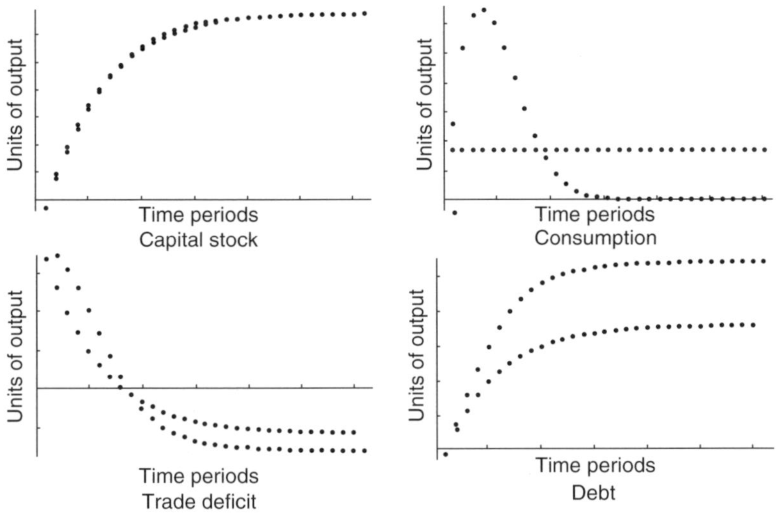

Figure 6.2 Simulated paths with learning and perfect foresight

indication that production will converge to a higher value than s/he had previously anticipated.

The model can be used to simulate different scenarios, depending on the initial conjectures of the representative agent. In Figure 6.2 we show the results for the case in which the agent starts with the belief that output will eventually rise 10 per cent above the value that the model generates for the new perfect foresight steady state, and where the initially expected speed of convergence is given by a parameter $\lambda = 0.95$, instead of the value (near 0.83) that approximates the behaviour along the perfect foresight path. These parameters are updated with a constant gain algorithm. In order to allow a comparison to be made, the graphs in Figure 6.2 show the results with both learning and perfect foresight. It can be observed that there is indeed convergence to a steady state, and that the values of the capital stock and aggregate output tend towards those that would apply under perfect foresight. Still, in the transition, the model with learning generates a cycle in consumption and a movement in the trade balance which differs noticeably from the perfect foresight path.

The simulation suggests that learning about the long-run trend using a 'reasonable' procedure can generate fluctuations in consumption (which would not be observed under perfect foresight) and may cause the trade balance to stay away for some time from a 'sustainable' path. In the model, the mistakes that are made in the transition have 'long-run' consequences, since they become embodied in the level of the foreign debt. One point to be stressed is that the estimates of wealth (and, therefore, of consumption) follow a non-monotonic movement. This implies that the original misperceptions are not corrected at once, but may get amplified for a certain time interval. The reason is that the agent, while being over-optimistic (in this case) about the present value of output, makes 'conservative' (and relatively accurate) one-step-ahead projections; in other words, the short-run behaviour s/he observes more than confirm his/her exaggerated perceptions of the future trend, until eventually the error is revealed.

This non-monotonicity can arise with other configurations of the initial parameters, but not all.[8] If the agent starts with a too-low estimate of $\bar{y}$, and initially predicts a too-slow convergence to the new steady state, wealth perceptions are, of course, over-pessimistic, and the individual will initially underpredict actual growth. This will lead to a revision of the parameters. If the corrections in the value of λ are relatively slow, it is possible that at some point wealth perceptions overshoot the sustainable value. In this case, there will be a 'delayed boom', which will in turn lead to a downward correction of consumption in the future; here again, the path is non-monotonic. If, instead, the agent initially expects a very rapid movement to an excessively high level of output, experience will rapidly tell him/her that his/her forecasts were biased: the convergence path of consumption would be monotonic from above. There are other cases (for example, with an initial $\bar{y}$ set at a too-slow level and a high λ), where consumption shows a smooth convergence from below.

There is therefore a multiplicity of possible behaviours depending on the parameters with which the learning starts. We do not consider this multiplicity to be a weakness of the analysis. On the contrary, it makes misperceptions more plausible, if it is assumed that agents not only learn from observing actual data, but that they can, at least qualitatively, also realize that the trajectory of the economy is itself influenced by learning processes. Suppose that the model generated a definite prediction of intertemporal disequilibrium irrespective of initial beliefs; say, its results showed that there would always be an initial boom and a future adjustment. Then one could clearly object that 'smart' agents should realize that they (and their neighbours) are overspending, which should induce a revision of plans. In this model, the situation is not so simple, implying that there is no easily identifiable way to revise (what will eventually turn out to be) a misperception.

In any case, the model can be extended without too much difficulty to incorporate non-traded goods. In Heymann and Sanguinetti (1998), it is assumed that good *N* (non-traded) is produced with traded inputs (and a Cobb–Douglas production function), while good *T* does not use *N* as a factor. This, in fact, 'decouples' the system: the production decisions of good *T* can be represented as in a one-good model. In addition, preferences are specified in a such a way that the share of each good in consumption expenditures is a constant. Therefore, with these simplifying hypotheses, in intertemporal equilibrium, total wealth is a (constant) multiple of 'traded goods wealth', defined as the present value of traded-goods output, net of investment and the pre-existing foreign debt.

In such a system, during a transition (caused, say, by a shock in the productivity parameter z), agents have to learn about the future value of traded-goods output for two reasons: to estimate their own future productivity (if there is an externality) and to estimate the future proceeds from the sale of non-traded output. We assume that agents are aware of this link between aggregate demand, the relative price of non-tradables and 'traded goods wealth'. Consequently, the learning procedure we sketched in this section for the one-good model is a central element of the scheme that generates wealth perceptions (and therefore, consumption decisions) in the framework with two goods.

In the two-goods setting, spending on non-traded goods is a function of perceived wealth; production of good *N* and the relative price of this good (that is, the inverse of the real exchange rate) would move together with the changes in wealth. Consumption cycles would then be associated with fluctuations in the real exchange rate and the production of non-tradables. Expectations biased towards pessimism (to change the example) would be associated with an 'excessively high' real exchange rate and a too-low production in non-traded-goods sectors.

4 Notes on credit fluctuations

The analysis of the previous section has concentrated on the expectations and decisions of producers–consumers. The credit market was represented simply through the exogenous interest rate, at which every agent could lend or borrow without restriction. In the model, debts were always repaid in full, and market participants planned on the basis of that assumption. The interest rate varied only with 'world conditions' (kept under the *ceteris paribus* assumption), independently of the behaviour of the economy to be modelled. Thus the volume of lending accommodated 'passively' the shifts in demand, and the state of expectations had no effect on the terms on which credit was supplied. Frustrated expectations led agents to revise their plans, and therefore brought about unforeseen adjustments in spending, but they did not cause any specific disturbance in financial markets.

No doubt that representation left out of the analysis important features of business fluctuations. The behaviour of credit markets is especially relevant for the types of cycle we are studying, which are driven by changing perceptions about the future performance of the economy: the expectations of lenders and the consequent movements in credit conditions clearly should matter in determining the movements in aggregate demand. More specifically, in the episodes mentioned in Section 2, one of the most prominent elements was the 'easing' of credit terms during the expansions (or, at least, during a good part of these phases), while contractions were associated with abrupt credit crunches and, sometimes, with big disturbances in financial markets.

Interest in modelling 'credit cycles' has revived in recent years.[9] This has placed in focus once more the interaction between real activity and financial conditions. While debtors may default on their obligations, changes in the size of collaterals and current cash-flows influence the ability of agents to finance spending and production. In this connection, we want to emphasize two simple points. First, credit terms depend on the anticipated magnitude of the future income of borrowers (or, what is equivalent for these purposes, the expected value of collaterals). Thus the supply of credit will be predicated on the beliefs of potential lenders regarding the evolution of income; such beliefs are derived from the learning performed by the agents. Second, lenders are particularly concerned about their debtors' income in 'bad states' (in which they default), while borrowers determine their demand for credit looking at expected income in the 'no-default' region; this asymmetry has potential consequences for the link between interest rates and real activity.

A well-developed analysis of credit and real markets would require the bringing together of the analysis of intertemporal choices on production, consumption, borrowing and lending over a more-or-less long horizon. This appears to be quite complicated. For this reason, at this point we shall use a very simple framework that is not fully integrated with the one presented in the previous section, but is useful in any case to illustrate the connections between output expectations, the supply of credit and the volume of spending.

The setup is quite standard (see Hodgman (1960), Jaffee and Stiglitz (1990)). We follow the usual practice in restricting the horizon to two periods. Given the aim of the exercise, it will be enough to consider a consumption loan model.[10] The demand for credit is generated by individuals endowed with exogenous flows of the single good in each period.[11] Output in period 1 is perfectly observed before decisions are taken, while future output is not known with certainty. Therefore, lenders and borrowers must make conjectures about output in period 2. Both parts of a credit transaction may differ regarding the probability distribution that they assume for the future income of the borrower.[12] However, once realized, the income of every individual in period 2 becomes public information.[13] We also suppose that the economy is small, and faces a parametric 'riskless interest rate' determined abroad.

Financial assets consist of bonds with a fixed interest rate in terms of the single good. If there are different types of borrower distinguished by some observable features, financial contracts can be written so as to discriminate between the types. We do not allow the existence of assets explicitly contingent on the borrower's income. However, in the case on which we will concentrate the analysis – two possible values for future income, in one of which there is default – the 'escape clause' of the contract operates like a contingency provision.

We suppose that there is a mass of risk-neutral potential lenders, so that, for every loan contract, the expected return equals the riskless 'world' return. Repayment of the loan takes place as follows. The consumption level of a borrower in period 2 cannot fall below a minimum value, $\underline{c}$. If actual income net of minimum consumption exceeds the contractual amount to be repaid, the lender receives the full value of the contract. Otherwise, the lender can appropriate the whole of income net of minimum consumption (that is, partial default is allowed).

We consider the case in which there are two states ('good' and 'bad') in period 2; in the good state output is $\bar{y}$, and $\underline{y}$ in the bad state. Let p be the probability of the good state; b the size of a loan made in period 1; r the contractual interest rate; and r^* the world interest rate. At this point, we shall assume that (from the point of view of the lender), p, $\underline{y}$, and $\bar{y}$ are independent of r. If there are different types of borrower, they are assumed to be perfectly distinguishable, so that there are no adverse selection effects à la Stiglitz and Weiss (1981).

The lender must expect a net return equal to the world interest rate. There are three regions. In the first, the amount borrowed is sufficiently small so that there is full repayment even in the bad state. This is true if $\underline{y} - \underline{c} > b(1 + r^*)$. Then the interest rate is simply r^*, because there is no default risk (if the borrower is assimilated to the country, there is zero spread attributable to 'country risk'). When the size of the loan exceeds the limit stated above, there is partial default in the bad state, and the interest rate rises with the amount borrowed, to account for that hazard. There is an upper limit $\bar{b}$, if $b > \bar{b}$, $b(1 + r^*)$ is larger than the expected income of the borrower net of minimum consumption. Then, at no interest rate can the lender anticipate recovering the opportunity cost of funds. Therefore, lending is restricted so that it will not exceed $\bar{b}$. The arbitrage conditions then imply:

$$
\begin{aligned}
&r = r^* && (a)\ if\ b(1+r^*) < \underline{y}^l - c\\
&b(1+r^*) = p^l b(1+r) + (1-p^l)(\underline{y}^l - \underline{c}) && (b)\ if\ y^l - c \leq b(1+r^*) \leq \bar{b}(1+r^*)\\
&\bar{b}(1+r^*) = p^l(\bar{y}^l - c) + (1-p^l)(\underline{y}^l - \underline{c}) && (c)
\end{aligned}
\tag{6.9}
$$

These equations determine the supply schedule for loans of a given 'type' (that is, for given attributes of the borrower as perceived by the lender). In the previous expression, the supra-indices attached to some variables indicate that they represent expectations formed by the lender. It is easy to see, but still worthy of note, that the arbitrage conditions in Equation (6.9) generate a supply of funds schedule that is independent of the value of income in the 'good state', when borrowing is not restricted. The value of $\bar{y}$ (as perceived by the lenders) does have an effect on the supply of loans, by changing the size of the credit limit $\bar{b}$, but it has no influence on the supply schedule below $\bar{b}$. Inside the region in which there is a chance of default, credit conditions (determined by the interest rate for a given loan size) depend only on the perceptions that lenders have about the income in the bad state: an improvement (say) in the expectations that lenders have of the 'worst case scenario' may lead to a sharp fall in the relevant interest rate even though agents have not revised by much their forecast of future income for the case in which the economy 'performs well'.

We consider now the problem of the individual consumer. This individual faces the interest rate, r, corresponding to his/her 'risk type'. In order to concentrate on the cases more relevant to the macroeconomic problems we are concerned with, we shall assume that current income is sufficiently low that the individual plans to be a borrower, and that his/her demand for loans is such that s/he would default on his/her debts in the event that the bad state occurred in period 2 (implying that consumption in that state would be $\underline{c}$, independently of the amount borrowed), but she would repay the loan in full in the good state. Then, the consumer maximizes expected utility, which is given by:

$$EU^i = u(y_1 + b) + \beta_p^i u(\bar{y}^i - b(1+r)) + \beta(1-p^i)u(c^i) \tag{6.10}$$

This implies:

$$u'(y_1 + b) - \beta p^i(1 + r)u'(\bar{y}^i - b(1 + r)) = 0 \qquad (6.11)$$

Given that consumption in the bad state is fixed, as long as the consumer stays in the region where there is default in such state, the demand for credit is independent of $\underline{y}$. By contrast, borrowing depends on $\bar{y}$. This result has a correspondence with the one obtained for the supply of funds: if there is a given probability of default, the supply of credit depends on the level of income in the bad state, as seen by lenders, while the demand schedule varies with the perception that borrowers have of the value of income in the good state. On the other hand, it is clear that the demand for credit depends negatively on the probability of the good state (keeping the interest rate constant), since a higher p increases the expected repayment.[14]

The supply and demand schedules derived from Equations (6.9) and (6.11) imply the following responses of market outcomes to changes in the variables considered as exogenous in this exercise:

- Naturally, an increase in current income (keeping expectations fixed) lowers the demand for credit. This results in a fall in the amount borrowed and a lower interest rate. If the increase in y_1 is sufficiently large, it can eliminate the default risk.
- A higher value of $\underline{y}$ (perceived by lenders) increases the volume of credit, by lowering the interest rate.
- An increase in $\bar{y}$ (anticipated by borrowers) also increases the volume of loans, but causes the interest rate to rise. This result, together with the previous one, indicates that, while optimism about income prospects has a positive effect on consumption and borrowing, the behaviour of interest rates can be quite different depending on the perceptions of agents on both sides of the credit market, and according to whether the change in expectations refers to an increase in the income to be generated if 'things go wrong' or to the outcome if 'all goes well'.
- A higher probability of the good state raises the supply of credit (and enlarges the credit limit), and reduces the demand at a given interest rate. The interest rate falls.
- A lower world interest rate clearly reduces the quoted rate and raises the volume of credit.

This very simple analysis can be extended in several ways. One of them would be to allow for the existence of asymmetric information about the probability distribution of individual incomes, in such a way that some agents face credit rationing. Lifting the assumption that the time horizon is only two periods long would open up several interesting possibilities, by incorporating the possibility of 'flexibility preference' effects, and by making the current decisions of borrowers depend on their forecasts of the future supply of credit. Also, there is no doubt that limiting the analysis to consumption loans is much too restrictive. Clearly, changes in credit conditions are transmitted to a large extent through the financing of investment and production; these effects make output depend directly on the expectations of lenders (see Kaufman (1996), Agénor and Aizenman (1997)).

At any rate, the results shown so far, elementary as they are, can be used to analyze some financial mechanisms in the context of business fluctuations. The channels through which expectations act on current spending will generally depend on how individuals perceive the probability distribution of future incomes. Although (for a given 'world interest rate') forecasts about the future wealth of borrowers determine both the supply and the demand for credit, there are conditions in which the 'financial sector' would appear to initiate a movement in spending, and cases where movements in the volume of lending would seem to respond to shifts in borrowers' attitudes. Changes in expectations about the level of income to be obtained in a 'bad' economic state would transmit their effects mainly through the supply of credit: the decisions of financial asset holders would then play an 'active role' in the determination of aggregate expenditure.[15]

This channel may be particularly significant, for example, in economies that stabilize after undergoing extreme instability: it seems likely that agents would remain at first quite uncertain about growth prospects, but change their perception of the 'worst case' scenario as economic conditions improve. Then the first reaction to be observed would be a sharp easing of the terms of credit, to which spending would respond.[16] The rise in domestic expenditure would come mainly from an induced effect of the expansion in credit supply. If, later on, the economy starts showing signs of a stronger trend in output, expectations about growth in the good state would be revised, leading to a rise in credit demand at given interest rates. In those circumstances, domestic spending would expand, while the interest rate may either rise or fall (depending, in particular, on whether the new expected growth path is associated with higher or lower variance of income). If there happens to be an overshooting of expectations (or, more generally, if for some reason there is a downward shift in expected future income), the way in which the adjustment takes place when agents revise their forecasts would vary according to whether it is the borrowers or lenders who start changing their minds about the growth potential, and according to whether the news to which the agents are responding modify the perceptions about the features of the 'best case scenario', or those of the 'bad state'. If this last case applies, the adjustment would start with a credit contraction.

5 Discussion

We have tried to build elements of an analytical framework that may help to understand some classes of large-amplitude cyclical movements, such as those that have been observed in Latin America in recent years, and were described briefly in an earlier section. Indeed, these fluctuations (or aspects of them) have been interpreted in different ways. In particular, several authors (for example, Maia and Ortiz (1995), Roldos (1995), Uribe (1997)) have developed models in which increases in aggregate demand, coupled with real appreciations and trade deficits, are rationalized as equilibrium responses to correctly perceived improvements in economic prospects. Another related group of arguments focuses on the incomplete credibility of policies: if agents expect that an exchange-rate based disinflation will be short-lived, they may plan to change the time profile of consumption, with an increase during the period in which the inflation tax is low, and a (pre-programmed) contraction when the unsustainable programme is abandoned and inflation rises again (see Calvo (1986), Kiguel and Liviatan (1992), Talvi (1995), Mendoza and Uribe (1996)).

Clearly, various patterns of movements in spending and relative prices can be obtained in perfect foresight models according to the impulse (present or future) acting on the system (see Heymann (1994)). These patterns include as possibilities fluctuations in aggregate demand and the real exchange rate. In addition, some variables may show sudden changes (for example, an abrupt fall in foreign reserves just before a devaluation, as in Krugman (1979)). But, in such models, the plans of agents are never disturbed.[17] In particular, the recession, if and when it comes, is part of a spending and production programme that agents have knowingly chosen from the start.

The perfect foresight models have shown that many economic configurations can emerge as a consequence of accurate expectations. However, this does not imply that all such configurations must be predicated on correct judgements; rather, those arguments can be taken as indicating that it may be hard to distinguish good from bad forecasts (so people may act on the basis of misperceptions without being able to realize it simply by observing the state of the economy). The fact that some set of future events may validate current plans does not mean that expectations are correct.[18] In the perfect foresight arguments based on lack of credibility of stabilization, for example, (eventually) successful programmes should not be associated with consumption cycles. But sometimes they are.

In any case, sharp recessions like those mentioned in section 2 seem difficult to reconcile with the absence of expectational errors. In fact, these contractions have not generally been interpreted as well-anticipated episodes. Recent literature has modelled crises as sunspot phenomena, that is, as events resulting from the co-ordination of individual expectations on the basis of some random shock that is not part of the economy's fundamentals (see Calvo and Mendoza (1996), Cole and Kehoe (1996), Sachs *et al.* (1996)). Although the sunspot models can rationalize the sudden drop in the demand for domestic financial assets that is usually observed in crises, the question naturally arises about how agents come to co-ordinate their expectations on a certain (more or less arbitrary) variable. In addition, the arguments do not specify whether one should assume that the co-ordination of expectations takes place 'spontaneously', without prior notice, once the shock that triggers the crisis has been observed, or whether agents have all the time been incorporating the (objective) probability of the particular shock (and the consequent run) into their plans. The second scenario does not appear too plausible; in the case of the first one, individuals would have misperceived the economy's behaviour by not taking precautions against the likelihood of a crisis.

An important set of literature has emphasized the influence of the movements in international interest rates on the recent fluctuations in Latin America (see Calvo *et al.* (1993)). It seems clear that changes in international credit markets had a strong effect in directing financial resources towards certain countries during some periods, and away from them at other times. In addition, perceptions of the creditworthiness of highly indebted economies may depend significantly on the level of world rates. Better terms of foreign financing, of course, induce increases in spending; in particular, the stock adjustment in household durables may generate wide swings in consumption expenditure. At the same time, it is not possible to analyze the effects of the changes in international interest rates without considering the behaviour of the demand for credit, and therefore also the income expectations of the domestic agents. Additionally, the effects of shifts in world rates would depend on whether they have been built into expectations:[19] the accuracy of wealth perceptions depends on whether future flows are properly discounted or not.

Our argument does not deny the role of international credit conditions, or the existence of contagion effects in financial disturbances. However, international impulses can only account for part of the cyclical behaviour (since different economies have performed quite differently for given international conditions), and phenomena such as crises and bank runs do not come 'out of the blue' (see Kaminsky and Reinhart (1996)): while such events need not be triggered by large changes in opinions about fundamentals, a state of scepticism about those fundamentals seems a necessary condition for them to happen.[20] The analysis we have presented here does not deal with all the aspects of the previously referred cyclical episodes: in particular, we have not studied the specific features of the 'crisis' periods. But the discussion in Section 2 indicated that there was indeed ample room for very large revisions in perceived permanent incomes. In turn (as was argued in Section 4), revisions of beliefs about the future performance of an economy can produce substantial changes in the terms on which its residents can obtain credit. It does not seem far-fetched to assume that changing expectations about future real growth and relative prices contributed to the fluctuations in spending in those cases.

In our framework, people may reasonably believe that an economic expansion is 'sustainable' while it is driven in part by inconsistent expectations, or symmetrically, they can underestimate growth prospects and therefore spend below their real possibilities. If mistakes are being made, they will be discovered only over time (and possibly, a not-too-short period of time). The potential for errors need not derive from the lack of sophistication of agents, but rather from the difficulties inherent in understanding the processes that drive the variables of interest. Similar difficulties apply to the analyst. Therefore, one cannot easily predict the cyclical evolution: if prediction were simple, it would in fact contradict the argument. However, this does not make the argument lack content. Rather, the (quite commonplace) point that sometimes the signals that the economy delivers need not have a clear-cut interpretation indicates that it may be wrong to rule out errors on the part of agents on pure a priori grounds – and it gives actual meaning to the learning that the analyst conducts.

Policymakers acting in an economic transition of some sort must decide on the basis of their judgement about how the economy will perform; this, in turn, implies determining a view of how private agents form their expectations (see Greenspan (1997), also Bomfim (1996)). The problem arises even when policies have very specific objectives (or are bound by some rule to aim for them): for example, fiscal authorities whose only concern is to 'balance the books' over a certain time period have to forecast future revenues; this means that they must try to identify the economy's trend, and attempt to find out whether or not the current evolution conforms to that trend. This will require 'choosing a mode of analysis', probably from among several alternatives. The choice will not necessarily be optimal; that cannot be known in advance. But a choice is made, nevertheless (as is the case with private agents when they define their plans), and it will have macroeconomic effects. It seems therefore reasonable that policies recognize this fact, taking into account both their own uncertainties and those confronting private agents.

Notes

1 The per capital GDP in dollar terms has shown very large movements (after correcting for US inflation): it reached almost \$14000 (in 1996 prices) in 1980, fell to \$5700 two years later, and was only \$3500 at the end of the decade (during the hyperinflationary period); in 1994, it exceeded \$8000. Of course, these figures simply result from applying the current exchange rates to the nominal value of GDP; they do not necessarily reflect 'sustainable' levels of income. But this is precisely the problem that agents face in these fluctuations: they observe that their income has a certain purchasing power over traded goods (which can be quite different from what it was some time before), and must decide whether it can be extrapolated into the future. The significance of the movements in 'dollar incomes' (and, more generally, in wealth perceptions) in the context of Argentine cycles is analyzed in Heymann (1983, 1984). For a discussion of the late 1970s/early 1980s episode, see also Dornbusch and De Pablo (1989).

2 The trend rate for the two previous decades (1955–74) has been estimated at 1 per cent per year (Hanson and De Melo (1985)).

3 It has been argued that wealth effects were significant during this period: 'The land and real estate boom led to the perception of a permanent increase in wealth' (Hanson and De Melo (1985)).

4 This simplification implies that the analysis leaves aside precautionary savings behaviour, and flexibility preference effects. In the initial stages of a transition, it is likely that agents will recognize that their forecasts are uncertain, and will therefore choose to delay commitments until they can form more reliable expectations. For the sake of simplicity, we concentrate here on how agents may make 'point projections' of their future income, and on the effects of such projections on market behaviour.

5 In equation (6.2) (${}_tW^i_{it}$) indicates the level of wealth of individual i in period t, as perceived by that individual in that period; r denotes the interest rate.

6 We use this formulation as a straightforward way to represent the (common-sense) assumption that the opportunities of a given agent depend on the aggregate performance of the economy. The influence of total output on individual production may derive from technology or from other effects such as 'thick market' externalities (see Howitt and McAffee (1992)).

7 We have used this property to solve the optimization problem (6.2)–(6.6). The first order conditions for this problem define a non-linear difference equation. We

obtained approximate solutions numerically as the roots of a system of equations, assuming that the steady state is reached after 40 steps.

8 It may be noted that, if one makes the learning start with a set of parameters such that the final level of output and the speed of convergence match those of the actual perfect foresight path, this path is almost exactly reproduced under iterations of the learning model: successive observations validate the initial parameters. This means that the learning algorithm applied to the function specified in Equation (6.7) does not 'generate errors by itself'.

9 See, for example, Bernanke and Gertler (1989), Greenwald and Stiglitz (1993), Lamont (1995), Kiyotaki and Moore (1997). The traditional literature on the cyclical behaviour of credit markets is vast and extremely varied (themes from this literature are reconsidered from different perspectives in Leijonhufvud (1968) and Minsky (1975)). The argument (common to the several lines of analysis despite their wide differences) that financial fluctuations (and, a fortiori, 'financial crises') originate from biases or inconsistencies in expectations separates that traditional body of literature from much of the recent one.

10 Our main purpose here is to study credit conditions faced by private agents. We assume that loan contracts can be enforced (provided the borrower has enough resources to fulfil his/her obligations). We leave aside the particular problems associated with 'sovereign debt'.

11 The exercise starts with no outstanding debt. It would be simple to include a predetermined amount of 'inherited' assets (liabilities) due in period 1: in this case, for the purpose of determining the size of borrowing in period 1, the analogue for period 1 'income' would be the flow endowment plus (minus) the value of those assets (liabilities).

12 The possibility of different conjectures includes as a special case that of asymmetric information, but is not restricted to that case, since agents need not interpret the same set of data equally.

13 This rules out, for the sake of simplicity, the existence of monitoring costs and, hence, of agency problems as in Bernanke and Gertler (1989).

14 It may be interesting to note that, if the instantaneous utility is logarithmic, consumption in period 1 would be given by:

$$y_1 + b = c_1 = \frac{1}{1+\beta p^i}(y_1 + \frac{\bar{y}^i}{1+r}) \tag{6.12}$$

The expression is analogous to that which applies under perfect foresight: consumption is proportional to a measure of wealth, with a coefficient that depends on the rate of time preference. Here, 'wealth' is defined in such a way that the present value of future income would be represented by income in the good state, discounted at the quoted interest rate. The intuition is that, given that the agent has chosen to borrow in the range in which there is default in period 2 if the bad state occurs, s/he effectively 'does not own', his/her income in that state (consumption will be $\underline{c}$ irrespective of $\underline{y}$); in the good state, the relevant interest rate is r, because the debt will be wholly repaid. Also, it can be seen that the probability of the good state operates like a variable that shifts the rate of time preference: the agent acts as if the 'rate of impatience' was higher the lower is p^i.

15 Our discussion here has dealt with credit markets without considering financial intermediaries. This is clearly an important omission. McKinnon and Pill (1997) discuss an 'overborrowing syndrome' focusing on the expectations formed by banks. In that paper, intermediaries can make exact predictions, while the public misreads the economy's signals by attributing an increase in the willingness to lend by banks to an improvement in fundamentals rather than correctly interpreting that the banks respond to a disincentive generated by deposit guarantees. In our analysis, there need not be an asymmetry in the capacity to make forecasts.

16 The shift in the supply of credit would be manifested in lower interest rates for given risk types, and probably also in the inclusion as potential borrowers of agents that were previously 'redlined'. It may be noted that, if this last effect is important, there can be an increase in the observed rate of default, a rise in the measures of interest rate differentials among different groups of borrowers, and perhaps even an increase in the average level of quoted interest rates, although the overall credit risk in the economy has shrunk, since presumably borrowers who were rationed out of the market will now have access to loans at comparatively high interest rates and will show relatively large probabilities of default.

17 Except for 'unexpected shocks' to which agents have been attributing zero probability, and will (it is implicit in the argument) again consider as practical impossibilities once they have absorbed the 'news' of one such event.

18 Moreover, the multiplicity of possible perfect-foresight interpretations of the changes in some economic variables also poses problems, since each specific model has different implications for the future path of the system: should an individual conclude that a rise in current aggregate consumption signals future inflation (as in the credibility-based arguments), or should s/he anticipate a higher total output? In addition, that same multiplicity goes against the often heard statement that introducing misperceptions into a model means that 'anything can be rationalized', and that this is not the case under the rational expectations assumption. When one is analyzing a certain episode (without knowing the future), a perfect foresight argument that rationalizes observed behaviour on the basis of expectations of some future event simply postulates that this event will in fact happen: one avoids a discussion about how the beliefs of agents may have been formed, and about whether the evolution of the system is likely to confirm those beliefs.

19 In this regard, it seems convenient to distinguish clearly between external, and 'exogenous' changes. In a rational expectations model, changes in the international interest rate should not qualify automatically as shocks: if the hypothesis is taken at face value, agents would form their expectations using a model that encompasses the 'systematic components' of the relevant variables belonging to foreign economies.

20 In some models, 'bad' equilibria exist in some economic configurations, and not in others. For example, Sachs *et al.* (1996) argue that balance-of-payments crises are possible for sufficiently low levels of the ratio of foreign reserves to the liabilities of the financial system. However, the value of this coefficient does not by itself determine the probability of a crisis. One could find cases where, say, a fall in the reserves/M2 coefficient may be interpreted as 'good', rather than 'bad' news; consider, for instance, a situation where the public has

(correctly) more optimistic views about credit risks, and shifts its demand from base money to deposits.

References

Agénor, P. and J. Aizenman (1997) 'Contagion and Volatility with Imperfect Credit Markets', Working paper, IMF, Washington, DC.

Bernanke, B. and M. Gertler (1989) 'Agency Costs, Net Worth and Business Fluctuations', *American Economic Review*, vol. 79, pp. 14–31.

Bomfim, A. (1996) 'Forecasting the Forecasts of Others: Expectational Heterogeneity and Aggregate Dynamics', Finance and Economic Discussion Papers Series, Federal Reserve, Washington, DC.

Calvo, G. (1986) 'Temporary Stabilization, Predetermined Exchange Rates', *Journal of Political Economy*, vol. 94, pp. 1319–29.

Calvo, G., L. Leiderman and C. Reinhart (1993) 'Capital Inflows and Real Exchange Rate Appreciations in Latin America: The Role of External Factors', *IMF Staff Papers*, vol. 40, pp. 865–7.

Calvo, G. and E. Mendoza (1996) 'Mexico's Balance-of-payments Crisis: a Chronicle of a Death Foretold', *Journal of International Economics*, vol. 41, pp. 235–64.

Calvo, G. and C. Vegh (1993) 'Exchange Rate Based Stabilizations under Imperfect Credibility', in H. Frisch and Wörgötter A. (eds), *Open Economy Macroeconomics* (London: Macmillan) pp. 3–28.

Cole, H. and Kehoe, T. (1996) 'A Self Fulfilling Model of Mexico 1994–1995 Debt Crisis', *Journal of International Economics*, vol. 41, pp. 309–30.

Dornbusch, R. and J. C. de Pablo (1989) 'Debt and Macroeconomic Instability in Argentina', in J. Sachs (ed.), *Developing Country Debt and the World Economy* (Cambridge, Mass. National Bureau of Economic Research).

Edwards, S. and A. Cox Edwards (1987) *Monetarism and Liberalization: The Chilean Experiment* (University of Chicago Press).

Evans, G. and S. Honkapohja (1993) 'Adaptive Forecasts, Hysteresis and Endogenous Fluctuations', Working paper, Federal Reserve, San Francisco.

Evans, G. and S. Honkapohja (1995) 'Adaptive Learning and Expectational Stability: An Introduction', in A. Kirman and M. Salmon (eds), *Learning and Rationality in Economics* (Oxford: Basil Blackwell) pp. 102–26.

Fernandez, R. (1985) 'The Expectations Management Approach to Stabilization in Argentina during 1976–82', *World Development*, vol. 13, pp. 871–92.

Frydman, R. and E. Phelps (eds) (1983) *Individual Forecasting and Aggregate Outcomes, Rational Expectations Examined* (Cambridge University Press).

Greenspan, A. (1997) 'Statement to the US Congress', 27 February.

Greenwald, B. and J. Stiglitz (1993) 'Financial Market Imperfections and Business Cycles', *Quarterly Journal of Economics*, vol. 108, pp. 77–114.

Hanson, J. and J. de Melo (1985) 'External Shocks, Financial Reforms, and Stabilization Attempts in Uruguay during 1974–1983', *World Development*, vol. 13, pp. 917–39.

Harberger, A. (1985) 'Observations on the Chilean Economy, 1973–1983', *Economic Development and Cultural Change*, vol. 34, pp. 451–62.

Heymann, D. (1983) 'A Study in Economic Instability The Case of Argentina', PhD. dissertation, University of California at Los Angeles.

Heymann, D. (1984) 'Precios Relativos, Riqueza y Producción', *Ensayos Económicos*, March.

Heymann, D. (1994) 'Sobre la Interpretación de la Cuenta Corriente', *Economía Mexicana*, vol. 3, pp. 31–59.
Heymann, D. and P. Sanguinetti (1998) 'Business Cycles from Misperceived Trends', *Economic Notes*, vol. 27(2), pp. 205–32.
Hodgman, D. (1960) 'Credit Risk and Credit Rationing', *Quarterly Journal of Economics*, vol. 76, pp. 258–78.
Howitt, P. and P. McAffee (1992) 'Animal Spirits', *American Economic Review*, vol. 82, pp. 493–507.
Jaffee, D. and J. Stiglitz (1990) 'Credit Rationing' in B. Friedman and F. Hahn (eds), *Handbook of Monetary Economics*, vol. II (Amsterdam: Elsevier).
Kaminsky, G. and C. Reinhart (1996) 'The Twin Crises: The Causes of Banking and Balance of Payments Problems', Mimeo, University of Maryland.
Kaufman, M. (1996) 'An Incursion into the Confidence Crisis-Credit Rationing-Real Activity Channel', Working Paper, Central Bank of Argentina.
Kiguel, M. and N. Liviatan (1992) 'The Business Cycle Associated with Exchange Rate Based Stabilization', *World Bank Economic Review*, vol. 6, pp. 279–305.
Kiyotaki, N. and J. Moore (1997) 'Credit Cycles', *Journal of Political Economy*, vol. 105, pp. 211–48.
Krugman, P. (1979) 'A Model of Balance-of-Payments Crises', *Journal of Money, Credit and Banking*, vol. 11, pp. 311–25.
Kydland, F. and C. Zarazaga (1997) 'Is the Business Cycle of Argentina "Different"?', Working paper, Federal Reserve, Dallas, Texas.
Lamont, O. (1995) 'Corporate Debt Overhang and Macroeconomic Expectations', *American Economic Review*, vol. 85, pp. 1106–17.
Leijonhufvud, A. (1968) '*On Keynesian Economics and the Economics of Keynes*, (Oxford University Press).
Leijonhufvud, A. (1981) *Information and Co-ordination* (Oxford University Press).
Leijonhufvud, A. (1993) 'Towards a Not-Too-Rational Macroeconomics', *Southern Economic Journal*, vol. 60, pp. 1–13.
Maia, J. and J. Ortiz (1995) 'Economic Openness, External Financing and Sustained Growth', *Estudios de Economía*, vol. 22, pp. 277–326.
Marcet, A. and T. Sargent (1989) 'Least-Square Learning and the Dynamics of Hyperinflation', in W. Barnett, J. Geweke and K. Shell (eds), *Economic Complexity, Chaos, Sunspots, Bubbles and Nonlinearity* (Cambridge University Press).
McKinnon, R. and H. Pill (1997) 'Credible Economic Liberalizations and Overborrowing', *American Economic Review*, vol. 87, pp. 189–93.
Mendoza, E. and M. Uribe (1996) 'The Syndrome of Exchange-Rate-Based Stabilization and the Uncertain Duration of Currency Pegs', Working paper, Federal Reserve, Washington DC.
Minsky, H. (1975) *John Maynard Keynes* (New York: Columbia University Press).
Obstfeld, M. and K. Rogoff (1994) 'The Intertemporal Approach to the Current Account', National Bureau of Economic Research Working paper No. 4893, Cambridge Mass.
Ortiz, G. (1991) 'Mexico beyond the Debt Crisis: Toward Sustainable Growth with Price Stability', in M. Bruno, S. Fischer, E. Helpman and N. Liviatan (eds), *Lessons of Economic Stabilization and Its Aftermath* (Cambridge, Mass.: MIT Press).
Rebelo, S. and C. Vegh (1995) 'Real Effects of Exchange Base Stabilization: An Analysis of Competing Theories', *NBER Macroeconomics Annual* (Cambridge, Mass: National Bureau of Economic Research).

Reinhart, C. and C. Vegh (1995) 'Nominal Interest Rate, Consumption Booms and Lack of Credibility: A Quantitative Examination', *Journal of Development Economics*, vol. 46, pp. 357–78.

Roldos, J. (1995) 'Supply-Side Effects of Disinflation Programs', *IMF Staff Papers*, vol. 42, pp. 158–83.

Sachs, J., A. Tornell, and A. Velasco (1996) 'The Mexican Peso Crisis, Sudden Death or Death Foretold?', *Journal of International Economics*, vol. 41, pp. 265–83.

Santaella, J. and A. Vela (1996) 'The Mexican Disinflation Program: An Exchange-Based Stabilization', Working paper, WP/96/24, IMF, Washington, DC.

Sargent, T. (1993) *Bounded Rationality in Macroeconomics* (Oxford University Press).

Stiglitz, J. and A. Weiss (1981) 'Credit Rationing in Markets with Imperfect Information', *American Economic Review*, vol. 71, pp. 393–410.

Talvi, E. (1995) 'Exchange-Rate-Based Stabilization with Endogenous Fiscal Response', Working paper, Interamerican Development Bank.

Uribe, M. (1997) 'Exchange-Rate-Based Inflation Stabilization: The Initial Real Effects of Credible Plans', *Journal of Monetary Economics*, vol. 39, pp. 197–221.

Vaz, D. (1997) 'On the Macroeconomic Consequences of Banking Crises: The Cases of Argentina, Chile and Uruguay', Mimeo, University of California at Los Angeles.

Comment

Pier Luigi Sacco
University of Bologna, Italy

1 Discussion

The main message behind the Heymann–Kaufman–Sanguinetti chapter (henceforth HKS) is that, even in a relatively simple theoretical framework, 'complex' adjustment to external shocks may occur, giving rise to a somewhat typical pattern under the form of a credit/spending cycle. At the heart of such complexity are the cognitive limitations of economic agents in tracing perturbations back to their roots and in taking immediately the most appropriate counteractions. In particular, HKS focus on the effect of a single, isolated shock. However, once one realizes that external shocks are seldom really isolated, the essential question becomes: how can we take account of agents' tentative reactions to perturbation processes with a realistic degree of complexity?

This is, of course, a very old theme in the history of economic analysis. The idea of a credit/spending cycle driven by agents' misperceptions is at least as old as Marshall (1879, 1887) – see also Delli Gatti and Gallegati (1992). Marshall's dynamic mechanism is based on the self-fulfilling character of price expectations that pump up profit expectations in the expansionary phase of the cycle, thereby boosting credit and spending, into an excessive credit exposition that forces credit contraction and a subsequent deflation process. In Marshall, as in HKS, the crucial point is that the reaction to the external shock caused by individual perceptions and decisions moves in the 'wrong' direction, thus eventually exacerbating adjustment costs. This basic mechanism has undergone countless variations in the history of business fluctuations theory (see, for example, Screpanti and Zamagni (1995) for a short review). Looking at agents' misperceptions, and more generally at bounded rationality as a primary source of business fluctuations, is a constant concern of economic theorists, running across and beyond the new classical macroeconomics revolution (see, for example, Leijonhufvud (1993), Minford (1997)).

Why, then, should economic agents do wrong in the first place? An answer to this question amounts to embedding it in the more general theoretical framework of learning processes. Although massive, recent research on learning is, however, still in its infancy and cannot provide illuminating, all-encompassing arguments in this respect. We must therefore base our reasoning on small amounts of non-systematic theoretical and empirical knowledge regarding the complexities of learning and of its effects on aggregate macroeconomic phenomena.

Once we take the issue seriously, we cannot but realize that HKS are making a first stab at a quite far-reaching line of research, and that the complex patterns of adjustment they illustrate in their model seem to be among the least paradoxical: after all, in the HKS model, eventual convergence to the 'fundamental' equilibrium is reached. Farmer (1995) surveys a large literature focused on the idea that macroeconomic equilibria themselves (and not only convergence processes) may be basically expectations-driven. Kurz (1997) goes on to deny any theoretical dignity to the very notion of 'objective' structural knowledge, upon which all rational expectations models are built to some degree, to argue that economic fluctuations are entirely endogenous and that individual beliefs may only be constrained by internal consistency conditions, and that volatility may be the normal state of things even for efficient economic systems (see also Leijonhufvud (1997)). The consequence is that, at a very basic theoretical level, it is enough that agents believe that the data-generating process they have to learn about is non-stationary for the resulting economic system to be completely non-stationary: the perception of dynamic complexity turns out to be self-fulfilling for economic agents with reasonable computational and cognitive constraints.

Indeed, it is the very idea of a reasonably articulated economic policy that provides enough room for economic agents to expect substantial complexity, if not perpetual change, in their economic environment: as shown by Kurz's 'operational' learning models, actual learning requires relatively long sequences of data generated by a stable underlying structure to achieve regularity and reliability of individual inferences, and policy shocks are in fact meant to change the underlying structure to some degree. This should not, however, induce theorists to think of policy shocks in entirely negative terms. One can certainly find, as has been done by, for example, Sargent (1986), paradigmatic examples in the history of economic policies in which policymakers tied their hands with easy-to-understand, credible pre-commitments to fixed policy rules obtaining huge stabilizing effects on a previously chaotic economy. On the other hand, it is hard to maintain that such a recipe should work in general (see, for example, Heymann and Leijonhufvud (1995)): it is perhaps more sensible to aim at a policy design planned in the light of the dynamic complexity of the pattern of adjustment of the economy, rather than in spite of (or against) it. Unless we constrain the decision-makers to reason in equilibrium terms by choosing objective functions that reflect preference for stability, and unless we constrain interaction among agents to occur under restrictive equilibrium conditions as in the Walrasian tâtonnement process, we must expect that the system dynamic will spend most of its time away from equilibrium (see Aoki (1996)): the correct benchmark for policy design and evaluation must have a substantial dynamic nature (see Saari (1996) for a radical point of view).

Given these premises, it is clear that, in perspective, a satisfactory modelling of the bounded rationality of agents will have to go beyond the statement of a fixed, 'mechanical' learning rule. Although boundedly rational, the cognitive mechanisms of agents can be complex and sophisticated. A clear case in point is the importance of analogical reasoning for boundedly rational inferences, an aspect that is emphasized, for example, in case-based decision theory (see Gilboa and Schmeidler (1995, 1997)). Agents' categorization of events is important for business fluctuations. If their past experience, and thus their mental framework of cases, is focused mainly on 'bad' states, agents will, say, tend to be pessimistic when they are called upon to interpret 'ambiguous' situations where data show clear signs neither of recovery nor of stagnation of the economic system; similarly, they could be very optimistic when facing an evidence of recovery that would be interpreted more cautiously by agents with a less biased background of experience, and so on. Categorization and framing effects are therefore likely to be quite relevant in explaining those 'inertia', 'euphoria' or 'panic' phenomena that are outstanding entries in the list of stylized facts behind business-cycle theories.

But analogical reasoning (just to stick to this one among the many 'hot lines' of research in bounded rationality) is difficult to grasp by means of traditional modelling approaches. Here comes, then, a new generation of models building on more flexible, self-adjusting classes of adaptive algorithms that can perform sophisticated inferences such as those of analogical reasoning and many more: neural networks (see, for example, Hertz *et al.* (1991), Sargent (1993)) and genetic algorithms (see, for example, Mitchell (1996), Bullard and Duffy (1998)). This is not the place for an extensive review of these new techniques, but it is relatively easy to conjecture that they will play a growing role in the coming research on bounded rationality in macroeconomic settings.

Our previous considerations suggest that we are witnessing a major point of departure from the established modelling practice about business-cycle fluctuations, and that the HKS model has a place in this innovative stream of research. We have reason to expect that this research will eventually discard new-classical-style 'equilibrium' reasoning in terms of an objective 'true' model of the economy, in favour of a more general approach that contemplates a variety of competing models, and thus of competing patterns of adjustment, each of which may become self-fulfilling under suitable, and possibly complex, conditions, only to become eventually self-defeating as agents learn enough to anticipate it systematically: in this view, one should never expect in principle the 'same' reaction from the economic system to the 'same' policies in 'similar' conditions. But this is far from being a frustrating state of things for economic policy: as argued by Bowden (1991), a sophisticated-enough policymaker could exploit it to his/her own advantage.

What we perceive as the economy's law of motion is, then, the self-organizing outcome of the interaction among individual subjective models and beliefs. In Aoki's (1996) 'field' model, for instance, agents endowed with different models talk to each other and tend to adopt models that induce the most rewarding actions, given the status quo. The actual law of motion will then depend on how the distribution of models (and of the corresponding individual actions) evolves over time; it is then far from obvious that the 'best' models (whatever this may mean) will eventually emerge. In the next section we shall present, for illustrative purposes, a very simple, original model that describes these sorts of effects, making relatively little use of mathematical technicality.

2 A simple model of the competition among economic models

Consider a 'large economy' theoretical setting in which a continuum of agents have to choose an action x from a set X; the actual consequence of x depends on the realization of an external variable y (state of nature) from the set Y. To choose the most convenient action x as a function of y, each agent is endowed with a subjective economic model M_i that uniquely prescribes some x given y: $x = M_i(y)$. Let q denote the distribution of the various subjective models across the population of agents; specifically, $q_i \varepsilon [0, 1]$ is the share of agents adopting model i with $q_1 + q_2 + q_3 = 1$. The payoff to an agent adopting model i will be given by $\Pi_i(x, \mathbf{q})$. For simplicity, it will be written in separable form, as a product between an idiosynchratic payoff coefficient $\pi_i(x)$ and a given function of $\boldsymbol{q}$, $s_i(\boldsymbol{q})$, namely $\Pi_i(x, \boldsymbol{q}) = \pi_i(x)\, s_i(\boldsymbol{q})$.

Consider, for simplicity, the case where only three alternative models are available and only three alternative states of nature y, y' and y'' are possible. When y is observed, the three models M_1, M_2 M_3 all disagree in the sense that they prescribe different actions x_1, x_2, x_3, yielding different payoff coefficients π_1, π_2, π_3. When y' is observed, models 1 and 2 agree, yielding the same payoff coefficient $\pi'_1 = \pi'_2$, whereas model 3 prescribes a different action yielding a different payoff coefficient π'_3. Finally, when y'' is observed, models 2 and 3 agree, yielding the same payoff coefficient, $\pi''_2 = \pi''_3$ whereas model 1 prescribes a different action, yielding π''_1.

Assume now that the dynamics of adoption of the various models across the economy are as follows: models which turn out to be relatively more rewarding given the current pattern of adoption are chosen by an increasing proportion of the agents, and the reverse for models that are relatively less rewarding. This assumption may be described in evolutionary game-theoretic terms by generic payoff-monotonic selection dynamics (see, for example, Weibull (1995)), and specifically by the so-called replicator dynamics that prescribe that shares q_i evolve proportionately to the difference between the model's performance and the average social performance given by the weighted average of the performances of the available models (where weights are given by their actual shares in the population). In other words, according to the replicator dynamics, models become more popular, the more they do 'better than average', and conversely. In mathematical terms, we have $dq_i/dt = q_i[\Pi_i - \Pi^*]$, $i = 1, 2, 3$, where d denotes a derivative and Π^* is the average social performance $q_1 \Pi_1 + q_2 \Pi_2 + q_3 \Pi_3$.

If we focus on the co-ordination scenario in which the function $s_i(\mathbf{q})$ is such that the payoff of a given model is increasing in the share of adopters of that model, and in the share of agents adopting models that agree with it at the given observed state of nature, one can write $\Pi_1 = \pi_1(q_1 - q_2 - q_3)p + \pi'_1(q_1 + q_2 - q_3)p' + \pi''_1(q_1 - q_2 - q_3)p''$, and similarly for Π_2, Π_3, where p is the probability of y, p' is the probability of y' and p'' of y'', with $p + p' + p'' = 1$. It is then relatively easy to check that, under the replicator dynamics, a multi-stable pattern emerges such that, if one starts 'close enough' to the equilibrium where all agents adopt model i, this model will eventually prevail. The ultimate success of a given model then depends essentially on initial conditions; that is, on how models are originally distributed across the population. One can show that the size of the basins of attraction of the three models is determined by the position of the interior stationary equilibrium $\boldsymbol{q}^*$ in the unit simplex; the further away $\boldsymbol{q}^*$ from the equilibrium in which model *i* prevails, the larger the basin of attraction of model *i*. Specifically, in the equi-probable case $p = p' = p''$, model 2 has the largest basin of attraction in that it is the one that is more likely to agree with some other model, exploiting the synergetic effect of the agreement: remember that, in co-ordination contexts, reward is proportional to the amount of co-ordination. The size of the basins of the various models may be modified in intuitive ways acting on the probabilities of the states of nature and on payoff coefficients.

The above result suggests that, in the simple framework of our 'minimal' description of the economy, the actual model that prevails depends essentially on the social pattern of opinions; that is, on how many agents agree on each specific model, and on the relative positioning of the models (that is, on how 'close' they are to each other in the space of available actions for economic agents), without any reference to any underlying 'objective' level of knowledge.

The implications of this social dynamic of models for macroeconomic adjustment issues are easy to imagine: think, for example, of the rival models as different views of the impact of public debt-financed government spending on individual wealth prospects (as a function of general macroeconomic conditions y). Depending on which view is prevailing across the economy, the macroeconomic effect of the policy shock as mediated by agents' perceptions and consequent actions will be quite different. Rather than being a positive theoretical endeavour, however, our argument is, of course, only a thought-provoking example that will, one hopes, stimulate further research along the lines discussed in this comment.

References

Aoki, M. (1996) *New Approaches to Macroeconomic Modelling. Evolutionary Stochastic Dynamics, Multiple Equilibria, and Externalities as Field Effects* (Cambridge University Press).

Bowden, R. (1991) *Statistical Games and Human Affairs* (Cambridge University Press).

Bullard, J. and J. Duffy (1998) 'A Model of Learning and Emulation with Artificial Adaptive Agents', *Journal of Economic Dynamics and Control*, vol. 22, pp. 179–207.

Delli Gatti, D. and M. Gallegati (1992) 'Credit, Confidence and Speculation: A Marshallian Perspective on Business Fluctuations', *Quaderni di Storia dell'Economia Politica,* vol. 10, pp. 451–83.

Farmer, R. (1995) *The Macroeconomics of Self-Fulfilling Prophecies* (Cambridge, Mass.: MIT Press).

Gilboa, I. and D. Schmeidler (1995) 'Case-Based Decision Theory', *Quarterly Journal of Economics*, vol. 110, pp. 605–39.

Gilboa, I. and D. Schmeidler (1997) 'Act Similarity in Case-Based Decision Theory', *Economic Theory*, vol. 9, pp. 47–61.

Hertz, J., Krogh, A. and R. G. Palmer (1991) *Introduction to the Theory of Neural Computation* (Redwood City, Calif. Addison-Wesley).
Heymann, D. and A. Leijonhufvud (1995) *High Inflation* (Oxford University Press).
Kurz, M. (ed.) (1997) *Endogenous Economic Fluctuations. Studies in the Theory of Rational Beliefs* (Berlin: Springer).
Leijonhufvud, A. (1993) 'Towards a Not-Too-Rational Macroeconomics', *Southern Economic Journal*, vol. 60, pp. 1–13.
Leijonhufvud, A. (1997) 'Macroeconomics and Complexity: Inflation Theory', in R. Viale (ed.), *Cognitive Economics*, Quaderni Lascomes (Milan: La Rosa), pp. 175–92.
Marshall, A. (with M. P. Marshall) (1879) *The Economics of Industry* (London: Macmillan).
Marshall, A. (1887) 'Remedies for Fluctuations of General Prices', *Contemporary Review* (March); reprinted in A. C. Pigou (ed.) (1925), *Memorials of Alfred Marshall* (London: Macmillan).
Minford, P. (1997) 'Macroeconomics: Before and After Rational Expectations', in B. Snowdon and H. R. Vane (eds.), *Reflections on the Development of Modern Macroeconomics* (Cheltenham: Edward Elgar), pp. 103–27.
Mitchell, M. (1996) *An Introduction to Genetic Algorithms* (Cambridge, Mass.: MIT Press).
Saari, D. G. (1996) 'The Ease of Generating Chaotic Behavior in Economics', *Chaos, Solitons and Fractals*, vol. 7, pp. 2267–78.
Sargent, T. (1986) *Rational Expectations and Inflation* (New York: Harper & Row).
Sargent, T. (1993) *Bounded Rationality in Macroeconomics* (Oxford: Oxford University Press).
Screpanti, E. and S. Zamagni (1995) *Outline of an History of Economic Thought* (Oxford: Clarendon Press).
Weibull, J. W. (1995) *Evolutionary Game Theory* (Cambridge, Mass.: MIT Press).

Comment

Jean-Luc Gaffard
University of Nice Sophia-Antipolis, France

Referring to Hicks's *Value and Capital*, Plosser (1989, p. 53) asserts that it is logically impossible to attribute an important portion of fluctuations to market failure without an understanding of all the sorts of fluctuations that would be observed in the absence of the hypothesized market failure. The view adopted by Heymann, Kaufman and Sanguinetti (HKS) in their chapter is, clearly, the opposite of this. In fact, they consider that there exist two distinct lines of reasoning: a standard line that is adapted to the analysis of smooth changes which do not lead the economy far from the steady state; and another that is better suited to the analysis of specific episodes characterized by strong changes in fundamentals. In the latter case, misperceptions about the future outcomes of current plans are considered as the real source of business fluctuations.

The contribution of this work towards a new analytical approach to business cycles, and its limitations, makes it possible to stress the analytical issues that economists interested in understanding business cycles should tackle in the future.

Day (1993) contrasted two kinds of dynamics: adapted equilibrium dynamics and adaptive evolutionary dynamics. The equilibrium approach focuses on the way economies work when agents are adapted optimally to their environment and react optimally to any shock. At the opposite extreme, the adaptive evolutionary approach focuses on 'the characterization of the way economies work when they work out of equilibrium' (Day (1993, p. 21)).

The HKS approach does not belong to the first class of models. But it does not really belong to the second either. It is only a step in the direction of building an adaptive approach. We intend to discuss this point to bring to light what such an approach should be. The so-called adaptive evolutionary dynamics should be an analysis that does not consist in adding restrictions (rigidities) to an equilibrium framework (Lucas (1980)). It calls for the building up of a completely new framework capable of taking into account all the elements of equilibrium processes.

The departure from equilibrium dynamics leads to 'algorithmic representation of both decision rules and learning procedures (including expectations formation)' (Leijonhufvud (1993, p. 5)). This is the kind of representation of decision processes that HKS propose to substitute for the standard optimizing behaviour. Misperceptions, expectations and learning mechanisms determine the profile of the evolution.

The first implication of focusing on sequentially articulated strategies should be that markets can no longer be represented as auction or bidding games in the sense that instantaneous price adjustments allow the markets themselves to clear systematically. Yet, in the HKS model, misperceptions do not prevent the market from clearing. The transitional increase in consumption spending causes a trade deficit associated with an increasing external debt. The only information that individuals process is the gap between the unknown steady-state output and the current output. Now, because the individuals' perceptions are not accurate, prices should fail to clear markets. Disequilibria should come to the surface through the appearance of stocks, which should be the relevant information to be processed by the agents.

An adaptive approach has a financial aspect. This point comes to light clearly in the HKS analysis. Changes in the perception of future income by lenders and borrowers are shown to be the significant channel through which spending is (over)stimulated. However, the main effect of misperceptions and changes in credit conditions is that the structure of production is no longer in line with the intertemporal plans of consumers. Analyzing such a situation requires the building of a theory of production which, in Hicks's words, is really 'in time'. As a matter of fact, the effective evolution of the economy does not depend only on the cognitive abilities of decision-makers but also on the complexity of the phenomenon of production. Misperceptions lead to wrong decisions. And wrong decisions result in new constraints which determine the range for future decisions. HKS's modelling does not consider such a sequence. Adjustment costs cannot stand for the real, irreversible effects of wrong decisions. As a consequence, the only effect of misperceptions is to delay the adjustment to a steady state that is determined exogenously. Indeed, mistakes are embodied in the level of foreign debt, but no feedback effects of an increasing foreign debt are brought to light. Therefore, the introduction of misperceptions turns out to be a simple way of replicating some stylized facts with a model, the stationary point of which is an intertemporal equilibrium. A better understanding of the role of misperceptions would require an appreciation of the importance of the time lag in building new productive capacity if the length of the construction phase not only involves additional costs but also has an effect on the final configuration of that productive capacity – that is, on the fundamentals which define the new steady state. Within this perspective, the analytical issues become substantially more complicated, but it is possible to deal with them by making use of a neo-Austrian type of model (Hicks (1973), Amendola and Gaffard (1998)).

Finally, an adaptive approach has some implications for economic policy. The HKS paper sets the debate 'Discretion versus Rules in economic policy' in a particular perspective. On the one hand, it leads implicitly to consider that economic policy must not consist of interventions that result in further shocks that aggravate misperceptions. On the other hand, it underlines the necessity for policymakers to carry out appropriate actions. What is true is that policy interventions must be consistent with the behaviour of individual agents. This had led Heymann and Leijonhufvud (1995) to talk of 'Rules and Discretion' instead of 'Rules versus Discretion'. For that, it would be necessary to go deeply into the foundations of economic policy. First of all, by definition, out of equilibrium there is no given configuration of the economy to be used as a benchmark for intervention. This makes the difference between an out-of-equilibrium approach and the so-called neoclassical synthesis. Moreover, out-of-equilibrium authorities do not possess complete information, and they do not possess it at the right moment. As a consequence, a policy of fine-tuning is not possible. And a policy that would result in adding new shocks to the existing other ones must be rejected. Economic policy should be aimed at solving co-ordination problems. This implies that policy interventions must be consistent with the expectations of individual agents. Any surprise must be avoided, and a gradual approach is required for any intervention.

By and large, the task assigned by Plosser to the economists has been carried out. We now have to put on our research agenda the task of going back to the disequilibrium analysis of business cycles. This is one of the messages implicitly delivered by HKS. Indeed, it must be clear that the task of building a complete out-of-equilibrium framework is a very difficult one. When pursued extensively it will lead to models of great complexity and variety. As Hicks put it, 'the "equilibrium" forces are (relatively) dependable; the "disequilibrium" forces are much less dependable', and he added: 'we can invent rules for their working, and calculate the behaviour of the resulting model; but such calculations are of illustrative value only' (Hicks (1985, p. 87)).

References

Amendola, M. and J.-L. Gaffard (1998) *Out of Equilibrium* (Oxford: Clarendon Press).

Day, R. H. (1993) 'Non linear Dynamics and Evolutionary Economics', in R. Day and Peng Chen (eds), *Non linear Dynamics and Evolutionary Economics* (Oxford University Press).

Heymann, D. and A. Leijonhufvud (1995) *High Inflation* (Oxford University Press).

Hicks, J. R. (1973) *Capital and Time* (Oxford: Clarendon Press).

Hicks, J. R. (1985) *Methods of Dynamic Economics* (Oxford: Clarendon Press).

Leijonhufvud, A. (1993) 'Towards Not Too Rational Macroeconomics', *Southern Economic Journal*, vol. 60, pp. 1–13.

Lucas, R. E. (1980) 'Methods and Problems in Business Cycle Theory', *Journal of Money, Credit, and Banking*, vol. 12, no. 4, pp. 696–715.

Plosser, C. (1989) 'Understanding Business Cycles', *Journal of Economic Perspectives*, vol. 3, pp. 51–77.

7
Monetary Policy and the Macroeconomics of 'Soft' Growth

Jean-Paul Fitoussi
Institut d'Études Politiques de Paris, France

After the Second World War, European construction and the fulfilment of the national economic policy objectives of European Economic Community (EEC) countries formed a virtuous circle: the pursuit of policy objectives was facilitated by European construction, and the latter was greatly helped by the achievement of both full employment and rapid growth. The EEC was a means to the ultimate ends of economic activity; that is, rising standards of living in a cohesive society that could offer all its members a job and an opportunity for progress. The question 'Why Europe?' had such a self-evident answer that it was not even raised.

With the 1990s, the context clearly changed dramatically. Full employment and growth and the European construction seem to be unrelated, if not conflicting, objectives. Building Europe seems to require structurally restrictive policies in a context of mass unemployment, low inflation and slow growth. People's expectations are no longer for rising standards of living, but for decreasing social protection within the framework of a leaner welfare state. Europe is no longer seen as the road to prosperity, the means for faster economic growth, but rather an end in itself, whatever sacrifices it might require of the citizenry. It may well be that this radical change has some rationale in the wake of the globalization of markets and the resulting intensification of competition, but this is not really explained, and people are still waiting for some explanation of why policies should be so restrictive in a context where inflation is no longer a credible threat. It may also be that the next steps in the building of Europe require a bigger investment, and hence some sacrifice of current consumption whose fruits will appear. But the sacrifices seem so unevenly distributed that there is now a widespread feeling that there will be permanent losers, and quite a large number of them.

One could argue that this problem is a classical problem in economic policy: if European construction becomes an independent objective, in its own right, then each single country will have one more objective than instruments to reach them. This will normally lead to policy dilemmas, which will be solved only when European construction (that is, monetary union) is achieved. In the interim, some other policy objective must be given up – say, growth – and if the remaining instruments are not adapted to the new, lower rate of growth consistent with European construction, this will lead to mounting disequilibria in public finances.

Ex post, it is now argued that the origin of the slump in Europe lies in the past activism of the European states, which is now crystallized in mounting public debts, huge budget deficits and high taxation. The 'eurosclerosis' explanation – which had already been invoked at the beginning of the 1980s – is rejuvenated, with, this time, public finance being the main suspect. Hence, the Maastricht criteria have had the merit of highlighting the impotence to which this evolution has led, and by now each government is convinced that it has to cut public expenditure enough to allow both a reduction in deficits and a decrease in taxes. Even if the debate about the causes of high interest rates is far from concluded, governments everywhere in Europe take as gospel the contention that the main cause of high interest rates is public debt.

It takes only a modicum of historical sensitivity, however, to see that alternative explanations are available, especially in periods of disinflation. That both short- and long-term real interest rates were at historically high levels in almost all countries in the early part of the 1930s is also an inescapable fact. And by now, no one would argue that this reflected insufficient saving: it has always been hard to prove the existence of excess demand in periods of declining inflation rates. If the supply-side recommendations of Robert Mundell – use restrictive monetary policy to fight inflation and expansionary budgetary policy to reduce unemployment – were implemented, however, such an outcome would be possible. (But in Europe something is lacking for one to argue that the same constellation prevails, namely a sufficient rate of growth in both output and employment.)

Of course, it is also possible to refer to structural factors to explain both slow growth and rising unemployment in a context of excess demand: in the presence of adverse supply shocks, wage inflexibility may lead to an increase in the 'natural rate of unemployment', a decrease in profitability and thus, through a permanent decrease in the investment ratio, to a lower rate of potential growth. A process of this kind was surely at work in the late 1970s and early 1980s, when oil shocks led to an increase in

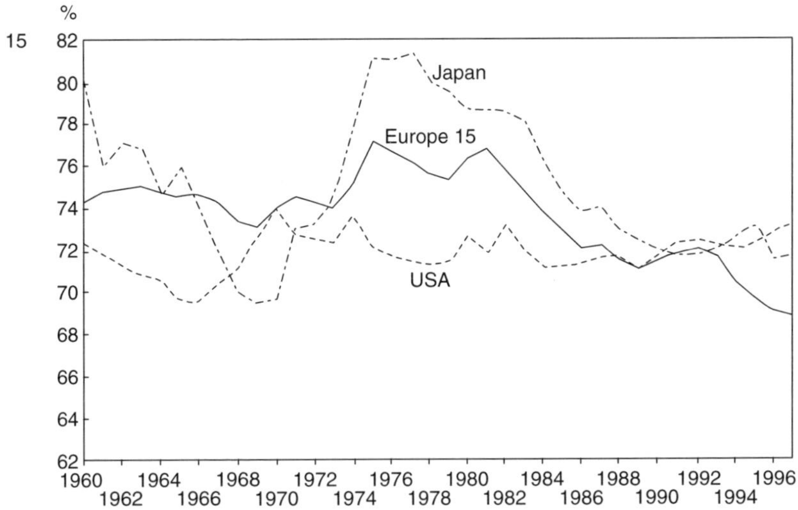

Source: EC.
Figure 7.1 Wage share in Europe, the USA and Japan

labour's share in national income throughout Europe. But since then this focus has been more than neutralized: the real price of oil has declined sharply – it is at the time of writing below its first-oil-shock level – and, perhaps more importantly, the share of wages has everywhere declined to well below that of the 1960s. Thus the wage share is now 8 points lower than in 1975, but strikingly, more than 5 points below the average value for the 1960s. It is hard, indeed, to make sense of the assumption of real wage rigidity to explain unemployment in a context where the share of profit is increasing.

There is no question that monetary policy since the end of the 1980s has been very restrictive, but the question of whether fiscal policy was too expansionary remains open. Of course, it is not easy to measure the tightness of fiscal policies and hence to give a definitive evaluation of the course of fiscal policy. There is no agreement among economists on the best way to measure potential growth, and hence structural deficits. But whatever increase there may have been around the turn of the 1990s, it has not prevented growth from slowing down and inflation from decelerating: five records were achieved in the 1990s: the highest level of unemployment in Europe since the Second World War; the lowest average rate of growth for a five-year period since the war; the lowest

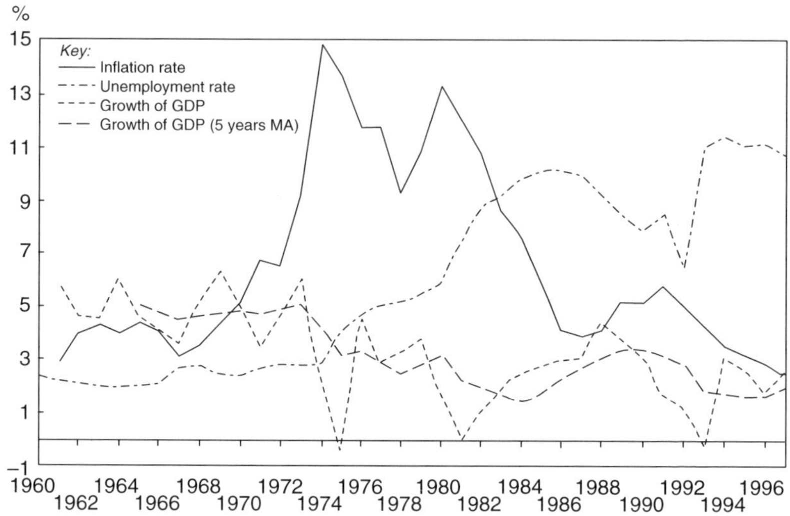

Source: EC.
Note: MA is monthly average
Figure 7.2 Inflation, unemployment and growth in Europe

inflation rate and wage share since 1961; and the highest real short-term interest rate in the post-war period.

It is thus difficult to sustain the claim that fiscal policy was unduly expansionary; it appears obvious that the overall policy mix was restrictive: whatever the laxity of fiscal policy, it was not enough to offset the restrictiveness of monetary policy. In a situation where the excess saving of the private sector more than compensates for the dissaving of the public sector, it is hard to maintain that the cause of abnormally high interest rates lies only in the mounting public debt.

1 Macroeconomic policies in Europe since the second oil shock

1.1 1979–87: a restrictive, but time-consistent policy-mix

The second oil shock happened at a time when, whatever the criteria chosen, inflation was a real evil. For the E15, the rate was 9.1 per cent in 1978. Moreover, even if for some countries unemployment was already a threat – having risen steadily since 1973 – it was, by late 1990s standards, very low, 4.9 per cent of the European labour force. It was clear that the

European countries had not yet absorbed the first oil shock. Besides, the course of macroeconomic policies was very expansionary: the short-term real rate of interest was negative in many countries; for the E15 averaged 1.2 per cent. But fiscal policy was also lax, as the structural deficit (measured by the OECD) was high: 4.0 per cent of GDP.

In such a context, it is easy to understand why the fight against inflation became a priority throughout Europe. All over the world, monetary policy became very restrictive, first under the leadership of the USA – which may explain, at least partially, the appreciation of the dollar in the first half of the 1980s, and from 1986 onwards, under European leadership. Real short-term interest rates have been consistently higher in the E15 than in the USA.

Germany has to be singled out as a case apart. First, at the onset of the second oil shock, it had both a very low inflation rate (2.7 per cent in 1978) and very low unemployment (3.1 per cent in the same year). It was the only country to have achieved a decrease in its unemployment rate. It had, of course, experienced an increase in the budget deficit following the episode of the 'locomotive' in 1978, but it was certainly in a better shape than any other European country. When the European Monetary System (EMS) was created (March 1979), it was obvious that Germany would be the leader of European monetary policy, as it had already achieved what was being targeted by the other countries. And it is worth emphasizing that, through the EMS, the fight against inflation has been less costly than it would otherwise have been, the other countries benefiting from the additional credibility because their currencies have the Deutsche Mark (DM) as anchor. This was thus the right strategy, since German nominal and real short-term interest rates remained lower than the US rates until 1988. In retrospect, it was a co-operative strategy. Each country in Europe was buying something it needed at a cheaper rate. Most were achieving disinflation, at a cost in terms of employment but a lower one (at least politically) than would have been the case if they had had to fight inflation individually. On the other hand, Germany was benefiting from the competitive advantage of its structurally lower inflation rate, while the rules of the EMS did not allow the other countries to devalue to compensate fully for inflation differentials. Thus Germany benefited in terms of employment and a current account surplus from an undervaluation of its currency. The other countries of the EMS accelerated their disinflation thanks to an overvaluation. This co-operative game was all the more necessary in that, for all European countries, the inflationary consequences of the second oil shock were amplified by the enormous real appreciation of the dollar during the first half of the 1980s.

This may explain why, in Europe, a restrictive monetary policy has not been even partially offset by an expansionary fiscal policy, as it has been in the USA. When the fight against 'real' inflation was raging, Feldstein (1986) blamed European unemployment on fiscal austerity: the shrinkage of public services and public-sector capital expenditure, and the maintenance of tax rates at pre-slump highs. The European austerity was often contrasted with the activist budget deficits run elsewhere: the USA and, earlier, Japan, in particular were in the red. With hindsight, we may now claim that fiscal policy in Europe was mildly restrictive until 1987. For the E15, the structural budget deficit as measured by the OECD declined between 1979 and 1987, from 5.1 per cent to 3.7 per cent of GDP. This evolution is all the more remarkable as it was paralleled by a steady increase in debt service, since actual interest payments by general government increased by more than 2 per cent of GDP for the E15. Hence, for the whole of Europe, the primary structural deficit had been reduced by more than 5 points of GDP, which means that by 1987, and continuing until the end of the decade, the structural primary budget was substantially in surplus.

Of course, if we consider development, country by country, the picture is varied, Germany being the country whose fiscal austerity was the most severe, but in Spain and Italy it would be difficult to even speak of austerity. But, on the whole, the proposition that fiscal policies in European countries ranged from highly restrictive to, at most, neutral holds during the 1980s.

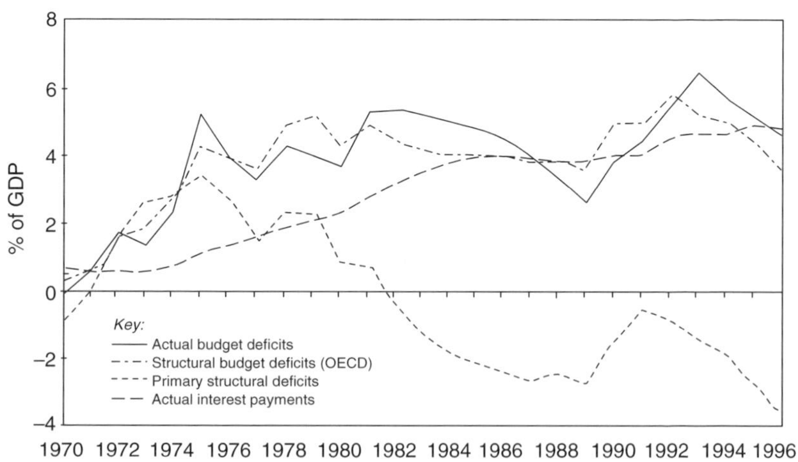

Source: OECD.

Figure 7.3 Public deficits in Europe

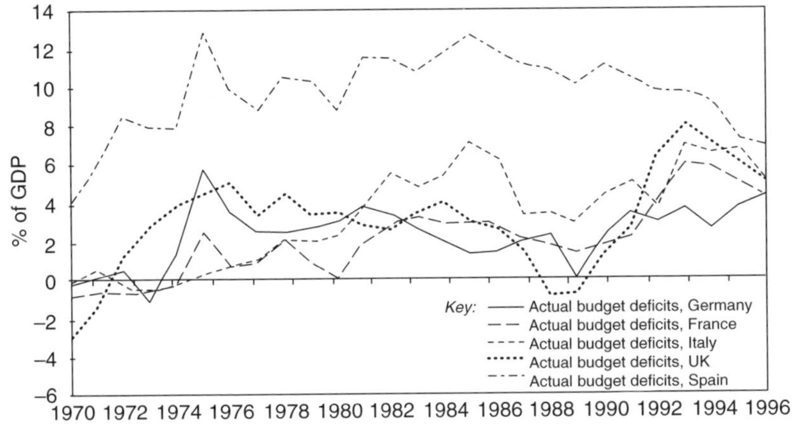

Source: OECD.
Figure 7.4 Actual budget deficits in Europe

In a nutshell, during most of the 1980s the policy mix in Europe was very restrictive – as it combined an increase in real interest rates of about 300–400 basis points and a reduction in structural deficits – but time-consistent, as monetary and fiscal policy were not in conflict with each other. Macroeconomic policy was, to say the least, not directed against unemployment, because it was busy elsewhere, attempting (successfully) to reduce inflation. Thus it should come as no surprise that, until 1986–7, unemployment was rising, approaching 10 per cent for the E15.

We may summarize this phase of European development by two propositions:

- Decentralized monetary union has a deflationary bias, of which the unemployment rate may be a systemic measure (Fitoussi and Flandreau (1994)), the reason being that union members have to align their policies to be consistent with the preferences of the most inflation-averse country. This was how the EMS functioned.
- But during this first period under review, one could argue that this deflationary bias was exactly the aim of most European countries. Indeed, all the countries in the world were looking for the least costly means of achieving a sizeable reduction in inflation. For Europe, the EMS was thus a convenient device.

1.2 1987–90: the years of recovery – was the inflation-threat an illusion?

Continuing to look at Europe as if it were a single country, it appears that the recovery of output begins in 1986, the year of the oil counter-shock. Of course, chronology is a matter of convention and it may be argued that Europe was in 1986 already in the upward phase of a cycle, since the rate of growth was higher than in 1982–3. But unemployment was still rising and the process was rather one of *soft growth* – that is, below potential, and did not show any acceleration until 1986. For the E15, growth peaked in 1988 and then decelerated steadily, turning negative in 1993. By 1990, one could argue that the rate of growth for the E15 was still above potential. Indeed, according to OECD calculations, the output gap (the difference between actual GDP and potential GDP) was positive for Europe between 1988 and 1991, showing a surplus of 1.2 per cent as late as 1991 (hard as it is to believe that a group of countries, the E15, growing at an average rate of 1.5 per cent, were characterized by a positive output gap).

On the eve of the counter-shock, the battle against inflation was almost, but not quite, won. For the E15, the inflation rate was at its lowest level since 1971 (5.8 per cent), in constant deceleration from 13.2 per cent in 1980. This pattern was common to most European countries, with, as always, Germany achieving the lowest inflation (1.8 per cent) in 1985. In this context, the sharp fall in the price of oil, amplified by the depreciation of the dollar, gave a strong supplementary disinflationary impulse: in 1985–6, the E15 inflation rate fell by about two percentage points, with the German rate becoming negative. Core inflation did not, of course, decrease that much: the implicit GDP deflator in 1986 was only half a point lower than in 1985.

But this sharp movement of the measured inflation rate would later lead to what may be called 'the European inflation illusion'. It was obvious that the contribution of the oil counter-shock to the disinflationary process would make people realize that inflation could return. And by 1988, indeed, the rate of inflation began to increase again for the E15, reaching 5.6 per cent in 1991. This picture obviously changes greatly if we measure the acceleration of inflation taking 1985 or 1986–7 as our starting point. Table 7.1 gives the measures of the increase of the rates of inflation for the E15 and each country in Europe.

Three conclusions emerge from this comparison:

(i) The rate of inflation in 1991 was below its 1985 level for Europe as a whole, and for the great majority of the countries;

Table 7.1 Increase in the rate of inflation during the recovery period

	1985–91	*1986–91*	*1987–91*
E15	−1.0	+2.4	+2.8
Austria	+0.1	+1.6	+1.9
Belgium	−1.7	+1.9	+1.7
Denmark	−2.3	−1.3	−1.6
Finland	−1.5	+0.7	+0.9
France	−2.7	+0.5	+0.1
Germany	+1.4	+3.7	+3.4
Greece	+0.2	−3.5	+3.1
Ireland	−2.3	−0.7	0.0
Italy	−2.9	+0.5	+1.5
Luxemburg	−1.0	+2.8	+3.1
Netherlands	+1.6	+3.7	+4.3
Portugal	−8.4	−0.8	+1.5
Spain	−1.9	−2.9	+0.6
Sweden	+1.9	+5.1	+5.1
UK	−0.2	+2.5	+1.8
USA	+0.6	+2.3	−0.5
Japan	+1.2	+2.6	+3.2

Source: EC.

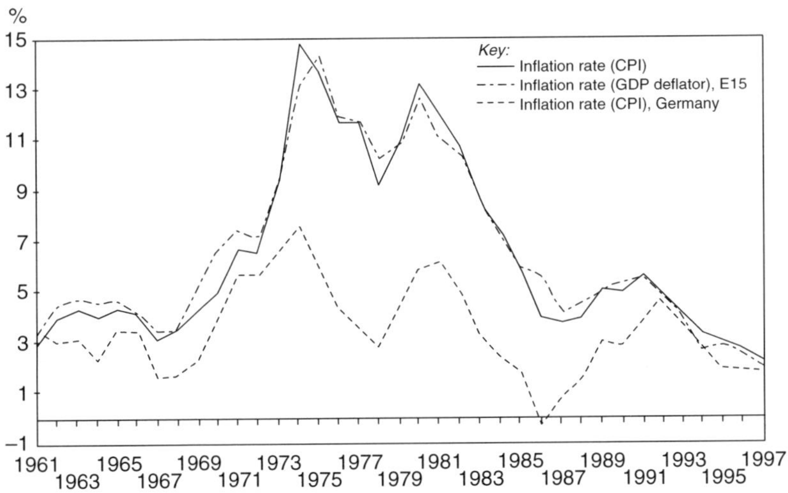

Source: OECD.
Figure 7.5 Inflation in Europe and Germany

Table 7.2 Impact of the oil counter-shock

	1985	*1986*	*1987*	*1988*	*1989*	*1990*	*1991*
Impact on average inflation rate in Europe	–	–1.2	–1.2	–0.8	–0.6	–0.5	–0.5
E15 inflation rate corrected for effect of oil counter-shock	6.1	4.9	4.5	4.5	5.8	6.3	5.6
German inflation rate corrected	2.2	1.1	1.4	2.1	3.4	3.2	4.1

Sources: Mimosa OFCE and EC.

(ii) Taking 1987 as the starting year, the increase appears to be very modest for the vast majority of the countries as well as for the E15; and

(iii) The only notable exceptions to this general picture are Germany and the Netherlands. In Germany, the rate of inflation was not only well above its 1987 level (by 3.4 points) but also perceptibly higher than in 1985 level (by 1.4 points).

We have simulated the disinflationary impact of the oil counter-shock for Europe as a whole using MIMOSA, the multinational model of Observatoire Français des Conjonctures Economiques (OFCE). It is then easy to calculate what the rate of inflation would have been without this shock. The result is given in Table 7.2, which shows that the disinflation process continued at least until 1988 for Europe as a whole, apparently ceasing in 1989–90. But taking into account the weight of Germany, and bearing Table 7.1 in mind, it may be safe to argue that the 'return' of inflation was a German phenomenon. One should add that it was not in fact a return, but rather the reflection of a new, historical shock, Europe-specific this time: German reunification. Figure 7.6, comparing the average rate of inflation in different subperiods from 1981 to 1997 for the E15 and for Germany, makes this point abundantly clear.

Hence one could hardly speak of a threat of inflation for Europe as a whole. Indeed, in 1992–3, while the German inflation rate rose to unusual levels (in 1992, it was just 1.3 points lower than what it had been at the 1981 peak immediately following the second oil shock), the E15 inflation rate continued to decrease.

At best, one could characterize this period as one of normal, very modest fluctuations in the inflation rate brought about by a large fluctuation in the rate of growth, as the latter had almost doubled in many countries. The puzzle is how such a large movement in output could have

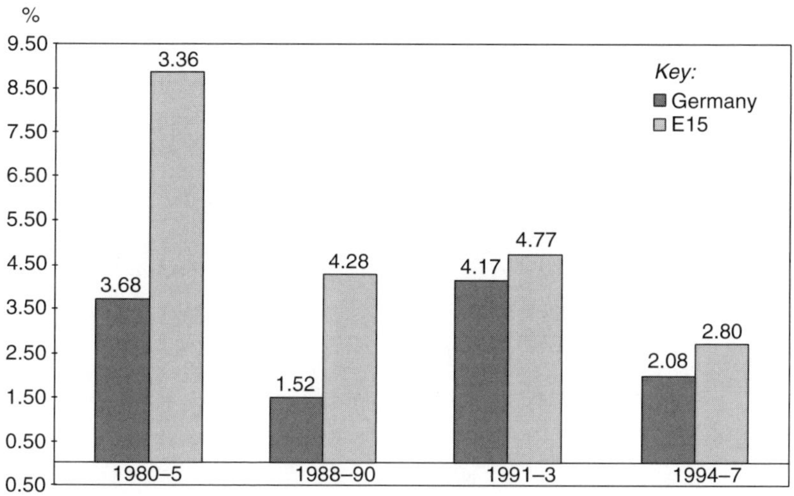

Source: OECD.
Figure 7.6 Inflation in Europe and in Germany 1981–97

been consistent with such a small variation in inflation. At the end of the 1960s, for example, a proportionately similar fluctuation in the rate of growth had been accompanied by a much larger change in the rate of inflation. The answer probably lies in the unemployment that has marked Europe since the mid-1980s; that is, the ample degree of slack in the labour market.

A question naturally arises: did this small increase in the rate of inflation justify so severe a move in monetary policy? Between 1986 and 1990, the real short-term interest rate (using the GDP deflator) rose by 280 basis points for the E15, and by 380 basis points in Germany. If we choose the CPI as a measure, the rise appears to be less dramatic, but still important. Besides, the average level of the real short-term interest rates was much higher in the period 1986–90 than in 1981–5. In fact, the acceleration in interest rates began in 1988–9 and lasted until 1992.

Two other factors about monetary policy may be emphasized before studying its consequences. From 1985 to 1995, the real short-term interest rate was consistently higher in Europe than in the USA. The same holds for the 1989–94 period for German comparative rates. Second (and more importantly?) between 1989 and 1993, real short-term interest rates were consistently higher than long-term ones for the E15. This was clearly not the case for the USA.

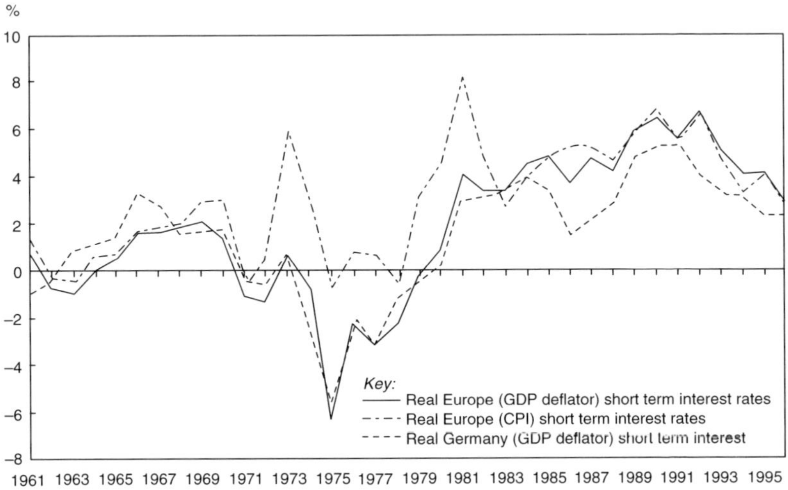

Source: OECD.

Figure 7.7 Short-term interest rates in Europe and Germany

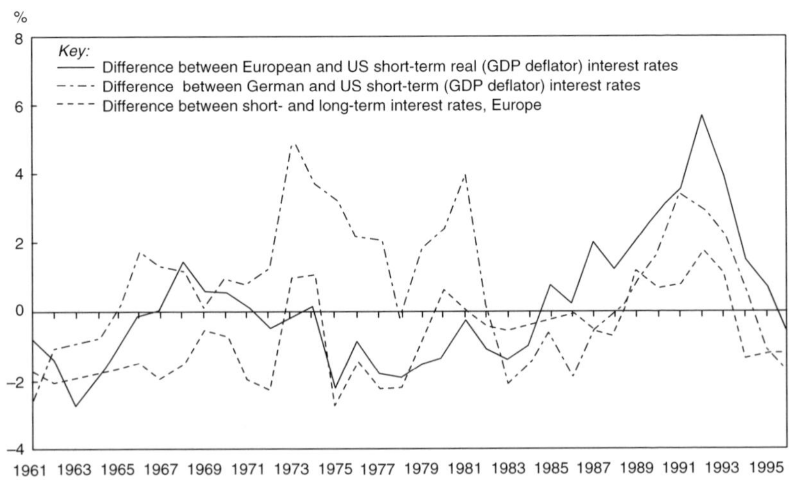

Source: OECD.

Figure 7.8 Interest rate differentials between European average, Germany and the USA

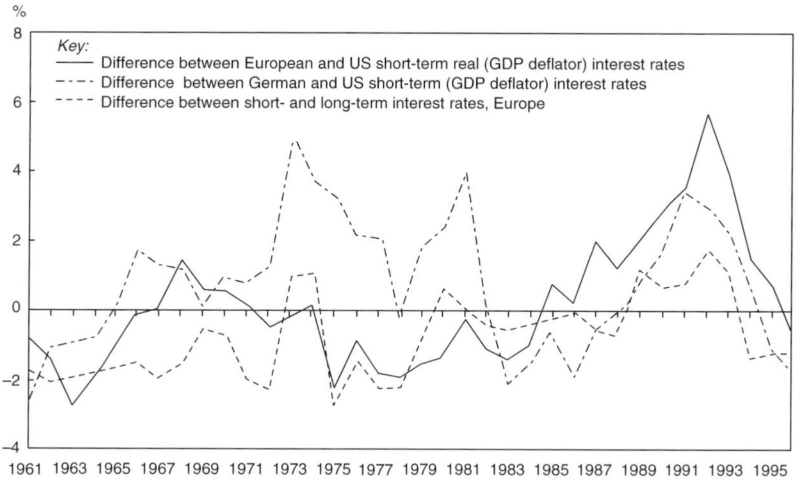

Source: EC, OECD.
Figure 7.9 Structural deficits and real interest rate-growth differentials in Europe

All these facts seem to indicate that monetary policy was the prime mover in the process that led Europe into a situation of slow growth. This interpretation is all the more plausible in that the structural deficits of European countries decreased until 1989, one year after monetary policy had become very restrictive. Indeed, in 1989, the OECD-computed structural budget deficit for Europe as a whole reached its lowest level since the second oil shock despite the huge rise in real short-term interest rates (which, based on the CPI, averaged 5.2 per cent between 1986 and 1989, about two points higher than in the first half of the 1980s).

1.3 The recession of the 1990s and after

We may interpret the preceding episode in two ways. One emphasizes the weight of the fear of inflation on the conduct of monetary policy: in many ways the belief in the return of inflation at the end of the 1980s was illusory, but the European countries, having paid such a high price to vanquish inflation, did not want to take any risks. The second emphasizes the mismanagement of the EMS at the turn of the 1990s. What is clear by now is that inflation was not at all an illusion for Germany. The German economy was clearly overheated, but this was not the case with the other countries. Given the EMS machinery, however, there was no way to avoid adopting German monetary policy. The rest followed inevitably: in 1990,

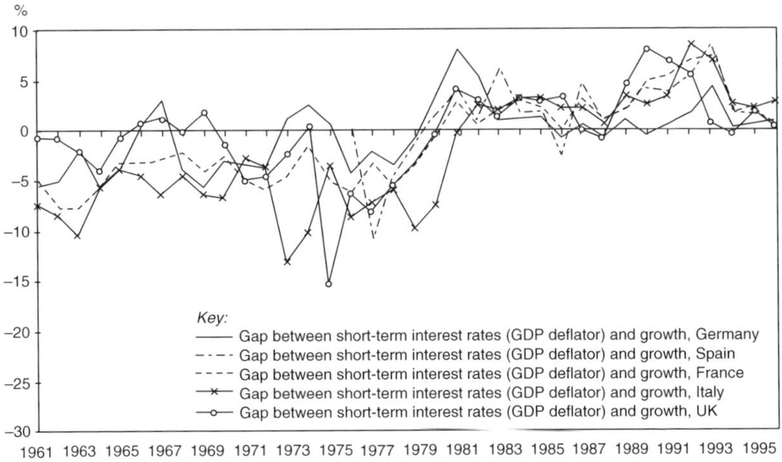

Source: EC.

Figure 7.10 Short-term interest rate growth differentials for selected European countries

European GDP growth began to decelerate – in virtually all European countries – but this deceleration did not bring any relief on the real interest rate front. The reasons are readily understood: both the inflation rate and the growth rate continued to increase in Germany, but not so in other countries. German growth was as high as 5.7 per cent in 1990, and 5 per cent in 1991. At the same time, inflation went from 2.8 per cent in 1990 and 3.8 per cent in 1991 to a peak of 4.8 per cent in 1992, and stayed as high as 4 per cent in 1993; 1992 and 1993 were the only years since 1961 in which German inflation was above the European average. The result is striking: the critical gap between the real short-term interest rate and the growth rate was negative in 1990 and around zero in 1991 in Germany, compared with 3.9 per cent for the E15. The situation was even worse for some of the major European countries.

In 1990, this critical gap was 5.0, 3.9 and 8.9 points for France, Italy and the UK, respectively. This reminds one of a trivial fact: one should not give the same monetary medicine to a country that is suffering from fever as to one with anaemia.

It is not clear whether it is the threat of inflation that led to the mismanagement of the EMS, or whether the latter was justified after the fact by the former. But what the sheer facts make incontrovertible is that there was mismanagement. Otherwise it would be hard to explain why real interest rates should increase at a time of declining inflation and growth.

More importantly, though, having a very restrictive fiscal policy as well would be hard to justify. Public deficits and unemployment were increasing because of a misconceived monetary policy that at the very least aggravated, if it did not cause, the slowdown of growth. It was clear that the extent of the slowdown was unexpected, as was the rise in real interest rates necessary to preserve the existing parities within the EMS. What government would be strong enough to add to the pains of the populace by announcing huge cuts in public expenditure, or major increases in taxes? Quite the reverse – governments would try to alleviate the pain, at least to some degree. Confronted by Europe's biggest employment contraction since the Second World War, they would not only let the system's built-in stabilizers work, but where possible increased social expenditure.

This is exactly what happened. Budget deficits deepened because there was no way out: fiscal policy had to bear the burden of adjustment in countries where this was possible. In other countries, such an option was simply not available, because the critical gap had reached values unseen since the 1930s: 7.8 percentage points for Italy, for example, where the deficit was already about 10 per cent of GDP. These countries had no choice but to change their monetary policy. Indeed 'the foreign exchange market' constrained them to do so.

There is some truth in the contention that European governments should have taken advantage of the resumption of growth at the end of the 1980s to reduce their structural deficits more willingly. Had they done so, the problem would now be less acute. But this contention misses an important point. There was no way of preventing the increase in the structural deficit in Germany, because this increase was the consequence of a country-specific shock – a truly autonomous, historical shock – indeed, a magnificent one: the reunification of a nation. Hence, there is something wrong in dealing with the increase in net public borrowing in Germany as if it were a structural problem: the country was investing in a very rewarding project – German reunification – whose long-term rate of return would certainly prove to be high. It was therefore perfectly rational to borrow to finance such an investment. In some sense, it is inappropriate to deal with what is a profitable investment – which had to be public in view of its collective impact and its externalities – as if it were an increase in the nation's structural deficit. That there is a discontinuity in the time series of 'structural deficits' at the very moment when this investment begins should therefore not come as a surprise. The

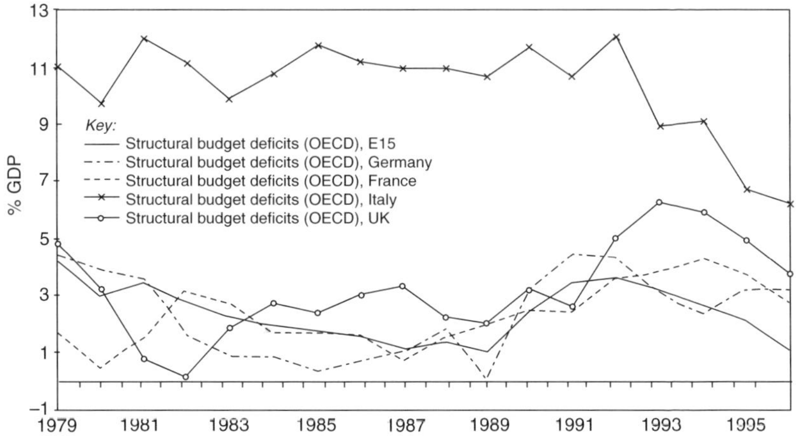

Source: OECD.
Figure 7.11 Structural deficits in Europe and Germany

macroeconomic nature of the calculation misses an important point: something completely new had occurred – a kind of regime shift – whose qualitative nature cannot be captured in a quantitative measurement.

Just looking at the figures, it appears that the increase in structural deficits beginning in 1990 is mainly the consequence of what happened in Germany; between 1989 and 1991, the German structural deficit increased by 4.5 points of GDP, while for Europe as a whole it increased by 2.4 points. At the risk of belabouring the point, one may add that, in the same years, gross fixed capital formation increased by 3 points in Germany and decreased slightly in Europe. In 1995, Germany was the only large country in Europe (and in the world) whose rate of investment was higher (by more than 2 points of GDP) than in 1987. For Europe as a whole it was a bit less than a point lower; for France, 1.7 points; for Italy and the UK, 2.8 points.

But whatever confidence one has in the measurement of structural deficits when something essentially new happens – and as the foregoing discussion indicates, our own confidence is very low – the evolution of the net borrowing position of European governments during this period means that the mismanagement of the EMS led to a completely mistaken, and unsustainable, policy mix in Europe. The policy mix was time-inconsistent, in such a way that it could have lead to the paradoxical monetary arithmetic described by Sargent and Wallace (1981): an over-restrictive monetary policy may generate inflationary expectations, because it implies slower growth and therefore a huge increase in the public deficit.

The story begins with a sizeable increase in real short-term interest rates in Europe at a time when there was no clear sign of acceleration of inflation, if we take full account of the effect of the oil counter-shock. (In 1989, the share of wages in the E15 was 2 points lower than it was in 1985.) The slowdown in growth to which it led did have an impact on the cyclical deficits at a time when it was difficult for governments deliberately to reduce the structural deficits in view of the increase in unemployment. This situation should have set some corrective mechanisms in motion: a decrease in the real rate of interest caused by the slackening in demand for money implied by the slowdown in activity, and thus a real depreciation of most European currencies. The first corrective mechanism would have rejuvenated internal demand; and the second, exports. But none of these effects was allowed into play. Instead, real interest rates continued to rise precisely to prevent currency depreciation.

There was only one country for which this policy mix was right – namely, Germany: the boom in investment, private and public, and the 'real' inflationary pressure brought about by German reunification should have led the DM to appreciate *vis-à-vis* all other currencies. The German policy mix was similar to that of the USA at the beginning of the 1980s, apart from two points: first, restrictive monetary policy and expansionary budgetary policy were truly simultaneous, whereas in the USA they had been sequential; and second, this policy mix was not a deliberate choice, as there was no other way to deal with the needs of German unification and the rebuilding of the eastern part of the country. Hence the DM should have appreciated strongly *vis-à-vis* the other European countries.

Instead, the non-German members of the EMS were caught in a trap: private demand could only fall in view of the greater restrictiveness of monetary policy, and there was no hope of a boost in foreign demand because of the real appreciation of their currencies. The only means of softening the hardship of the recession was fiscal policy. So there is no mystery in the simultaneous increase in deficits and unemployment throughout Europe.

But once again, this policy mix proved unsustainable: it led to the exit of some countries from the EMS in 1992, to a change in the system's rules in 1993, and to the worst recession Europe has known since the Second World War. That, in a year of economic contraction, 1993, the real short-term interest rate was as high as 4.6 per cent for the E15 will certainly

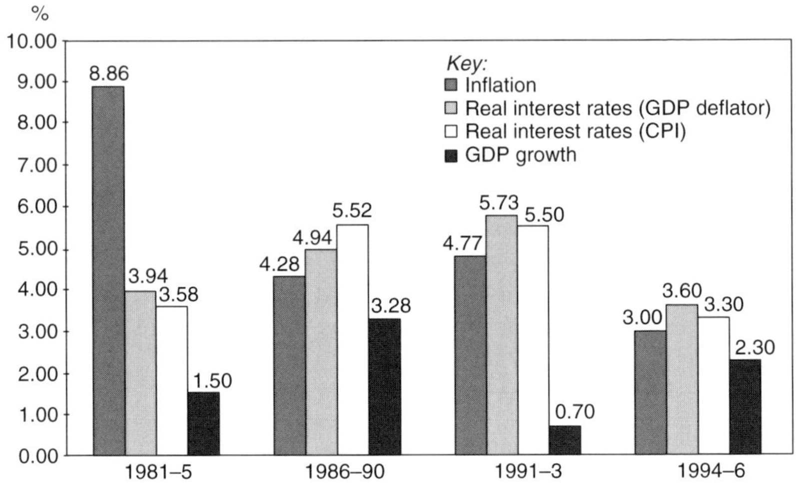

Source: EC.

Figure 7.12 Inflation, real interest rates and growth in E 15

remain a curiosity in economic history. Figures 7.12 and 7.13, summarizing the evolution of inflation, real interest rates and growth from 1981 to 1996, give an idea of the violence of the recessive shock on all European countries apart from Germany.

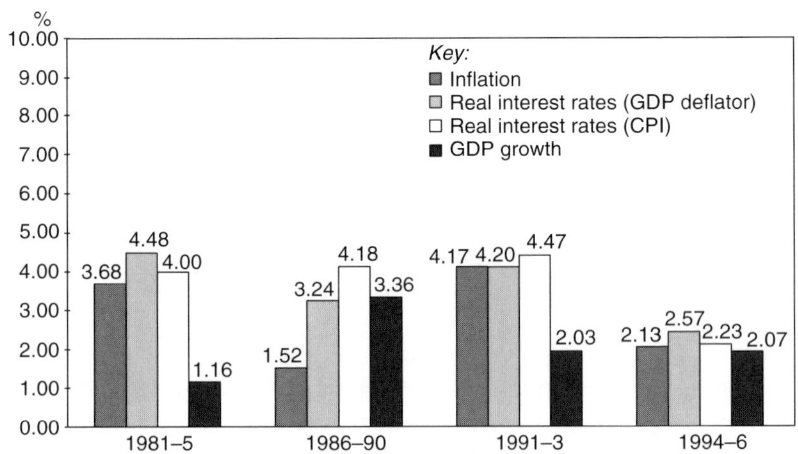

Source: EC.

Figure 7.13 Inflation, real interest rates and growth in Germany

By 1994, it was obvious that what was needed was a complete turnaround in the policy mix for the whole of Europe. Obvious, but difficult to get through the paraphernalia of the discourses on economic policy. Another inversion was, in effect, taking place in the minds of governments and technocrats: interest rates were held to be so high because of the large public deficits. First cut deficits by increasing taxes and/or decreasing expenditure, one will then be rewarded by a decrease in short-term interest rates at which one was aiming. This attitude has, if anything, delayed a much-needed change in economic policy: it is hard to get fiscal deficits down when interest rates are still considered to be too high. In fact, it took almost two years to get interest rates down, two years and a transitory (one hopes) interruption of what was expected to be a period of recovery.

2 The European unemployment problem in the 1990s: the anatomy of soft growth

The preceding section emphasized the role of monetary policy in Europe in building the 'stock problem' – mass unemployment and mounting public debts – in which Europe became trapped. That does not mean that the rise of unemployment in Europe since the early 1980s can be blamed on demand factors alone, or that it had no structural roots. For one thing, demand-management policies may have structural consequences; and for another, one can hardly refute the argument that the equilibrium rate of unemployment – call it the 'natural' rate or 'NAIRU' – has risen during this period. Hence some theoretical notes are in order.

2.1 The unemployment problem: theoretical notes

The various theories that seek to explain the unemployment problem may be interpreted as different diagnoses of a single illness. Each provides its own analysis of the rise of unemployment, and offers remedies that are related to the assumed nature of the disease.

2.1.1 General equilibrium analysis

In the framework of a general equilibrium model which describes a set of interdependent markets, nothing authorizes us to look for the origin of any disequilibrium in the market. The price vector may differ from its equilibrium level for a number of reasons, of which only a few may have to do with the malfunctioning of the labour market. It remains true that the sheer existence of involuntary unemployment implies that some prices are 'false' in the Hicksian sense, but this does not imply that the price of labour has to adjust, or that it is the only price that should adjust.

More often, the search for efficiency will lead to reallocation in *several* markets (Malinvaud (1977)). Consider, for example, inefficiencies arising from asymmetric information or market incompleteness. In this case, equilibrium prices will generally not be efficient. For example, this may lead to a situation where real wages are high and some agents are unemployed. But this does not mean that high real wages 'cause' unemployment, because both variables are endogenous (Solow (1986)). If, for example, prices and wages both exhibit downward rigidities, unemployment and high real wages may result from restrictions in the money supply. Indeed, it may well be argued that such a situation was probably responsible for the recent deterioration of employment prospects in Europe (Atkinson *et al.* (1994)).

More generally, the very nature of problems associated with information asymmetries suggests that it is precisely in the markets assigned to co-ordinate intertemporal decisions that rigidities and inefficiencies are most common. Equilibrium interest rates might not coincide with full employment, since investment decisions (which in turn determine labour demand by firms) are made on the basis of signals sent by these typically inefficient markets, it is only too natural to expect that they lead to distortions. As a result, the burden of adjustment will fall upon other markets. For example, a high rate of interest, by generating a reduction in profitability, will in turn produce a contraction of real wages if full employment is required.

The basic insight was spelt out in Fitoussi and Phelps (1988). The Fitoussi–Phelps monograph traced the slump in Europe in the 1980s to the rise of long-term rates of interest that were at historic highs from 1982 onwards. This increase was itself assumed to be the consequence of the change in the policy regime in the USA – a change in both monetary and fiscal policy.

The theoretical models developed to study the effects of this change carry the implication that a rise in the real rate of interest causes firms to raise the supply price of output at a given level of wages – as in the case of an adverse supply shock. Each of these models focuses on a different effect of the real rate of interest, but all go in the same direction. Hence the supply-shock mechanism operating through different kinds of investment may be considered emblematic of a polymorphous collection of real interest-rate effects on unemployment.

In effect, the demand for labour is a function of real wages (as in traditional approaches) *and* of the rate of interest that determines the price of the asset that firms seek to accumulate. Intuitively, this corresponds to the 'customer' asset. If a firm expects an increase in the value of its customers, it will seek to expand its customer base (or 'stock') by lowering the selling price of its product *vis-à-vis* its competitors. This will produce an increase in its production and in its demand for labour.

The capital market is the essential transmission mechanism, since asset prices are an inverse function of interest rates. High interest rates lower asset prices and thus reduce the demand for labour. This produces an increase in the equilibrium rate of involuntary unemployment.

The reasoning may be put in terms of straightforward profit maximization in an imperfectly competitive environment. In such a setting there is a trade-off between present profits and market shares (or, equivalently, between present and future profits), controlled by the real rate of interest. Hence desired mark-ups of individual firms are positively related to real interest rates. For an increase in the real interest rate to generate unemployment, some degree of wage rigidity or stickiness is required, otherwise the increased mark-ups of firms would be accommodated by a cut in real wages at the existing level of employment.

If we accept such a theory, the policy conclusion is straightforward: in the presence of unemployment, the policy mix should never involve too expansionary a fiscal policy, nor too restrictive a monetary policy. This finding is quite important, especially in view of the policies adopted in Europe during the 1980s, where typically neutral fiscal policies and very restrictive monetary policies prevailed. The situation deteriorated further following German reunification, since when the policy mix in Europe has been exactly the opposite of what was required: short-term real interest rates have been historically high, as have budget deficits. As a result, potential growth prospects have deteriorated and income inequalities have widened.

In a nutshell, the foregoing reasoning has underscored the point that, in Europe, passive macroeconomic policies *vis-à-vis* unemployment (but very active ones for monetary stability) have shifted the burden disproportionately to the labour market, to budget deficits, and hence the social protection system. Or, to put things differently, the symptom of the European problem has changed, but not the illness that generated it: until the beginning of the 1980s it was double-digit inflation; now it is double-digit unemployment and abnormally slow growth. A rate of growth persistently lower than its potential leads as a result to the 'good' – increased competitiveness through disinflation, slowdown of imports through weak internal demand – but also to the 'bad' – increased unemployment, and fiscal and social deficits. If restrictive monetary policy is pursued nevertheless – and despite the fact that the effective rate of inflation is below its target level – the only way out is to cut public and social expenditure. This is the route now being taken – if not in fact, at least verbally – by most European governments. Apparently, the fact that, when conducted simultaneously by all countries, this policy is at least in part self-defeating, does not dissuade most governments and international organizations from advocating it.

2.1.2 Partial equilibrium analysis

Hands-off policies are seen as the only way to enhance flexibility in the labour market: too high a level of social protection has weakened incentives to work *and* at the same time driven up taxes and the cost of labour. In terms of modern analysis of the labour market, both the demand and the 'surrogate supply' of labour have shifted adversely – that is, to the left. Hence unemployment is structural, and the only solution is deregulation through a decrease in social protection. The increases in numbers of jobless and in social deficits are part and parcel of the same problem, but now the direction of the causality is not, as was argued before, from the former to the latter, but the reverse: from the extent of social protection to the extent of unemployment. When it is pointed out to the advocates of a hands-off policy that significant deregulation has already taken place in most European labour markets without any boost to employment, they answer that what matters is not deregulation *per se*, but rather *relative* deregulation. In their view, globalization has changed the rules of the game, and if flexibility is badly needed it is to enhance competitiveness in the mature industrial countries to cope with increased competition from the emerging economies.

To put things bluntly, their answer amounts to saying that inequalities in industrialized countries, and especially in continental Europe, have not increased enough to cope with globalization. Yet there is a puzzle in this answer, because the data are not as consistent as it would seem at first sight. To clarify this point, a comparison between Europe and the USA is in order, as America is held up as being paradigmatic of a free labour market. Two striking, very well-known facts emerge from this comparison:

(i) an astonishing parallelism in the evolution of the rate of inflation in the two countries since the start of the 1960s; and
(ii) a clear divergence in the evolution of the rate of unemployment from about 1975, much of the increase in European unemployment occurring between 1975 and 1985. At the time of writing the rate of unemployment is at its 1963 level in the USA, and five times higher in Europe.

La cause est entendue: much, if not all, of the increase in European unemployment is because of an increase in the NAIRU – that is, to a malfunctioning of the labour market. Otherwise, if the unemployment rate in Europe was above its natural level, disinflation would have been much more severe, and the European inflation rate would have diverged from the US rate.

Usually, an increase in the natural rate of unemployment, when the economy is subject to an adverse supply shock, can always be traced to some kind of real wage rigidity. There follows a profit squeeze, a fall in the rate of investment, and thus an increase in the equilibrium rate of unemployment. A process of this kind seems to have characterized Europe between the first oil shock and the beginning of the 1980s, since during this period the share of wages in national income rose. But since 1982 the process has been more than reversed (as we have already noted), the share of wages has decreased strongly and continues to do so, and as early as 1984–5, it was already below its pre-first-oil-shock value. This has not been the case in the USA, where the wage share stayed roughly constant during that period. Clearly, something else is needed to make this type of explanation convincing.

There is even a kind of recent laboratory experiment that contradicts the hypothesis of an increase in natural rate of unemployment, namely the case of the depreciating countries in Europe since 1992. If the natural rate thesis were valid, these countries would have enjoyed, at best, a temporary gain in competitiveness, because of the inflationary effect of depreciation through real wage rigidity. Gordon (1996) shows that the contrary has been true. He compares the performances of the depreciating countries in Europe (Italy, Portugal, Spain, Sweden and the United Kingdom) to those of the appreciating countries (Austria, Belgium, France, the Netherlands and Switzerland). Germany is excluded because the strong surge of inflation there until 1992 – see above – would have exaggerated the extent of disinflation in the period 1992–5, which is precisely the period of the experiment. Gordon's conclusions are straightforward: 'both groups of countries enjoyed an acceleration of nominal GDP growth, a deceleration of inflation, and thus an even greater acceleration of GDP growth. But there the similarities stop. The acceleration of nominal GDP growth in the depreciating countries exceeded that in the appreciating countries by 1.3 percentage points. *Yet none of this was absorbed by inflation; inflation actually decelerated more in the depreciating countries than the appreciating countries*. And as a result the acceleration of real GDP growth in the depreciating countries exceeded that in the appreciating countries by 1.7 percentage points' (Gordon

(1996, p. 34)). This is clear evidence that the actual rate of unemployment is above its natural level, and that another explanation has to be found.

The Fitoussi–Phelps hypothesis on the unemployment effect of the rise in real interest rates has also been tested recently against more conventional explanations, of which the preceding is a good example (de la Croix and Lubrano (1996)). The authors conclude that, effectively for the European countries they have studied, real interest rates and unemployment are co-integrated, the former causing the latter, while they found traces of another variable with comparable impact on the unemployment rate, including the real wage.

2.2 Anatomy of soft growth

'So what?', one might respond to the foregoing argument. There are good reasons why interest rates are so high, such as the increase in public debts since the beginning of the 1980s. Everybody knows that high real interest rates are a bad thing, but financial markets are sovereign and there is little governments can do to escape from their tutelage. Central banks all over the world are just doing what is necessary to avoid the increase in long-term interest rates that would follow a surge in inflationary expectations.

To understand what is true and what is dubious in the above argument, we have to analyse *the dynamics of slow growth.*

2.2.1 The changing balance of power

It would be misleading to speak of a market as if it were a person capable of making decisions and imposing his or her tutelage on governments. The market is a method for allocating scarce resources, and when it is perfect the allocation is optimal. Financial markets, in particular, are seen as being efficient; that is, as leading to an optimal allocation of saving to investment opportunities. But we have already emphasized that these markets are assigned a practically impossible task: co-ordinating the intertemporal plans of economic agents. This means that most of the time they are out of equilibrium. In such a situation the short side of the market will dominate, and the long side will be rationed. At the time of writing there is strong evidence that financial markets are dominated by 'creditors' – a generic term for those who possess the capital, or those who act on their account. In effect, financial deregulation and globalization have multiplied the investment opportunities without multiplying the amount of loanable funds. So there is some truth in the contention that, at the world level, there is a potential insufficiency of saving.

Besides, deregulation has increased the liquidity of the market and, together with exchange rate flexibility, it allows the operators to follow short-term strategies with long-term financial assets. What has increased is not only the degree of spatial mobility of capital, but also time mobility throughout the spectrum of maturities of financial assets. In a market in a permanent state of flux it is difficult to say what is causing what: is the long-term interest rate causing the short-term one, or vice versa? As there is some evidence that money illusion determines, at least partially, the behaviour of real rates at higher maturities (see Atkinson *et al.* (1993)) and that short-term interest rates strongly influence the determination of exchange rates, it seems that the potency of monetary policy has increased strongly since the beginning of the 1980s, and that it bears some responsibility for the huge increase of real interest rates, and hence in the change of the balance of power in capital markets.

But this change in the balance of power in the financial markets will spread to other markets. Mass unemployment, in particular, is the sign that labour markets are dominated by firms; that is, that the demand for labour constitutes the short side of the market. Hence the bargaining position of wage-earners is weak.

Domination of the 'creditors' in financial markets and of firms in the labour market are the main characteristic features of this time. They structure the future and lead to the mechanics of soft growth. By soft growth, we mean a situation where the rate of actual growth is persistently lower than its potential, hence a situation exists where unemployment is above its natural rate and exhibits a tendency to increase.

2.2.2 The dynamics of soft growth

'Creditors' and firms do not in reality share the same interests. The business sector should normally be a net debtor, so these two groups are rather in conflicting positions. But in this conflict the 'creditors' are winners from the outset, thanks to globalization and the enormous investment needs throughout the world.

Hence firms will seek, as a normal strategy, to gain autonomy *vis-à-vis* financial markets by increasing their profit margins to self-finance their operations. In a world where long-term real interest rates are high, and short-term interest rates high and also volatile, it is better not to be indebted. Moreover, high real interest rates amount to a depreciation of the future. Hence profit margins must be widened, not only to re-establish profitability, as in conventional equilibrium theory, but also to reflect the fact that the future is more heavily discounted. This may explain why, particularly since the beginning of the 1980s, self-financing has been very high in many countries of Europe, in fact above 100 per cent. In France, in particular since 1992, the business sector, for the first time since the

Second World War, has had a net creditor position! What could happen, when those in charge of building the future (that is, of investing) become net lenders?

The business sector can proceed globally to such an adaptation, and increase its profit margins (cash flow) only by economizing on both investment and labour. This leads unavoidably to unemployment – wages cannot have the flexibility that is assumed in a perfectly competitive market – and, with the help of the dynamics of unemployment, to wage moderation – that is, a situation where wages lag behind productivity. In other words, downsizing is a constraint on the behaviour of firms. Hence the social game becomes deeply unbalanced, because one of its players – the workers – is too weak. The constant threat of unemployment makes their situation too precarious.

This precariousness is contagious. It hurts first, and most importantly, unskilled labour but then spreads to the middle classes and small firms. The problem of small firms is precisely that they are small and have limited possibilities of shedding labour. They thus cannot avoid calling on the 'creditors'. But the banking system has little confidence in their ability to reimburse. Those who have little collateral will thus be credit-rationed. Moreover, in the constellation of soft growth, asset prices have to fall, because the rate of interest is too high. Hence the banking system will also eventually get into difficulties. This may constitute a revenge of sorts, but it is a cold comfort. The fact that the predator has lost weight is no relief for a prey who is starving to death. But the difficulties of the banking system will increase the intensity of credit rationing in the economy.

As a consequence of mass unemployment, wage moderation and the increase in precariousness of a growing portion of society, consumption is structurally weak. The household saving rate will be higher than in a normal growth environment. But there is no growth without tensions – and tensions are what 'creditors' fear above all. Tensions may lead to inflation, and for lenders inflation is the prime evil. All in all, the present balance of power is the most convenient for them. A very sharp increase in employment is good news for society as a whole, but, objectively, bad news for those who benefit from the present balance. It signifies that this balance is changing; so there is nothing astonishing if such news leads to a decline in financial markets.

The forces governing the mechanics of soft growth cannot but lead to a weaker state. In an economy, all agents cannot be creditors at the same time. Some debtors are indispensable. Of course, one may imagine a situation theoretically where all agents are net lenders to the rest of the world. But this implies that the competitiveness of the economy is so great that external demand more than compensates for the structural weakness of internal demand. Except for very special cases, such a configuration cannot be consistent with an overvalued currency. And if the process of soft growth is triggered by a high rate of interest (in absolute terms and relative to other countries), it normally also leads to an overvaluation of the currency. (This, in stylized terms, has been the case in Europe since at least the beginning of the 1990s.)

So who are the debtors? Governments, of course. The process which leads to their indebtedness is straightforward. The weakness of economic activity reduces tax revenue at the very moment that it increases social expenditure through mounting unemployment. Moreover, the high interest rates and low growth ensure that debt service will be substantial, further widening deficits. Public deficits have to be large because, in a way, governments substitute for firms as normal debtors. And to avoid too fast an increase in the deficits, governments (like the business sector) try to decrease public investment. To describe the same phenomenon in a different way: the private sector is increasing its demand for safe financial assets and the public sector is constrained to supply them. Thus the process of soft growth leads almost unavoidably to an indebted state, and hence to the need to downsize the state itself. Whatever the causes, this occurs at a time when, apparently, there is no way out but to pursue hands-off policies – that is, to deregulate further the labour market and to downsize the welfare state. Structural reforms appear all the more necessary, in that macroeconomic policies are ill-designed and, through the supply side effects of the real rate of interest, have adverse structural consequences.

The problem is the classical one of the dynamic inefficiency of capitalism: distorted income distribution may lead to over-accumulation or to under-accumulation – that is, to sub-optimal growth. Excessive income inequality, encapsulated in too great a positive differential between the real rate of interest and the growth rate leads to under-investment, through under-consumption. The phenomenon is aggravated by credit rationing, which is the normal consequence of an abnormally high level of interest rates, and by a lopsided balance of power on the labour market. If structural reforms increase income inequalities, this may perhaps lead to an increase in employment, but it will obviously strengthen the trend to under-investment and to the aggregate inefficiency of the system.

What are the alternatives?

We can identify at least two other possibilities. First, the government tries to escape the tutelage of the 'creditors' by trying (as do firms) to cut expenditure and/or to increase taxes. Shrinking the deficit will reduce its net borrower position. For various reasons, however, this is not easy. First, public and social expenditures do not have the flexibility of private ones: cuts have to be explained and accepted, at least in a democracy. Second, they are the reflection of a social contract that cannot be changed as frequently as a private one. And third, it requires a very strong faith in the Ricardian-equivalence theorem to take the risk of a drastic reduction in the public deficit at a time of mass unemployment and slow growth. Of course, one may count on a more pedestrian effect: that the decrease in interest rate allowed by the abrupt fall in the deficit will lead to an increase in both private investment and consumption. But for that to happen, one has to be sure that the high level of interest rate is not mainly caused, originally, by a constraint on the exchange rate. Finally, the programme of restructuring public finances has to be designed in such a way that it will have at least neutral consequences on the degree of inequality.

In the second scenario, one first gets monetary policy right by reducing short-term interest rates durably, in the hope that private-sector self-financing will decrease, allowing for a reduction in public deficits. But, because part of the deficit is structural, the government will also take advantage of the expansionary monetary policy to proceed further with the restructuring of the public finances (in the case of Italy, for example).

Superficially, these two scenarios seem to amount to the same thing, but in fact they are profoundly different. In the situation in Europe at the time of writing, timing is crucial. To begin with, restrictive fiscal policy may produce a smaller reduction in the budget deficit, since part of the *ex ante* reduction will not show up *ex post* because of the likely decline in public receipts. Now it will be a relief if interest rates fall mainly as a consequence of slower growth – and hence slack demand for money and credit. This is because such a slowdown could lead the government to reconsider its own budgetary policy. It is thus all the more crucial to begin by getting the rate of interest down, because it takes time for monetary policy to affect activity.

The problem is to be clear about the threat of inflation that such a policy may entail. As we saw in the first part of this section, this threat was not truly present for most European countries at the end of the 1980s. But even now there are many reasons why inflation will be no threat again for many years to come.

The most important reasons are structural. The factors that generated inflation in the 1970s and early 1980s have completely disappeared: the Vietnam War, the end of the Bretton-Woods system, and the oil shocks, though the price of oil may be constrained by the entry of Russia and other oil-producing CIS members on to the international economic scene. An emerging structural factor will be increasingly important, namely the globalization of goods markets. The heightened competition to which this leads has a deflationary impact – firms believing that they may raise their prices in the future are becoming the exception; all over the world, the expectations and strategy of firms are, on the contrary, for price cuts – and perhaps more importantly, on the price of labour. Unskilled labour has already been affected and in the future medium-skilled labour and even skilled labour will also be affected.

Two other factors already referred to will also play a major role. Mass unemployment, with the new balance of power it has produced, has had a structural effect on the bargaining power of labour. To get a feel for the importance of this factor, just think of the answer we would give to the following question: what would happen to inflation if an oil shock of the same magnitude as the first one occurred? We have already observed that the share of wages in national income is now well below the level of the 1960s in Europe, and that it is likely to continue to decline; these facts will help in answering the preceding question.

Finally, the structural deficits of European countries have been decreasing for several years – in common with all the OECD countries, in fact.

For all these reasons, the battle against inflation must be terminated, because the phenomenon has disappeared, and there is indeed little to be won in a fight against a ghost. The country will be exhausted, with no energy left to confront real problems. As Lester Thurow (1996) has put it: 'It is well to remember that in 1931 and 1932 as the US was plunging into the Great Depression, economic advisers such as Andrew Mellon, Secretary of the Treasury, were arguing that nothing could be done without risking an out-break of inflation – despite the fact that prices had fallen 23 per cent from 1929 to 1932 and would fall another 4 per cent in 1933.'

References

Aglietta, Michel and Merih Uctum (1996) 'La consolidation budgétaire en Europe', *Economie internationale,* no. 65, 1st quarter, pp. 37–61.

Artus, Patrick and Jean-Paul Fitoussi (1989) 'Fondements de la politique budgétaire: quelques développements récents', *OFCE Working Papers,* No. 1989–23, September.

Atkinson, Anthony B., Olivier J. Blanchard, Jean-Paul Fitoussi, John S. Flemming, Edmund Malinvaud, Edmund S. Phelps and Robert M. Solow (1993) *Taux d'intérêt et chômage,* in Report of the International Policy Group of the Observatoire Français des Conjonctures Economiques (OFCE) (Paris: Collection *Références*/ OFCE).

Atkinson, Anthony B., Olivier J. Blanchard, Jean-Paul Fitoussi, John S. Flemming, Edmund Malinvaud, Edmund S. Phelps and Robert M. Solow (1994) *Pour l'emploi et la cohésion sociale*, in Report of the International Policy Group of OFCE (Paris: Collection *Références*/OFCE).

Blanchard, Olivier J. and Jean-Paul Fitoussi (1998) 'Croissance et chômage', *Conseil d'Analyse Economique*, La Documentation Française, no. 4.

Creel, Jérôme and Henri Sterdyniak (1995) 'Les déficits publics en Europe: causes, conséquences ou remèdes à la crise?', *Revue de l'OFCE*, no. 54, July, pp. 57–100.

Croix, David de la and Michel Lubrano (1996) 'Are Interest Rates Responsible for Unemployment in the Eighties? A Bayesian Analysis of Cointegrated Relationship with a Regime Shift', in *Advances in Econometrics*, vol. 11 (Greenwich, Conn.: JAI Press).

Drèze, Jacques and Edmond Malinvaud, (1994) 'Croissance et emploi: l'ambition d'une initiative européenne', *Revue de l'OFCE*, no. 49, April; English version 'Growth and Employment: The Scope of a European Initiative', *European Economic Review*, vol. 38, no. 3–4, pp. 489–504.

Feldstein, Martin (1986) 'US Budget Deficits and the European Economies: Resolving the Political Economy Puzzle', *American Economic Review*, vol. 76, no. 2, pp. 342–46.

Fitoussi, Jean-Paul and Marc Flandreau (1994) 'Le système monétaire international et l'Union monétaire européenne', *Revue de l'OFCE*, no. 51, October, pp. 167–81.

Fitoussi, Jean-Paul and Edmund S. Phelps (1988) *The Slump in Europe: Reconstructing Open Economy Theory* (Oxford: Basil Blackwell).

Gordon, Robert J. (1996) 'Macroeconomic Policy in the Presence of Structural Maladjustment', Paper presented to the OECD Conference on 'Interactions between Structural Reform, Macroeconomic Policies and Economic Performance', Paris, 18–19 January.

Le Bihan, Hervé and Frédéric Lerais (1998) 'Simulation Properties of Mimosa, a Multi-country Macroeconomic Model', Mimosa Working Paper, no. 98–01.

Le Bihan, Hervé, Catherine Mathieu and Henri Sterdyniak (1996) 'L'austérité budgétaire en Europe et la croissance', *Lettre de l'OFCE*, no. 153, July, pp. 1–4.

Malinvaud, Edmond (1977) *The Theory of Unemployment Reconsidered* (Oxford: Basil Blackwell).

Solow, Robert M. (1986) 'Unemployment: Getting the Questions Right', *Economica*, vol. 53 (210S), pp. S23–34.

Thurow, Lester (1996) *The Future of Capitalism* (New York: Morrow).

Comment

Erich W. Streissler
University of Vienna, Austria

1 Real interest rates in the long run

I completely agree with Fitoussi that, at present, real interest rates are among the most important determinants of investment, of economic growth in general, and thus of employment. In fact, at low levels of growth, real interest rates seem to dominate investment decisions, while at high growth rates they are dominated rather by the rate and structure of the change in demand (an accelerator-type explanation). I also share with Fitoussi a belief in the central tenet of Keynes's General Theory, that nominal interest rates are, at least in the short run, primarily determined by a stock equilibrium on financial asset markets, and that therefore real interest rates need not also clear the labour market in a flow equilibrium.

Where I differ from Fitoussi is in the answer to the question: what determines the level of real interest rates? I do not agree that, in the long run, monetary policy is their main determinant. A subsidiary, but closely-related point is lack of agreement between us as to the long-run effects of nominal exchange rate depreciation; and possibly even as to the point whether, in the long run, monetary policy can influence the real exchange rate at all.

I greatly admire Fitoussi's wealth of insightful quantitative description. But disagreement is possibly because his descriptive exercises appear to me to be full of prescriptive intent. And then the disagreement may be because we have different notions of 'the long run'. Because of the length of time that learning, and even expectation formation, seem to take with regard to many phenomena of macroeconomics and many of the ultimate consequences of economic policy, and in particular because convergence to the theoretical equilibria takes so long – as the exchange rate literature of the 1990s has shown – I understand by the long run a time span of about ten years or more. But as Fitoussi intends to discuss 'soft growth', and economic growth is a long-run concept, I take it Fitoussi is also speaking about such a long run.

Closely related to the questions of the long-run consequences of monetary policy and of the consequences of the long run, is the ambiguity of the term 'restrictive monetary policy', as used by Fitoussi. Does he take restrictive monetary policy to mean a policy designed for an effective transition from an historically high inflation rate regime to a low inflation rate regime; in other words, a policy of constantly lowering the rate of inflation? If so, there is no disagreement: for at least with a large volume of nominally fixed contracts and/or with sticky expectations, such a policy will, of course, cause high nominal interest rates, and on historical evidence also high real interest rates. Furthermore, most probably a real exchange rate appreciation. Thus, it will possibly have strong real effects in lowering growth and increasing unemployment. But to my mind such a policy of lowering inflation is, by its very nature, only temporary. Or does Fitoussi take restrictive monetary policy to mean a policy of permanently keeping inflation at a negligible level – for example, in the zero to 2 per cent range of measured inflation and around a mean of 1 per cent, which the Bundesbank considers as no inflation, because measured inflation tends to overestimate the loss in real purchasing power by about 1 per cent (Tödter and Ziebarth (1997, p. 47))? Then I see no increase in real interest rates brought about by such a policy. Thus our disagreement can be pinpointed in the following way: if 'restrictive monetary policy' means keeping the rate of inflation permanently at a negligible level, and keeping it steadily at such a level with very little variation, I see no long-run effect of such a policy in raising real interest rates but, if anything, rather a slight real interest rate *decreasing* effect. I therefore do not understand why such a 'restrictive monetary policy' can be said to be a cause of 'soft growth', that is economic growth below its potential level and with substantial under-utilization of resources, in particular with high unemployment. Thus I completely disagree that its opposite can be the correctly understood policy aim of a majority of European countries; in fact, I do not understand how it could be the correctly understood long-run policy aim of any single European country participating in the euro to have anything but such a stable negligible inflation rate policy for the coming common European currency. The desire for an expansionary monetary policy is a desire for short-run real benefits at long-run cost, arising in particular from a higher real interest rate and greater uncertainties in the long run.

2 The experience of small countries close to Germany

One tends constantly to be surprised to see how much economic thought is conditioned by historical experience and by momentary quantitative constellations. Possibly, humankind is even genetically preconditioned to over-generalize from present observations.

In reading the – of course, extremely well substantiated – data presented by Fitoussi for 'Europe as a whole', I feel as if I were coming from another planet, and not only from another European country, Austria. As is well known and quoted in the international literature as an interesting example (Isard (1995, pp. 27 ff.)), Austria's currency has been closely linked to the Deutsche Mark (DM) since around the mid-1970s, and extremely closely so since 1980, with the Austrian Schilling fluctuating relative to the DM within only one-seventh of a percentage point (7.03 to 7.04 Schilling to the Mark) in the 1990s. A similar policy has been followed by the Netherlands, only slightly less so by Denmark, and, relative to the Belgian franc, even more strictly so by Luxembourg. These small countries may be insignificant as such; but their experience has already come close to what most European countries will go through within a common European currency setting, and therefore it is of more than parochial importance. Having known no autonomous monetary policy since the mid-1970s (in other words, importing German policy whatever may happen), one is, of course, more likely to believe in the long-run insignificance of monetary policy. In other words, one tends to read the copious economic literature on the long-run neutrality of money with a much greater degree of belief.

In fact, for these countries – Austria, the Netherlands, Denmark (given in the order of the closeness of their link to the DM) and, in another constellation – Luxembourg, monetary policy seems to have been not quite neutral in the long run, but has, if anything, deviated somewhat in the opposite direction from that suggested by Fitoussi: Luxembourg has the lowest unemployment rate in Europe, followed by Austria with, at the time of writing an unemployment rate of 4.5 per cent (but with less youth unemployment than even Luxembourg). The Netherlands and Denmark also show unemployment rates far below the European average. Luxembourg, Denmark, Belgium and Austria (in that order) show the highest purchasing power adjusted real per capita national income levels, achieved in the case of Austria since the late 1970s and in the 1980s. Calculated since the 1980s, Austria showed the lowest average real interest rate in Europe – lower than Germany. An important econometric exercise

(Handler (1989)) has shown that Austria probably has a positively inclined Phillips-curve with respect to expected inflation.

Of course, German policy has not in fact achieved a negligible average inflation rate within this period; nor was the margin small in which its rate of inflation fluctuated. Though not showing good monetary policy practice, it was, however, at least the best autonomous policy in Europe. And it should be noted – against Fitoussi – that as far as it was good policy for Germany (which may be seriously doubted for around 1990), it was good policy not only for Germany – it was, evidently, even better policy for Austria, the Netherlands and Denmark, because these countries suffered much less unemployment and also showed up better than Germany on other economic indicators. It seems to me a very important European experience that those countries that merely adapted to the monetary policy of another country showed the best economic performance, but, of course, only if they stuck to it for a very long time.

Finally, the whole mystique of Austrian policy since the mid-1970s was centred around the idea that real economic success could be achieved by having, on average, a currency-appreciating policy – that is, linking the Schilling to the generally appreciating DM. To demonstrate credibility of its so-called 'hard currency policy', Austria even appreciated by 4.5 per cent relative to the DM in 1979–80, causing a credibility recession in 1981 (that is, zero growth in that year). Appreciating the Schilling with the DM was even quaintly termed by Seidel (1979), 'Austro-Keynesianism' though, as Haberler (1982, pp. 67 ff.) rightly remarked, the name 'Austro-Monetarism' would, in fact, have been more appropriate. In any case, this policy showed no longer-term negative real effects, either on growth or on employment, which makes it easier for an Austrian to believe that nominal exchange rate changes are also neutral in the long run, if not that appreciation is once again slightly beneficial. It may have helped, however, that in the 1990s (and also before that) the Austrian manufacturing industry witnessed a strong real depreciation relative to Germany. From 1986 to 1996, hourly-paid labour productivity of Austrian manufacturing industry increased relative to Germany by 2.0 per cent a year, and industrial hourly-paid unit labour cost fell relative to Germany by 1.3 per cent a year – altogether an astounding 13 per cent (Guger (1997, pp. 480–1)). Against this background, it may be easier to understand that trade union politicians introduced the first steps towards the appreciation policy around 1975 (see Frisch (1976) for an economic rationale), while industrialists opposed it. And taking into account the high degree of competitiveness of the Austrian economy, they may have been quite correct, as appreciation may have had short-run favourable effects on the

Austrian wage share without having negative effects on employment. At least in 1981, the year of the credibility recession after the appreciation relative to Germany, the Austrian wage share reached its highest level, of more than 75 per cent. The slight decline from then on to some 70 per cent can be explained, partly – in another explanation than that given by Fitoussi – by the dying out of this short-run appreciation effect.

3 Effects of a stable monetary policy

Coming from this empirical background, I would therefore argue that, in the long run, a stable monetary policy achieving a negligible rate of inflation on average, with negligible variation at that, will not increase the real rate of interest, but rather achieve the lowest real interest rates possible, taking account of real factors. For the theoretical underpinnings of this statement, I would above all rely on the strong empirical regularity that a lower average rate of inflation is highly correlated with a lower variability of inflation, and that therefore a low expected rate of inflation entails also a low expected value of its variance. I would then argue that a stable monetary policy aiming at a steady negligible rate of inflation (1 per cent within a zero to 2 per cent corridor) would eliminate a risk premium in the real rate of interest caused by price level uncertainty and individual nominal price uncertainty. I would argue that such a policy would minimize the real costs of nominal contracts, which are unavoidable because of the high transaction and control cost of writing real price (indexed) contracts; and it would furthermore minimize the real costs of learning new prices (Noussair *et al.* (1997)).

As to the additional costs of correctly anticipated inflation, I would point to the increase in taxation of capital due to inflation in our usual nominal value tax systems. In order to equalize net real interest rates around the world, countries with higher average rates of inflation have to have higher gross real interest rates in order to compensate for the higher effective capital taxation. I am aware that minimum inflationary costs might be possibly bounded slightly away from zero inflation – and certainly well away from zero nominal interest rates; but I think an 'optimum' average inflation rate will be very close to zero.

As to the exchange rate, I think that a nominal appreciation policy is, if anything, once again in the long run more likely to be on the beneficial side for growth and employment. It has been argued that appreciation stimulates productivity growth; and, for the case of Austria, some empirical verification of this has been found (Marin (1986)). This would imply something like an aspiration-level theory of innovation: innovation being more likely when competition, above all international competition, increases. Though admittedly of limited plausibility, such an argument is not wholly absurd.

4 'Fundamentals' behind real interest rates

In so far as there was an actual increase in real interest rates in the 1980s and 1990s in European countries I would also ask, much more than does Fitoussi, whether that was not caused more by basic real forces and not the temporary effects of monetary policy at all. Have the 1980s not seen the switch of increasing numbers of emerging nations to export-led growth, and thus to the opening up of new opportunities for investment the world over? Have not first the South East Asian countries (including China), then South America and then, from 1989 onwards, Central and Eastern Europe, shown an increased investment demand at high rates of return? Would such additional investment opportunities at given or, in the case of the USA, even continuously falling saving rates, not push up real interest rates everywhere? Was it not the sign of well-functioning and not of badly-functioning 'capitalism' and well-functioning and not badly-functioning investment markets, if capital was shifted out of the rich, old European countries – and of Japan – by higher real interest rates to meet such a demand? To my mind, in parts of his argument, Fitoussi only makes clear that German reunification not only pushed up French real interest rates, but also French unemployment. In fact, it has, of course, long been realised that the whole of Europe was negatively hit via higher interest rates because of German reunification and the fall of the Iron Curtain, and the only countries emerging as net winners were those whose additional exports to Central and Eastern Europe had a stronger positive impact than the negative impact of higher interest rates. Evidently, France was not one of the net winners.

5 Questions of a political economy nature

I now turn to a series of wider implications only hinted at by Fitoussi's chapter. My questions here are all of a political-economy nature.

It is frequently stated that by having a common currency countries lose an important policy instrument; and that they are then ill-suited to deal with external economic shocks. I am very sceptical about the latter argument. Within a currency union you soon learn that most shocks are, in fact, endogenous; and by pure necessity you learn to adapt much better to those that are external: for example, oil price movements. (In fact, the currency appreciation policy was introduced in Austria in order to deal better with the first oil price shock in 1974–75, and with a smaller real loss).

But I am also sceptical of the first statement too. The idea that there can never be enough policy instruments arises basically from the notion of the all-wise and benevolent economic dictator. In fact, in the real world, having many instruments can cause great uncertainty as to when to use which, and to what extent; it can cause political conflict and strife between various politicians and parties; and in consequence can cause much uncertainty among economic agents. In other words, the idea that the extension of the choice set cannot be anything but advantageous because it makes it more likely that a higher level of satisfaction can be achieved depends crucially on the assumption that the process of choice as such is without cost. If, however, a more complex choice set also increases the costs of making a choice, it may be better to have only a restricted choice. The decrease in the number of admissible policies may be more than compensated by the greater ease and clarity of making a choice, and by the economic agents' better understanding of what the policies are likely to be.

So why not take monetary policy as an outside datum and no longer try to influence it? This is the idea of the 'nominal anchor' of a basic currency taken one step further: the advantage of having a whole sphere of policy (that is, monetary policy), as a given 'anchor' against which other policies are adjusted.

6 A policy for depreciating the euro?

Rightly or wrongly, French politicians are perceived above all in Germany and Austria as demanding a higher than negligible inflation and a currency depreciation policy for the euro. Merely asking for such a policy can be politically dangerous, and very costly in terms of financial market reactions.

It is politically dangerous because it has already forced a plebiscite on Austria regarding the introduction of the euro which, unimportant as such on a European scale, might lead to a similar plebiscite in Germany. At the time of writing, the majority of the Austrian population seems to be against the euro because of inflationary fears, so it is very fortunate that the plebiscite is not likely to succeed, largely because it has been introduced by the wrong party, towards which there is much opposition. In Germany, fortunately, a plebiscite would require a change in the constitution, which is always a difficult matter. But there the real danger is that the German Constitutional Court might declare it unconstitutional for Germany to take part in the euro, which would demolish the whole project. According to this Court it would be unconstitutional for Germany to take part if the euro were likely to become a more inflationary currency than the DM (a preliminary decision to this intent has already been made); because this would be an infringement of the inviolability of property rights guaranteed to the German people by their constitution. Financial market reactions to the likelihood of a more inflationary euro may easily lead to temporarily higher real interest rates, the very type of development that Fitoussi deplores. It probably contributed to the devaluation of the DM relative to the US dollar. Fitoussi pointedly asks questions such as: Who are 'the financial markets', after all? What is the political power behind a few financiers? And should governments take into account such nonentities? As long as there exists full capital market integration and full convertibility in Europe, capital market sentiment has, however, strong real effects, whatever the political power behind capital markets.

Nor should one underestimate the political voting power and the impact of the value judgements of the economic agents behind the capital markets. Today capital markets are dominated by so-called institutional investors, but these are only pension funds under another name. Behind them is the vast number of 'old age' pensioners, frequently nowadays not at all very old and politically very active. Low inflation in many European countries meant that pensioners frequently have large real savings which in turn means that, for them, keeping inflation low has become the paramount economic aim: here is the constituency for strict monetary austerity. In how many countries of Europe does there still exist a political majority for more employment creation and less 'softness' in growth?

7 Is there a 'Europe as a whole'?

This brings me to my final point. 'Europe as a whole' is a fine statistical concept, admirably used by Fitoussi. But how much reality has it in terms of political decision-taking or, if you will, in terms of a transitive, or even a definable, social welfare function? The paramount economic value in Germany or Austria seems to be guarding the purchasing power of money. Austria, which expected to have, on average, an appreciating currency, has issued much foreign-denominated debt, particularly in yen and Swiss francs; it is therefore highly interested in euro appreciation (Fitoussi, to my mind, and from the standpoint of Austrian appreciation policy, greatly overestimates the size and stability of a political coalition in favour of depreciation of the euro, in particular as the trade of EU-Europe outside its borders is less than 10 per cent of GDP, and many European exports are so high-tech that their price elasticity is low relative to moderate price or exchange rate changes.) Italy, with its high internally-financed government debt is, above all, interested in low nominal interest rates, which by the Fisher relationship can once more very well mean low inflation rates. Higher employment may be paramount in France or Spain; and so on. It appears to me very likely that preferences as to economic aims are to a marked extent not single-peaked within European nations, and even less so *between* European nations. Furthermore, because of differing historical experiences, preferences are likely to be only partial orderings, better defined only relative to those possibilities that have in fact been experienced. This would be to argue that no social welfare function for 'Europe as a whole' can be defined; and, furthermore, even as far as social welfare functions for each European nation can be assumed to exist, that politicians are unlikely to be able to judge what they are (this happens frequently already for their own country and even more so for other countries with which they have to deal).

It has been suggested to me that, in the future European common monetary policy, it would be, as always, better to play a co-operative game than to play a Nash equilibrium strategy. But, according to the above argument, neither of these would be feasible. For there would be no well-defined payoff matrix of players; and the beliefs about payoffs, as far as they can be defined, are not likely to be mutually consistent. Perhaps in time each would learn about the other's payoffs and beliefs, so that in future decades policy games might become possible; but, I think, not at the time of the introduction of the common currency. 'Europe as a whole' does not exist in terms of policy formulation.

Which only means that the European central bank is likely to be uncontrollable politically by a council of ministers, who will seldom agree. Thus, I expect a European central bank, which will follow strictly its statutory economic aim – namely, a negligible rate of inflation – and will follow this aim unimpeded by concerted political pressure. It is only to be hoped that not too much talk about the need of an expansionary monetary policy in order to fight 'soft growth' will force it to engineer too much of a credibility recession initially.

Postscript (April 1999)

This Comment was written in late 1997. Meanwhile, the euro has been introduced and the political activities against its introduction, discussed in Section 7 above, which posed a real threat at the time of writing, have come to nothing. It was the German minister of finance, Oskar Lafontaine, rather than French politicians, who campaigned more actively for a 'looser' monetary policy. The euro has depreciated substantially against the US dollar, which may partly be caused by lingering fears, even after the demise of Lafontaine, that it would prove to be more inflationary than the DM; but it seems more likely to be related to the very low real as well as nominal long-term interest rates – lower than in the USA. Thus low, not high interest rates have become typical in Europe, contrary to Fitoussi's fears. The argument that inflation will have negative real effects because of the fiscal drag of taxation has recently been well restated by Feldstein (1997); and it has been shown empirically by Shiller (1997) that in many countries there now is no winning constituency for higher inflation, even if it brings lower unemployment.

References

Feldstein, Martin (1997) 'The Costs and Benefits of Going from Low Inflation to Price Stability', in Romer and Romer (1997), pp. 123–56.

Frisch, Helmut (1976) 'Eine Verallgemeinerung des skandinavischen Modells der Inflation: Mit einer empirischen Analyse für Österreich', *Empirica*, vol. 2, pp. 197–218.

Guger, Alois (1997) 'Relative Lohnstückkosten der Industrie gesunken', *Monatsberichte*, Österreichisches Institut für Wirtschaftsforschung, vol. 70, pp. 477–83.

Haberler, Gottfried (1982) 'Austria's Economic Development after Two World Wars: A Mirror Picture of the World Economy', in Sven W. Arndt (ed.), *The Political Economy of Austria* (Washington and London: American Enterprise Institute), pp. 61–75.

Handler, Heinz (1989) *Grundlagen der österreichischen Hartwährungspolitik–Geldwertstabilisierung, Phillipskurve, Unsicherheit* (Vienna: Manz).

Isard, Peter (1995) *Exchange Rate Economics* (Cambridge University Press).

Marin, Dalia (1986) 'Exchange Rate and Industrial Profits: Austria's Revaluation Policy in the 1970s', *Applied Economics*, vol. 18, pp. 675–89.

Noussair, Charles N., Charles R. Plott, and Raymond G. Riezman (1997) 'The Principles of Exchange Rate Determination in an International Finance Experiment', *Journal of Political Economy*, vol. 105, pp. 822–61.

Romer, Christina D. and David H. Romer (1997) *Reducing Inflation – Motivation and Strategy* (University of Chicago Press).

Sargent, Thomas J. and Neil Wallace (1981) 'Some Unpleasent Monetarist Arithmetic', *Federal Reserve Bank of Minneapolis Quarterly Review*, vol 5, no .3, pp. 15–31.

Seidel, Hans (1979) 'Die Österreichische Wirtschaft – Entwicklung, Erfolge und Probleme', *Quartalshefte dex Girozentrale*, vol. 14(1), pp. 35–75.

Tödter, Karl-Heinz and Gerhard Ziebarth (1997) 'Preisstabilität oder geringe Inflation für Deutschland – Eine Analyse von Kosten und Nutzen', *Diskussionspapier* 3/97, Volkswirtschaftliche Forschungsgruppe der Deutschen Bundesbank, Frankfurt am Main.

Shiller, Robert J. (1997) 'Why Do People Dislike Inflation?', in Romer and Romer (1997), pp. 13–69.

Index of Names

Subject Index